THE BOWERY BOYS

THE BOWERY BOYS

STREET CORNER RADICALS AND THE POLITICS OF REBELLION

PETER ADAMS

Westport, Connecticut
London

Library of Congress Cataloging-in-Publication Data

Adams, Peter, 1953–

    The Bowery Boys : street corner radicals and the politics of rebellion / Peter Adams.
      p. cm.
    Includes bibliographical references and index.
    ISBN 0-275-98538-5 (alk. paper)
1. Bowery Boys (Gang). 2. Gangs—New York (State)—New York—History—
19th century. 3. New York (N.Y.)—Social conditions—19th century. 4. New York
(N.Y.)—Politics and government—19th century. I. Title.
HV6439.U7N393 2005
364.1'06'6097471—dc22   2004028071

British Library Cataloguing in Publication Data is available.

Library of Congress Catalog Card Number: 2004028071
ISBN: 0-275-98538-5

First published in 2005

Praeger Publishers, 88 Post Road West, Westport, CT 06881
An imprint of Greenwood Publishing Group, Inc.
www.praeger.com

Printed in the United States of America

The paper used in this book complies with the
Permanent Paper Standard issued by the National
Information Standards Organization (Z39.48-1984).

10 9 8 7 6 5 4 3 2 1

For Genevieve and Elliot

Contents

Acknowledgments

Writing often can be a solitary task; it is one of the distinct pleasures of the craft. That said, there can be no doubt that the research and writing of any book involves the aid, comfort, and support of many people. I am particularly indebted to the outstanding staff of the Library of Congress, who were generous with their time and the resources of what is truly one of America's greatest treasures.

The librarians and staff of the New York Historical Society, New York Public Library, Georgetown University Library, Brown University Library, and Catholic University Library were equally generous and helpful in leading me to the materials assembled for this project.

A number of people took the time from their busy schedules to offer valuable suggestions to focus and otherwise improve what started out as a very rough manuscript. Fred Heller, Syd Jones, Mark Adams, and Eric Sollinger offered their suggestions, resources, and moral support—all of it much appreciated. The one person whose contribution mattered more than I can ever give thanks was Maureen, my wife and best friend, who continues to guide me through those most uncertain pages of all—life itself. To her I say simply, *Ex Amore, Vita.*

Introduction: The Bowery Boys' New York

L
ike many studies of the New York Bowery Boys during the middle of the nineteenth century, this one started with Herbert Asbury's *Gangs of New York*, and as in any treatment of the subject, the first order of business was to separate myth from reality. Written in 1927, Asbury's lively account of Manhattan's underworld is filled with anecdote and a healthy dose of exaggeration. Martin Scorsese brought the *Gangs of New York* to the screen in 2002, introducing America to an urban subculture prone to being understood one-dimensionally. True, plenty of drunken mayhem occurred in the filthy streets and dark warrens of the city's lower east side during the three decades before the Civil War, and there was a conflict between Catholic and Protestant that could rival the battles of Belfast; but there was also a political dimension to the Bowery Boys under its charismatic leader Mike Walsh.

In part, this book is a biographical treatment of Walsh, who took the Bowery Boys into the principal debates over class and power in antebellum New York and New England. With his political faction, the Spartan Association, Walsh expressed the views of the Far Left of the Jacksonian democracy of the 1840s and early 1850s. Antebellum New York, as it developed into this country's commercial capital, gave rise to uniquely American variations of radical political thought. It was, of course, a unique place. The city was a mixture of wealth and abysmal poverty, high society and saloon brawls, mansions and immigrant shantytowns of jerry-rigged log cabins.

Mike Walsh organized the Bowery Boys into a political insurgency that challenged Tammany Hall to open its doors to the burgeoning industrial proletariat. (Courtesy of the Library of Congress)

The character of the city was shaped in part by a dramatic growth in population—from 200,000 in 1830 to 371,000 in 1845 and up to 630,000 just ten years later. The lower wards of the city (those below Canal Street) became increasingly working class and immigrant as wealth and opportunity migrated northward up the island of Manhattan. In 1842, the city saw the construction of 912 new buildings, but by 1845 that number rose closer to 2,000 new buildings in a single year. The price of land also began its upward climb, which saw no end in sight through the twentieth century, even among the shantytowns. For example a lot on William Street near Wall Street was sold for $51,000 in 1834 and quickly resold for $120,000 just two years later.[1]

Throughout the antebellum years, Manhattan streets were paved over farmland and old Indian trails at a quickening pace, yet many people remained without a decent roof over their heads. By 1864, the *New York Times* estimated that close to 20,000 squatters, who paid no taxes or rent, were scattered throughout New York City. Most of the city's shanty dwellers were Irish or German, with some living on Dutch Hill, a steep precipice at First Avenue and Fortieth Street. This squatters' colony was a home to people who lived in the most primitive conditions, tending livestock and working in nearby quarries and manure heaps.

City services, from schools to health care and fire and police, could hardly keep up. This was a city of volunteer fire brigades who battled each other for control of a hydrant as buildings burned; it was also a city of police ill-equipped to impose law and order. As the *New York Herald* observed in 1843, "The city is virtually without any municipal government." In 1844, as a committee of the Common Council reported that "lawless bands of ruffians stroll the city," police protection was still in the hands of the Watch Department, which consisted of only about 1,200 night watchmen, hardly adequate for a city of that size.[2]

Literally moonlighting, most night watchmen had day jobs and spent their time on duty sleeping in their small, telephone booth–sized shelters. Young men often made sport of tipping these boxes over, with the unsuspecting night watchman inside. Even as early as 1835, one newspaper asked, "Is our police [force] not sufficiently strong and well organized? What defect in our political system are we to attribute the power of mob law? We are on the verge of anarchy and the rule of law is at an end." With the police so ineffective, many New Yorkers were prepared to arm themselves.[3] Crime was so ubiquitous in much of the city that frontiersman Davy Crockett, during his visit to New York, commented, "I would rather risk myself in an Indian fight than venture among these creatures after night."[4]

Threats to public health were poorly understood or inadequately addressed in a city where thousands lived in cramped, poorly ventilated underground cellars that often flooded with refuse from the streets above. As late as 1857, nearly three-fourths of New York, including some of the most densely populated sections, lacked sewers. People were increasingly packed into tighter spaces; between 1820 and 1850 the number of residents occupying a typical city block went from 157 to 272.

In his colorful and offbeat account of the underside of mid-nineteenth-century New York, *Secrets of the Great City*, Edward Martin's description of life among the city's poor is typical of many contemporary accounts.

> These buildings seem overflowing with human beings.... The cellars are so dark that one unaccustomed to them cannot set foot before them without a bright light. They are filled with wretched inmates.... The walls are lined with bunks or berths and the woodwork and bedding are alive with vermin. Thousands of children are born in these foul places every year. They never see the light of day until they are able to crawl into the streets.[5]

Health conditions for children were worsened by the consumption of swill milk, a cheap product from cows fed on the waste products of distilleries. Less than one-half of children born in New York in the 1850s survived to the age of ten. Diseases like cholera were prevalent throughout the city, not just in the poorest neighborhoods; between July and October 1832, as many as 3,500 people died in an outbreak of Asiatic cholera, and in the 1849 epidemic, 1 percent of New York's population died.

Speaking for the immigrant and common laborer, Mike Walsh was familiar with the chronic overcrowding and unhealthy living conditions that distinguished life in working-class New York, calling it the "cause of more vice and misery, more suffering in every way than all other causes put together." The Bowery Boy described "buildings extended until a single inch of yard is not left, thus cutting off all chances of light or air—entirely destroying ventilation." Walsh also warned of the hazards of "slender-built tenements, which are occupied before the mortar used on the foundation is thoroughly dry." Sparing no descriptive, the leader of the Spartans saw the infant mortality rate as a "wholesale slaughter of the poor," noting quite accurately that one-third of the deaths in New York in 1846 were children under the age of five.[6]

Poverty and misery aside, antebellum New York had no shortage of entertainment. In the lower wards of the city were pits for every conceivable gladiatorial contest—between dogs and rats, men against men, and even bear wrestling at McLaughlin's Bear Pit at First Avenue and Tenth Street. Bowery Boy Ned Buntline, in his 1848 exposé of urban life, describes a working-class Manhattan where "every house serves the double purpose of brothel and dance hall ... [with] rooms filled with ill-dressed men, and painted, bloated women drinking, dancing, shouting and carousing."

Another feature of the city was its immense German beer gardens that could accommodate up to 1,500 guests. One of the most famous, the Vauxhall Gardens, attracted a working-class patronage: "a favorite spot for mass meetings and the stamping grounds of the buncombe orators." Not surprisingly, P. T. Barnum found the Vauxhall a perfect place to begin his career with the famous mermaid hoax.[7]

New York was then, as it is now, a city of theaters. Castle Garden was the site of the New York performance of one of the first international superstars, Jenny Lind, dubbed the Swedish Nightingale. Barnum sponsored her 1850 U.S. tour, which drew thousands of fans to the docks to greet her arrival, including an escort of twenty volunteer fire companies.

Gotham was a city of free-flowing liquor and ample access to prostitutes, who entertained their customers out of dance halls, upper-class houses called bagnios, or on the streets. Just at the crossroads of Anthony, Leonard, Orange, and Centre streets, near the notorious Five Points, more than a dozen houses of prostitution operated in the 1830s and 1840s. Martin implies that child prostitution was not uncommon, and there were numerous reported cases of white slavery in which women as young as fourteen were raped and forced into prostitution.

This was an environment that nourished the gang subculture emerging in the 1820s and flourishing in the working-class wards of the city until their eclipse just before the Civil War. Contemporary reformers understood the relationship between the emergence of politically active gangs and the conditions that bred more than just physical disease. John Griscom, an early advocate of establishing a system of health inspectors, made a direct connection between the living conditions of the working classes in lower Manhattan and the New York gangs who aimed their ire at the city's privileged. "In times of riot and tumult," said Griscom, "the disturbers of the peace [are] from the cellars and alleys where they have never been taught to respect themselves, much less others."[8]

With a lifestyle and culture separate from middle-class society, most Bowery Boys were in their teens and early twenties, as the number of young, single workingmen in New York's manufacturing districts increased markedly in the first half of the nineteenth century. Richard Stott, in his study of nineteenth-century New York culture, notes that in 1820 those aged 16 to 45 made up 47 percent of the city's population, but by 1850 that age group represented 57 percent of the city.

Charles Loring Brace, who chronicled the life of New York's underclass, estimated there were as many as 10,000 homeless children roaming its streets in 1852. With so many adolescents on the streets, New York's educational system could reach only about half of school-aged children. Brace, who opened the first lodging house for street boys in 1854, described the homeless youth as an "unconscious society" prone to violence and potentially, to revolution. Brace called this the dangerous class, embittered at a city that ignored their profound poverty.[9]

Not all the young men who called themselves Bowery Boys were at the bottom of the economic ladder. Many were shipbuilders, carpenters, butchers, and printers. Some owned property or were master butchers or tradesmen, making them middle class. Others were struggling journeymen or factory laborers, radicalized by an industrializing economy that created a new but less prosperous urban proletariat.

These were the young men lionized by Walt Whitman: "the splendid and rugged characters ... the firemen of *Mannahatta*, the target excursionist and Bowery Boy." Mike Walsh echoed the great poet's words with his own description of a vibrant city, "New York is to the union what ... ancient Rome was to its vast empire—what the heart is to the body ... and as she throbs fast or slow, healthy or unhealthy, the whole union has to keep time to her."

While Whitman was not a member of Walsh's Spartan Association, he admired Walsh for his tough-talking defense of the common man. Both men projected virility and masculine comradeship. Whitman derided the "impotent, loose in the knees" aristocrat just as Walsh praised political men of action, "with their backbone straight."

Over the years, the Bowery Boy became part of the mythology of a freewheeling city—the original urban legend. New York's Bowery Boy was a distinctive social type in dress, slang, and mannerism. Referring to the Bowery Boys who followed Butcher Bill Poole in the mid-1850s, the *New York Tribune* cautioned that "as long as gambling, drunkenness, prostitution, prize fighting and their associate evils continue, we shall have these characters." The group had a strict code of conduct, as evidenced in a small article in Walsh's newspaper, the *Subterranean*. When a couple of the "b'hoys" attacked an unnamed, but "prominent," New Yorker "contrary to orders," Walsh promised, "we will attend to them next week."[10]

The Bowery Boy's hair was cut short in the back and slicked down in the front with a thick grease or soap; ringlets of hair were pasted down in front of the ears. These were the soaplocks, a word that became synonymous with the Bowery Boys. Butt-ender was another word that meant Bowery Boy, a reference to his ever-present cigar. His speech was the beginning of the New York working-class accent that evolved through the nineteenth and twentieth centuries. In dress, the Bowery Boys, like many other gang members, wore the red shirt of the fire brigades. The rest of his outfit was a gaudy street look that

AND OTHER PLACES. SCENES AND INCIDENTS. THE KILLED AND WOUNDED.

The original urban legend, the Bowery Boy was a distinctive New York type with slang, dress, and manners that helped define the city's working-class culture. (Courtesy of the Library of Congress)

included a black frock coat; plenty of jewelry; and heavy boots ideal for brawling, rushing to a fire, or an afternoon of target practice.

Of course, the mythology of the Bowery Boys originates from the b'hoys
themselves and was embellished by each generation, including Herbert
Asbury's description. There was the apocryphal career of firefighter Mose
Humphreys. Humphreys was made famous by the actor Frank Chanfrau, who
played Mose as a cigar-chomping stereotype of the b'hoy at the Bowery
Theater to crowds of appreciative working-class New Yorkers in 1848. The
play, *A Glance at New York*, ran for 70 nights; but one play was not enough to
tell the whole story of Mose, his buddy Sikesey, and the Bowery gal Lizzie.
There were sequels: *Mose in a Muss* and *Mose in California* during the gold rush.
Mose was romanticized as a city-bred Paul Bunyan with amazing strength,
boots soled with copper studs, a butcher's cleaver, and a keg of beer swinging
from his belt. He could swim the Hudson in two strokes, jog around Manhattan
in six hours, and thrust a lamppost like a battering ram at his adversaries.

A real Mose Humphreys was likely a celebrated member of the Lady
Washington engine company, one of the many volunteer fire brigades that
served as a vehicle for gang intimidation and power. In typical Bowery Boy
style, he may also have worked by day as a journeyman in a print shop. According to various contemporary and later accounts, Lady Washington
Company met up with the rival Peterson Company on the way back from
a fire in the summer of 1836. They clashed, as often happened between fire
companies, and a riot ensued, as other brigades rushed to the scene to take
sides. Mose was defeated, and the Lady Washington engine was captured
and vandalized. Mose's heroics in this battle soon became legend, but in
defeat, he left New York for as far away as he could go: running a pool hall
in Hawaii and organizing Honolulu's first fire department.

While Mike Walsh and his young partisans called themselves Bowery
Boys, it would be a mistake to identify the Bowery Boys as a specific group
at a specific time. There were several gangs who referred to themselves as
Bowery Boys under different leaders during the antebellum years, but
Walsh is distinguished by his success in leading the Bowery Boys into the
political and social struggles of the newly industrialized working class. The
Bowery Boys who followed Walsh under the banner of the Spartan
Association, which he organized in 1840, were deeply politicized; they
were what the *New York Tribune* called, the "adolescent shoulder hitters
and politicians [who] take their first lessons in rowdyism."[11]

Walsh was not alone in harnessing the disaffected youth of the city to
political ends, but he was the most effective and the most volatile. His was
the prototype of the politicized gang, a model imitated by a variety of
clubhouses in the poorer wards of New York City and other urban areas.
The working-class gang as an organized faction "was [Walsh's] great technical

contribution to American politics," according to Arthur M. Schlesinger Jr. in *Age of Jackson*.

Walsh articulated the frustration of those crowded into factories and sweatshops—immigrant or native-born—whom he called the shirtless democrats and subterraneans, signifying their status as the proletarianized underclass, denied the fruits of the market revolution and the levers of political power. This was a working class, he said, "submerged, buried and trodden under foot." For Walsh, the new capitalism that drove America's fast-paced industrialization produced a "gloomy, churlish money-worshipping spirit of the age" that "has swept nearly all the poetry of life out of the poor man's sphere."[12]

The Bowery Boy mobilized this undisciplined working class youth to challenge the power structure and the symbols of the moneyed aristocracy, whether that be in an attack against British stage actors or an election-day riot aimed at the entrenched leaders of the Democratic Party at Tammany Hall.

Historian Sean Wilentz, in his *Chants Democratic*, writes that for a short time, Walsh was able "to usurp the role of the one great political representative of the city's wage earners and struggling producers.... Walsh came to consider himself the only man two-fisted enough to lead the city's lower classes." Walsh, Wilentz says, was unique in molding these young Bowery Boys into a political movement that, while not wholly socialist, certainly advanced a forceful critique of America's emerging industrial capitalism.

Dabbling in uniquely American variants of socialist thought, the Bowery Boys found an ally in George Henry Evans, one of the foremost intellectuals of the Jacksonian left. Evans recognized Walsh's ability to pack a hall with cheering followers ready, if necessary, to transform New York's downtown streets into the barricades of revolutionary Europe. Walsh, joining Evans and other early labor activists, was at the center of the effort to build the first true industrial unions in America.

Arriving in New York from Ireland as a small boy, Walsh learned quickly the art of politics on the lower east side. Persuasive, a good mimic, and intelligent, Walsh was proud of his acquired street smarts and persistent rebelliousness—traits admired by his Bowery Boy and working-class followers. He was a passionate speaker who coined the phrase "vote early and often," as well as that quintessentially New York label "shyster." If these terms credited to him are any indication, Walsh was certainly regarded by many New Yorkers as a bullying opportunist and self-promoter.[13]

Educated for a short time at St. Peter's School in New York, Walsh claimed to have spent several years of his youth as a deck hand on a Mississippi riverboat. Recalling his experiences, likely inflated, Walsh said, "I happen to know something about the people of this land ... working bareheaded and barefooted." Fact and fiction are hard to separate in Walsh's life; he also purported to have fought in the Indian wars in Florida and to have lost a brother at the Alamo. As one contemporary remarked, "of all the singular and eccentric men" of New York, "I doubt if ever there was a more peculiar, popular, brilliant and yet, on the whole, a more impractical creature than Michael Walsh."

Eccentric would be an accurate assessment; he was an original character who lived by his own motto, "any dead fish can swim with the stream, but it takes a real live one to go against the current." Walsh preferred to sleep outdoors in city parks during the summer saying it was good for his health, and he often spoke of unconfirmed assassination attempts by his political enemies. With a violent temper, the leader of the Bowery Boys in 1844 was convicted and fined on assault charges; Walsh's only regret was that he had not "cut off both of his ears at the time."[14]

He was the author of less-than-memorable poems, such as one recalling the cholera outbreak of 1832, as well as self-published short stories that featured a character he called Billy Bisbee. In one, "Billy Bisbee's Account of the Florida Campaign," Walsh describes the harsh life of the soldier and condemns the dishonest recruiting tactics of the armed forces as it induced working class youth to fight in the Indian wars of the southeastern United States during the 1830s. While young Billy Bisbee was promised an exciting and rewarding military career, he found himself in the worst drudgery as an infantry soldier in hostile Seminole territory. After deserting, Bisbee, reflecting Walsh's views on authority, vowed never again to "place my body at the disposal of any number of tyrannical despots."

Walsh was a practical joker who once convinced hundreds of tavern patrons that a wealthy acquaintance just back from the California gold rush was waiting at a local hotel to hand out gifts and free drinks. Once, when an ex-tavern owner running for office took on more pretentious airs at a campaign rally than the Bowery Boy could tolerate, Walsh was eager to take him down a peg. In the audience, the heckling Walsh would interrupt with calls of "a pitcher of ice water at table twenty-five." The Bowery Boys approved of Walsh's straightforward style saying, "If he loves, he loves ardently; if he hates, it is with inveterate hatred."[15]

Despite a penchant for hard drinking and boorish behavior, Walsh could be capable of insights that reveal an intellectual curiosity and acuity. Knowledge, he confided, can crush "the vestiges of superstition and tyranny beneath its chariot wheels." He also expressed the optimism of the Young America movement's doctrine of Manifest Destiny, correctly predicting that "the diffusion of the English language I regard as one of the great signs of the times."[16]

Yet ever mindful of the anti-intellectualism of his constituents on the streets, Walsh belittled a formal education and the bookishness of the upper classes. It is "far better to know the men among whom one lives than to know of men who have been dead 3,000 years," he said. For the Bowery Boys of the lower east side, the best lessons in life were learned in the streets, not the classroom. As Walsh explained, "I would not barter away all the practical knowledge I have received in lumber and ship yards for all the Latin that was ever spoken in ancient Rome. I'd rather speak sense in one plain and expressive language, than speak nonsense in fifty."

And expressive in the English language he was, referring to himself as "the immortal, independent Mike!, the poet and philosopher—the incorruptible patriot—the President of the Spartan Band—the orator and star of Tammany Hall—the champion of the shirtless, the advocate of the houseless—the idol of the Subterraneans." With a love of high-sounding martial titles, Walsh bestowed ranks from Napoleon's army to his partisans; he had a devoted following, and "captivated the poor of his ward," as Gustavus Myers writes in his 1917 *History of Tammany Hall*.

Clearly, Walsh was a demagogue armed with pointed language and wit, who could bring his shirtless democrats to their feet at the first utterance; telling, for example, mill workers in Fall River, Massachusetts, that the "nabobs in England do not oppress and grind the face of the poor more than is done in this country." Walsh reserved some of his most stinging criticism for Horace Greeley's *New York Tribune* and others in the reformist and middle class press, calling them "mental prostitutes, mere maggots of society, scribbling vermin."

While falling far short of the revolutionary zeal and discipline of the Parisian or Berlin workers of the 1830s and 1840s, New York's politicized gangs nonetheless frightened the merchant elite. With their paramilitary fire brigades and associated gun clubs, New York's working-class youth often appeared as a threatening army in waiting.

Like many of the political clubhouses challenging Tammany's grip on power, Walsh's Spartan Association needed its own newspaper. Bowery Boy leaders, such as Walsh, Ned Buntline, and Edward Strahan, were particularly adept at using the press to direct worker dissatisfaction on the streets. Walsh's *Subterranean*, Strahan's *Progressive Democrat*, and *Buntline's Own* were the prototypes of the underground newspaper that would advance unconventional ideas throughout the rest of the nineteenth century and into the twentieth. Published between 1843 and 1847, the *Subterranean* was irreverent, irresponsible, and viewed by middle-class New Yorkers as insurrectionary and scandalous. Walsh called it "the most radical paper on earth," and his founding partner was George Wilkes, who later published the sensationalist tabloid, the *Police Gazette*, and became an enthusiastic propagandist for Marxism during the 1870s.

Walsh merged the *Subterranean* with George Henry Evans's *Working Man's Advocate* for several months in late 1844. The combined newspaper was devoted to the National Reform Association, which Walsh and Evans founded to advance their plan to settle industrial workers in the American West. Drawing workers from the overcrowded factories and giving them the tools to plow the land would act as a safety valve in a city ready to explode with hungry disaffected laboring men.

As a young apprentice, Walsh learned the printing trade, which prepared him for his career as a journalist, first writing for the *New York Aurora* between 1839 and 1842. Walsh served briefly as the Washington correspondent for the *Aurora*, which was under Walt Whitman's editorship at the time. As a journalist, Walsh was far from an objective observer of political events. Leaving New York for his Washington assignment, Walsh was escorted to the train station by a contingent of sixty well-armed Bowery Boys.

Once in Washington, Walsh interviewed President John Tyler—an interview that was as much about the "immortal champion of the subterraneans" as the president. Indicative of Walsh's style and pretensions, he describes how he slowed his pace as he approached the White House, not wanting anyone to think that he was too anxious for his dinner with Tyler. He spent a few minutes first on the mansion's grounds imagining himself president "with two bright luscious-looking young ladies putting naughty, though very pleasing, thoughts into my head." Walsh's dinner with President Tyler in December 1842 was more subdued than his erotic fantasies of life in the White House, but he came away with a positive impression of the president, describing him as "a pure patriot ... He's one of the [Bowery] b'hoys which is the highest compliment that can be paid to any man."[17]

Walsh was certainly smart enough to know when it was time to drop the role of political outsider and rabble-rouser. He finally made his peace with the Democratic Party in 1851 and was elected to the U.S. Congress the following year. He served one term, likely the only member of Congress who never took the trouble to become a U.S. citizen. In Congress and during his three terms in the New York State Legislature, the leader of the Bowery Boys continued to press a remarkably progressive agenda, calling for fair labor practices, the ten-hour day, an end to child labor, and plain English in court proceedings and legal documents. "My influence," he said, "is only to be obtained in favor of a thing that is right and calculated to benefit the working classes."

Politics in antebellum New York was an incomprehensible puzzle to Connecticut patrician Oliver Wolcott; "a labyrinth of wheels within wheels, understood only by the managers." Mike Walsh and the Bowery Boys represented one corner of that labyrinth, a radical insurgency that threatened the public order and existing class relations.[18]

The Bowery Boys: Shirtless and Unterrified

Even in his jail cell, looking out from Blackwell's Island onto the East River, the leader of the Bowery Boys could cajole, inflame, and mobilize his devoted followers on Manhattan's lower east side. In November 1843, Mike Walsh was at the peak of his popularity, having organized young factory workers and unskilled laborers as foot soldiers in the political clubhouse he named the Spartan Association or more informally, the Spartan Band.

To these men, Mike Walsh had "arisen from the ranks of the mass of the people ... [and] wrung from the oppressed millions the light of liberty." Walsh's Bowery Boy was a blend of gang member, insurgent Democrat, and labor radical at a time when the city's workers were losing ground to factories and sweatshops.

Jailed on libel charges, Walsh was enraged with what he often described as the "miserable worn-out hacks of politicians" at the top of New York's Democratic Party. To the faithful in the mostly poor and immigrant Sixth Ward, Walsh was no less than Tammany's political prisoner. Certainly the Democratic Party establishment wanted this troublemaker and his inflammatory newspaper, the *Subterranean*, off the streets after a year of political violence that reminded some of the dangerous radicalism arising in European capitals. To New York's "respectable classes," democracy itself was threatened by well-organized, working-class toughs in America's largest city.[1]

Although safely behind bars, Walsh was treated to cigars, schnapps, and dutiful couriers who carried his dispatches back to the offices of the

Subterranean. "He was living gloriously ... holding court ... [making] the prison resound with much wit, fun and philosophy," said one observer. The object of Walsh's libel was Levi D. Slamm, a rival in the battles that were fought ward by ward, street by street among various factions vying to crash the gates of Tammany Hall from below. Walsh accused Slamm of selling out his political faction in exchange for Tammany patronage and printing contracts for his newspaper. For Walsh, the young factory lads struggling to survive on consistently poor wages were often betrayed by "worthless, selfish, and dishonest leaders" like Levi Slamm.[2]

Almost three years later, Walsh was sentenced again to six months on Blackwell's Island on yet another libel charge. This time the Spartan Association was strong enough to win his release through an outpouring on the streets. Walsh's transgression seemed mild; he was sued by furniture dealer John Harspool, who had received a contract to furnish President James K. Polk's White House. Walsh accused Harspool of exploiting his workers while "amassing a princely fortune" and of sending the White House secondhand furniture from one of his several brothels.

Summoning thousands for a rally at City Hall Park in April 1846, the Bowery Boys and Spartan Association demanded Walsh's immediate release. The front page of the *Subterranean* on April 4 informed New Yorkers, "We consider the present infamous persecution of Mike Walsh a blow aimed at the honest laboring portion of this community." Facing violence in the streets or a well-organized political backlash, Tammany's entire delegation to the state legislature persuaded Governor Silas Wright to pardon Walsh midway through his sentence.

Governor Wright, on the advice of frightened Tammany leaders, waited until after the city's spring elections before releasing the Bowery Boy from behind bars. They were familiar with the mayhem Walsh could raise on Election Day. Returning to the banks of the East River in a raucous celebration, Walsh was hailed by the gangs of New York as the "champion of the poor man's rights." It was obvious that the Democratic Party in New York could no longer ignore the Bowery Boys or their Spartans. Within just five months, Walsh was literally carried into Tammany Hall and nominated for a seat in the state legislature.

One of those pleased to see Walsh freed and escorted triumphantly through the doors of Tammany Hall was Walt Whitman, who counted himself among the subterranean democrats. Whitman gave poetic voice to Walsh's primitive notions of democracy and his attacks on the aristocracy. So Whitman wrote in *Democratic Vistas,* "As circulation is to the air, so is agitation and a plentiful degree of speculative license to political and moral sanity. Vive the attack—the perennial assault."

One of Whitman's poems, "Lesson of the Two Symbols," appeared on July 15, 1843, in the first issue of the *Subterranean*. When Walsh died in 1859, an obituary in the *Brooklyn Daily Times* was likely written by Whitman, who referred to the leader of the Bowery Boys as a man of "original talent, rough, full of passionate impulses ... but he lacked balance, caution—the ship often seemed devoid of both ballast and rudder." Those passionate impulses resonated well with the b'hoys who manned the volunteer fire brigades or joined the ranks of the newly proletarianized workers struggling to find a place in a rapidly changing economy.

As historian Sean Wilentz observes, Walsh was neither a common ward heeler nor a cynical rabble-rouser, but the assembler of a coalition dedicated both to advancing his own political fortunes and to social reform. He represented "a new and curious figure in New York politics, the radical Bowery Boy politician" with his "restless search for a political voice and a public persona."

In some cases the Bowery Boys fought Catholic immigrants; in other instances they sought common ground with Catholic workers in opposition to the class enemy or the Tammany power structure. For Walsh, the ultimate opportunist, his alliance with Catholics could shift depending on the mood of the men in the streets, but he was consistent in his attacks on the closed clubhouse at Tammany and its operatives "who preside like cankers over our party."[3]

The job of breaking Tammany's hold on the Democratic Party, Walsh said, belonged to the subterranean democrats who were armed with a powerful weapon—the ballot.

During the three decades before the Civil War, the intersection of the New York gangs and the political life of the city came on Election Day. Several factors accounted for this. New York State, between 1821 and 1826, extended the vote to all white males over age twenty-one; voting was no longer limited to property holders. The expansion of suffrage at a time of rapid industrialization also created the first generation of workers with the vote. If capitalism was enriching the few, the ballot was broadening the social power of the many, says historian of antebellum New York politics Amy Bridges. This meant that social and class conflict in America's major cities became politicized.

Edward Mallon, a leader of New York's tailors during the strike of 1850, echoed Walsh's sentiments that America offered a road to power that was closed to disenfranchised European workers, declaring, "There was one weapon the workingmen had in their hands by which they could triumph over capitalists and money.... It was more powerful than the gun or the chain behind the barricades of Paris. It was the ballot."[4]

With wider suffrage, popular movements like the quasi-socialist Working Men's Party of 1829 and later, the Spartan Association, could fight for the allegiance of the emerging immigrant and laboring-class voting blocs. The city's conservative political leaders, such as Chancellor of the State James Kent, feared that with the ballot, the rising tide of industrial workers and Irish immigrants would be empowered to establish a revolutionary regime in America without firing a shot.

Often these tensions overflowed into the streets, as factions struggled for supremacy. The first large-scale manifestation of political violence in New York occurred in 1834; it was the first direct election for mayor, and it brought thousands of working-class voters into the political process. In addition, many of these voters were immigrants recently naturalized by Tammany specifically to cast their ballots for the Democratic Party as many times as they could during the three days of polling. Finally, strains between the two major parties were high, with the Whigs opposing what they considered President Andrew Jackson's strong-armed rule against banks and the commercial class. For mayor, the Whigs put up Gulian C. Verplanck, a former Democrat. Verplanck had the strong support of the city's manufacturers and merchants. The Democratic Party chose a committed Jacksonian, Cornelius Lawrence.

The rioting started in the poor and largely immigrant Sixth Ward on April 8, the first day of balloting. Tammany Democrats attacked Whigs at a central polling place with knives and clubs killing one and wounding twenty. The mob, which included city aldermen among the leaders and young gang members as foot soldiers, destroyed ballots and ransacked the building. Whig leaders appealed to the mayor for help but were rebuffed. The next day the Whigs organized into armed detachments and took positions at polls throughout the Sixth Ward. In addition, U.S. infantry troops loyal to President Jackson were deployed.

On April 10, the ballot boxes of the Sixth Ward were taken to city hall under guard, as thousands of partisans of both parties remained in the streets to hear that Lawrence was elected mayor by just over 200 votes. The Whigs, however, carried the Common Council. Violence again broke out in a crowd massed between Broadway and the Bowery; this time the mayor declared a state of emergency. Gun shops on Broadway were cleaned out as the Whigs marched on the state arsenal, only to be stopped by U.S. soldiers on horseback.[5]

The 1834 street battle was only the beginning of this militant style of politics; elections through the rest of the antebellum period were continually marred by fraud and violence. A new breed of ward politician was harnessing the energy of working-class gangs to vote "not merely once but twice or thrice if necessary . . . taking possession of a poll and holding it all day," according to one contemporary observer.[6]

Because of the absence of any kind of voter registration law or other oversight, ballot box stuffing, repeat voting, and other types of fraud were endemic at the polls. Even when a voter registration law was introduced in 1840, Democrats and Whigs quickly circumvented it. Both parties routinely hired repeat voters, who would come to the polls with some discrete identifier like an ink mark on the ear. A state law that imposed fines of up to $250 for voter fraud and intimidation was unenforceable in a city with a largely ineffective and corrupt police force.

Both Democrats and Whigs, who were fighting for power at the ward level and for control of the city itself, tapped the restless gangs of New York to accomplish this brazen fraud. Even Whigs had to admit that "the horde of ruffians owes its origin and long impunity to the two great political parties."[7]

Yet it was the Democratic Party, with its roots in Andrew Jackson's more inclusive and muscular democracy, that attracted the immigrants and laborers who became the backbone of the working-class gangs. Historian Amy Bridges notes that the Democratic Party's emphasis on the assertiveness of the common man invited the participation of groups like the Bowery Boys into the political process.

David Grimsted, in his study of rioting and disorder before the Civil War, says Jackson's "transformation of the presidency … helped create a sense of power justly residing in the hands of each man rather than in the state." Jackson's public persona, so different from his predecessors, "made him seem the anarchic hero," writes Grimsted, who reminds us that Jackson himself did not look favorably at this democracy of the streets.

Referring to the Democratic Party's recruitment of gang members to intimidate voters or raid polling places, former mayor and diarist Philip Hone accurately predicted these very gangs would soon aspire to power themselves. The politicians of Tammany Hall "have used these men to answer a temporary purpose, and [they] find now that the dogs they have taught to bark will bite them as soon as their political opponents."

Mike Walsh made his entrance into city politics during a chaotic Democratic Party nominating meeting on October 28, 1841, and like Hone's analogy of the dog taught to bark, the Bowery Boy leader was unleashed and headed for Tammany's throat. The Spartan Association crashed the party caucus, demanding Walsh's inclusion on the regular Tammany ticket as a candidate for State Assembly.

Walsh addressed Tammany leaders for about an hour "in a style of furious oratory," until the meeting degenerated into a shouting match and fistfight. Tammany refused to nominate Walsh, choosing instead a more reliable Democratic Party regular. The Spartan Association then mobilized hundreds of supporters at an outdoor rally, further angering Tammany

Democrats who saw this as yet another example of disintegrating party
discipline and factionalism out of control: the internal dissension "that
mother Tammany has failed to silence." Running for U.S. Congress against
Tammany as an independent on the pro-Catholic Carroll Hall ticket, Walsh
threw the race to the Whigs.[8]

Walsh, now excluded from Tammany councils, organized his own Spartan
ticket the following spring during the city's annual elections for Common
Council. Unsatisfied with just challenging Tammany on the ballot, Walsh
recruited fellow Bowery Boy and professional bare-knuckles boxer, Yankee
Bill Sullivan, to set the Spartans on an election-day rampage.

On April 11, 1842, they attacked polling places and roughed up voters
in the Sixth Ward and then engaged in a brawl with a Tammany-aligned
Irish Catholic gang, the Faugh O'Bhallas. By the early evening, the streets
were clogged with thousands of rioters, and the police were quickly
overwhelmed. Several people had been beaten severely, and downtown
homes were looted. Walsh's Bowery Boys took refuge in the Sixth Ward
Hotel at Centre and Duane Streets, defending it against an attack by more
than 300 Irish.

While the fight centered on control of the Democratic Party, it also
became a confrontation between Protestant and Catholic. So enraged
were the Bowery Boys by the assault from the Faugh O'Bhallas that they
proceeded to sack the home of Catholic Bishop John Hughes, which was
protected by parishioners. By nine o'clock that evening, the mayor had
ordered out the National Guard to protect St. Patrick's Cathedral on
Prince Street, but peace was not restored until midnight.

The mayhem started in what was dubbed the "bloody Sixth" Ward, but
there were widespread accusations in other lower Manhattan wards of
ballot tampering and repeat voting by regular Democrats, Whigs, and insurgents. Typical of the extreme methods employed to steal an election,
prisoners from Blackwell's Island were set free for the day by Tammany
operatives to vote as often as they could.

In some of the wards where fighting and intimidation occurred, such as
Walsh's Sixth, the Whigs prevailed as they reaped the rewards of a hopelessly
fractured Democratic Party. As a result, Tammany stridently demanded
new elections; the victorious Whigs, of course, resisted. A "transparent
sham," railed the Whig New York Tribune, which asked Tammany, is this
"Latin America or the land of Washington and Jay?" By May, the Whig-
controlled Common Council and the Democratic Mayor Robert Morris
were headed for a dangerous stalemate.[9]

With the council chambers guarded by more than 200 police, Mayor
Morris refused to recognize the newly elected Whig aldermen of the Sixth
Ward. He ran the May 16 session of the council with the incumbent

Democrats still in place. It was not until May 31 that the state supreme court, siding with the Whigs, forced Morris to swear in the new aldermen. The court found that the number of ballots destroyed or tampered with would not have changed the Whig victory in the Sixth Ward.

Many New Yorkers put the blame for this riot on Tammany itself, which since 1834, had openly utilized gang members as political enforcers and street fighters. Now the tide in the streets was turning against the Democratic regulars, and young workingmen were swearing allegiance to new and unstable political forces born in the poverty and discontent of the lower east side.

In particular, the *New York Tribune* pointed to Mayor Morris's weak response to the disturbance—saying he was unable to rein in the forces he and his Tammany predecessors had let loose. "Morris allowed the gangs full sway and was popular accordingly," writes historian Gustavus Myers. Or was Morris playing a devious game in using the gang warfare and disarray as a pretext to contest Whig victories. "Why were no arrests made of persons known to have been involved? Walsh was foremost in the fray yet there was no attempt to bring him to justice," the *Tribune* speculated. "It is because the mayor knows the chief rioters were of his own party."

But the *Tribune*'s conspiracy theory that united the mayor and Walsh against the Whigs is unlikely. Instead, Morris was in over his head and powerless to control the Bowery Boys now organized as a threatening political clubhouse. Walsh was in no mood to work with the regular Democrats who blocked his nomination for office in 1841 and again in the spring of 1842. Denouncing Morris as an enemy of the working class, Walsh pledged to support only those committed "fully to the interests of the laboring classes and the promotion of pure republicanism."[10]

The Spartan Band was not the only upstart political clubhouse vying for the laborer's loyalty in New York's lower east side wards during the 1840s. Many were led by rank opportunists who forged brittle alliances that crumbled easily in a saloon melee, and the self-promoting Walsh was certainly no exception. Ward-level politicians Levi D. Slamm and Isaiah Rynders also emerged from neighborhood gangs to battle each other and Tammany on the fringes of the two-party system. As a result, the two-party system in New York looked more like a patchwork of minor parties formed around rival street fighters. "We have six or seven third parties here [New York City] and we want to know which is the true one, which has the right hand?" the *New York Herald* asked.

This variety of working-class factions, with their fluid affiliations and ties to the city's gang subculture, prompted the *Herald* to describe a political landscape inhabited by "regulars and irregulars, regular-irregulars, irregular-regulars, old Democrats, young Democrats, old Hunkers, young Hunkers, indomitables and subterraneans of every description." Tammany Hall was faced with dozens of candidates competing for power in elections for city and state office, with all of the contenders claiming to represent workingmen and the true Party of Jackson.

Sober-minded observers of New York's chaotic politics worried that this persistent party factionalism could threaten the very existence of the Democratic Party in the city. "It would not surprise us to see the party split into fragments," one political commentator predicted.[11]

Walsh, with just under a hundred core Spartans, was able to drain enough votes from the regular Democratic Party ticket to hand the Whigs unexpected victories in 1841 and 1842. The concern was not only for contests in the city, but close races statewide that could be thrown to the Whigs, while the Democratic vote in the city remained divided. Additionally, the Democratic Party leadership was worried that Walsh was coming perilously close to putting his hands on more than $250,000 in salaries and patronage available to anyone who controlled the city's delegation to Albany.

The Bowery Boy had to be either defeated or tamed through a trade of his revolutionary ardor for a place inside Tammany. For Walsh, there was no accommodation with a Democratic Party interested more in its own privileges than the struggling factory worker. As he told New York Democrats crowded into Tammany's meeting hall, "you have been boasting in your newspapers and barrooms that I should not speak here. I'm now here in defiance of you all—yes in defiance ... of all your power, patronage and corruption."

That defiance continued to ring loudly in Tammany's ears as the presidential election year of 1844 approached, and Democratic Party caucuses were split based on their choice of a candidate for nomination. Most Democratic Party regulars were behind former President Martin Van Buren, a principled Free-Soiler whom Walsh particularly disliked.

Walsh's Spartans also backed presidential contenders, as did all the city's political clubs, in the hopes that if their man won the White House they would be rewarded with the most coveted patronage prize—positions in the New York Customs House. With more than 700 appraisers, clerks, weighers, and inspectors, the customs house paid exceptionally well, ample reward for those responsible for getting out the vote on Election Day.

Through the spring and summer of 1843, Walsh attempted to build a strong anti–Van Buren coalition in the city, in the hopes of denying the former president delegates to the New York state nominating convention in Syracuse. Both President John Tyler and John Calhoun courted the insurgent Democrats, and Walsh joined these forces to attack Tammany's favorite.

Mike Walsh briefly pledged his support to the Whig president for nomination on the Democratic Party ticket. But the Bowery Boy was motivated less out of enthusiasm for President John Tyler, above, than a loathing for Tammany's choice in 1844, Martin Van Buren. (Courtesy of the Library of Congress)

Although Tyler was a Whig, his nomination by that party seemed un-likely. Tyler, who assumed the presidency after the death of his predecessor William Henry Harrison, was out of step with a Whig Party dominated by Henry Clay. As the Whig *New York Tribune* suggested, Tyler opposed the party platform but "had no definite policy of his own to recommend." The Spartans cynically and briefly lent support to the incumbent president in the hopes of securing some customs house positions, but Tyler's opportu-nity inside the Democratic Party quickly evaporated. The Bowery Boy threw his full support behind Calhoun by the summer but was unable to

LOCO FOCO SCRAMBLE FOR COLLECTORS LICENSES.

Democratic Party politics in New York were characterized by patronage and favoritism. Licenses and government appointments, including those at the federal Customs House, were often traded for votes. (Courtesy of the Library of Congress)

outmaneuver Tammany, which secured the votes to endorse Van Buren at the New York State Democratic Party convention that August.

The anti–Van Buren forces were not finished, their anger not quite spent. They took their protest against party insiders to City Hall Park in October 1843, as Tammany Democrats gathered to choose candidates for the fall's state contests. Walsh demanded the Democrats grant the Spartans a place on the ticket. Chasing Tammany leaders and the police off the rostrum, Walsh, in typical style, asked if a coroner was present to declare the old party dead. The anti–Van Buren force "generated by the subterraneans," the *New York Herald* wrote, "comes into the world a full-grown babe with its fists doubled up and ready to strike everybody and anybody."[12]

Realizing Walsh's power to draw working-class votes from the regular Democratic column as well as wreak havoc in the streets, party leaders were finally prepared to offer the Bowery Boy a seat at the Tammany table if he would disband his unruly Spartans. Walsh refused to compromise. Seeing that the meeting was in the hands of the Bowery Boys, Tammany operatives hastily organized a separate caucus in another corner of the park. Anarchy reigned in the park, and Spartans taunted the police with shouts of "bloody police suckers;" the *New York Herald* asked how a political party divided into several violent factions can hope to govern.

The two sides nominated their own slates, with Walsh heading the Spartan ticket as a candidate for state senator, and fellow Bowery Boy David C. Broderick named for state assembly. In addition, the Spartan slate included Brooklyn cabinetmaker John Commerford for state assembly. Commerford brought strong labor credentials to the Spartan ticket; in 1835 he had led the New York City General Trades' Union, the first large-scale labor federation in America. Commerford was a prominent intellectual voice in the Spartan Association, later joining Walsh and George Henry Evans in the land-reform movement. Like Walsh and Evans, Commerford advocated a more equitable distribution of wealth in America and cheap land for settlement in the West.

Walsh's Spartans failed on Election Day 1843; by refusing to renounce gang warfare, Walsh played to the fears of many Democrats who saw in the Spartans the victory of mob rule. Party meetings too often degenerated into brawls, as the Bowery Boys stole ballot boxes and beat up newspaper reporters in broad daylight. In one caucus, Walsh shoved other speakers from the platform and loudly declared, "I don't play second fiddle to any man." It would be another three years before Tammany and the Spartans would begin to see the mutual benefits of compromise and accommodation.

One reason for Tammany's weakness in the face of this destructive factionalism was a general retreat of the so-called respectable classes from ward-level politics. As Whig intellectual Horace Greeley described it, the withdrawal of the merchant classes from the political life of the wards created a power vacuum, with the majority of citizens not even voting, "leaving the office seekers, grog shop keepers and hired rowdies a substantial control of our elections."[13]

As commercial possibilities grew in the expanding industrial economy of the 1840s, merchants abdicated ward-level political power to the professional politicians and clubhouses whose power base was increasingly working class. These laboring-class activists, with little economic opportunities, found the rough and tumble of local politics a path to upward mobility. The occupations of alderman and assistant alderman shifted in the 1840s from the merchants and lawyers of just two decades earlier to workingmen.

Historian of labor politics Edward Pessen, in his studies of wealth and power in antebellum America, shows a dramatic decline in the number of wealthy and eminent families on the New York Common Council through the 1830s. In 1826 the wealthy had comprised two-thirds of the city's aldermen, but that proportion fell to one-half by 1831, and to about two-fifths in 1840.

This is not to say that the levers of power in New York were handed to the working class. Pessen notes that although their numbers diminished significantly on the council during the 1830s and 1840s, the wealthiest 2 percent were still well represented in city government. The mayoralty, for example, was occupied mainly by men of wealth such as Philip Hone

in 1826, publisher James Harper in 1844, and merchants like sugar baron
William Havemeyer in 1845.[14]

At the ward level, conditions were different. Merchants and other
middle-class New Yorkers were ill-prepared to do political and often physical battle with the new breed of working-class politicians who were aligned
with gangs, fire companies, and target clubs. Democratic Party nominations were often held in saloons or even brothels in the rougher neighborhoods, intimidating the "respectable classes" from attending party caucuses
or voting.

Votes were traded for drink or cash, and meetings were packed with
men "who would cut their own mothers' throats for $10," editorialized the
New York Tribune. As Mike Walsh told the readers of the *Subterranean* at the
opening of the fall election cycle, "This is truly the season of caucuses.
Every grog shop, oyster box, barber shop, alley and charcoal wagon is the
scene of a caucus after dark."

Consequently, the Democratic Party was unable to curb its rebellious
factions and instill discipline at the neighborhood and clubhouse level.
Tammany had little organization at the streets and no effective year-round
presence in the wards until Mayor Fernando Wood's highly centralized
administration in the middle 1850s. With meetings frequently disintegrating into brawls and knife fights involving dozens of combatants, Democratic Party regulars often fled to a safe house to carry on political business.
Elections at the ward level could be hijacked by a small force of bullies
dispatched from a couple of firehouses.[15]

Tammany, no less than the Spartan Band, aggressively recruited workingmen to its ranks. However, Tammany leaders and aldermen, once
elected, were more interested in lining their own pockets than addressing
the concerns of their lower east side constituents. Aldermen and assistant
aldermen on the Common Council, with scant accountability, created their
own corrupt fiefdoms, with gang members serving loyally as enforcers on
the streets. The aldermen's principal activity was the distribution of about
$1.5 million in patronage a year by the mid-1840s.

The size of the political landscape grew too rapidly for Tammany to respond organizationally, as more wards were carved out of an expanding
metropolis. In 1808 there were nine wards represented by eighteen aldermen and assistant aldermen. By 1826 the city was divided into twelve wards
with twenty-four aldermen and assistant aldermen, and enlarged to seven-
teen wards a decade later with thirty-four representatives.

With this steadily climbing population, especially in the working-class
and immigrant wards of the city, Tammany was faced with a shortage of
the patronage jobs so important to building party discipline and loyalty at
the neighborhood level. The patronage resources available to a growing

number of aldermen were inadequate by the 1840s. In the first decades of the nineteenth century, the number of patronage jobs amounted to about 1,500, but by the 1840s, the number of positions grew by only 500, while the population of the city tripled from under 100,000 to more than 300,000. Aldermen did try to increase the number of city jobs with such creative but largely ineffective tactics as reducing salaries to make room for more employees. Tammany increased the pace of work on the Croton Aqueduct in the 1840s, giving rise to the term "pipe laying" to mean employing men on public works for partisan gain.

A corrupt and weak police department was yet another factor that encouraged ward-level politicians to enlist gangs to ensure the vote went their way. Police regularly received bribes or promotions from their local alderman to ignore or even aid gang members as they ransacked a polling place or bullied voters. The state legislature found in 1840 that some police officers were earning thousands of dollars a year in under-the-table payments from ambitious politicians who had their hands in the city treasury. Bowery Boy George Wilkes, writing in his *Police Gazette*, said police corruption in New York "has arrived at a mark which has never been exceeded even by the Turkish method of adjudication."

In his *History of Tammany Hall*, Gustavus Myers writes that aldermen of the Common Council freely employed "their gangs of lawbreakers at the polls" to secure an election victory. And because these aldermen controlled police appointments, voter fraud went unpunished as "policemen instantly became deaf, blind, and generally invisible." Wilkes referred to the "arrogant and overbearing conduct of members of the police force" who pressured voters to cast their ballots for the very aldermen who appoint them to the force. "The hour that the police are brought to bear on the political rights of the people, [their] usefulness and integrity wanes."

Demagogic politicians, whether from Tammany Hall or the rival clubhouses like the Spartans, could pack polling places by opening jail cells on Election Day with impunity. A grand jury investigation in 1846 found that politically-appointed prison officials routinely released convicts so they could vote illegally. The convicts, who were brought to the city by ferry the night before, were even given lodging, police protection, free drinks, and a set of clothes for their election-day outing. As few as thirty convicts voting dozens of times in a particular ward or wards could influence the results of a citywide election.

The *New York Tribune* wondered if politically motivated gang warfare could be suppressed "when these sneaky aldermen prowl around station houses for the sole purpose of discharging their partisan bullies [who] have fallen into the hands of the police." The problem became so severe by 1852, with more than one hundred gang members freed by their aldermen in just three months, that the police commissioner told his force to disobey any orders from aldermen to discharge a prisoner. Faced with inadequate police protection and politicians who protected gang members, many New Yorkers felt it was a time to arm themselves or be subject to intimidation on practically every street corner.[16]

Reformers warned that Tammany politicians, as well as challengers like the Spartan Band and Isaiah Rynders's Empire Club, "threatened to turn the art of government into the rule of the strong-armed tough." In 1843, the *New York Herald* observed that in America's largest city, "violence of the ruffians and government of the mob is supreme."

Mike Walsh's Spartans were without a doubt one of the more serious threats to the stability of the Democratic Party. Walsh insisted disingenuously that he was not the problem but represented popular anger and frustration with the corrupt and exclusive clique running Tammany. While Walsh said it would be politically popular "to chant down with the standing army—abolish all police," he claimed to recognize the need for law and order and proposed to take the appointment of police officers out of the Common Council and put it into the hands of a stronger executive. "Corrupt aldermen are often kept in office for years by illegal votes. The remedy is plain; take from the aldermen all patronage, all appointments for office."[17]

Above all, Walsh phrased his challenge to Tammany in the provocative language of class warfare. Walsh called Democratic Party nominations "an insulting and ridiculous farce," stacked against honest workers in favor of party insiders "who are continually sticking themselves at the head of everything ... manufacturing public opinion by the cart load and shoving it down your throats."

He described Tammany caucuses that ignored the voters and consisted of backroom deals, intimidation, and bribes to the highest bidder. The poorest were bribed with drinks and herded to rigged meetings by their employers who were often rewarded later with city contracts. When it suited Tammany, the working class was the "bone and sinew of the country," Walsh said, but they "use us until there is nothing but bone and sinew left."

Walsh declared there was only one solution: a revolution from below. "We must purify our own party." To purify the party was to remove the opportunists and the greedy, who only sought elective office for personal gain—those "that make a trade of politics" and concoct rules of the game so complicated and secretive so as to exclude "the mass of people." In colorful language that was the signature of the *Police Gazette*, fellow-Spartan George Wilkes told his readers that "a knot of mutton heads can secure the election of a candidate and then govern him to answer their private ends, regardless of public good."

Purifying the party also meant opening Tammany to the growing numbers of factory workers and unskilled laborers who were crowding into the city's manufacturing district in Walsh's core Sixth and Fourteenth wards. It was in these wards that hundreds of sweatshops turned out clothing and shoes, employing the city's native-born and immigrant poor.

Walsh told these newly proletarianized factory hands that cracking the political system had to start at the local level—in the Democratic Party clubhouses of the working-class wards. Get involved, he urged them. "Don't stand with folded arms. Go to your primary meetings, not to act as automatons and to say yes or no as you are told, but to act like freemen."[18]

To rid the system of closed-door nominating meetings controlled by Tammany operatives, Walsh and his Spartans advocated a system of direct primary elections in the wards. In typical fashion Walsh said the "brainless and unprincipled nonentities" chosen for the Democratic Party slate to local and state office betrayed the working class by serving "the secret caucuses of Tammany." Wilkes predicted that direct primary elections would "put an end to the bargaining and selling" of votes. "As matters are conducted now the fighting crowds dictate to the masses the representatives of the state and nation."

As an angry outsider looking in, Walsh attacked a system of useless but lucrative patronage jobs that rewarded "unprincipled political favorites." He exposed a scheme in which newspapers promised their endorsements to council candidates in exchange for city printing contracts or even cash payoffs. "I will yet ride over all this rotten opposition like a balloon over a dung hill," he predicted.

Walsh promised those on the lowest rungs of the economic ladder that their hard work in defense of the party of Jackson would be rewarded. "Tammany Hall belongs to us," not the Democrats that campaign for the laborer's vote "only to [turn] round and frown upon us as though we were beneath them" after Election Day. For the leader of the Spartans, "no man can be a good political Democrat without [being] a social democrat, [serving] to elevate the downtrodden masses beneath you."

Pointing to Tammany leaders huddled at one end of City Hall Park during the chaotic 1843 party caucus, Walsh asked his followers, "Are we to bark like dogs for our masters alone? ... We have stood by that [Democratic] party in the shade of adversity and now we are told we have no voice in its councils. It is because we are poor that such a decision [was] made." Walsh preferred that purification of the Democratic Party come through the ballot; if not, he and the Spartans advocated change in terms that sounded to many like a call for armed revolution. "We are not to be trampled with impunity," warned the leader of the Bowery Boys. "Like the pendulum of the clock, we will not stop in the middle, but will bound with the same force to the opposite side."[19]

Walsh was reflecting more than a decade of anger among the city's industrial proletariat at a Democratic Party leadership unwilling to cede power to a new generation of working class advocates. As early as 1829, New York laborers sought a political solution to their economic distress with the Working Men's Party. However, that experiment in third-party labor politics, largely engineered by George Henry Evans, was quickly co-opted and neutralized by the Democrats and even the Whigs. After the failure of the Working Men's Party, labor radicals led a rally in 1834 to demand a Workingmen's Committee inside the Democratic Party, with representatives selected from each ward. When that was defeated by the party regulars, these anti-Tammany Democrats walked out to form the Locofoco wing in 1835. With a platform based largely on opposition to monopolies and government preferences to business, the Locofocos attracted labor activists such as Ely Moore and Levi Slamm. The Locofocos return to the Tammany fold after 1837 was treachery, Walsh said. He told his "subterranean democrats" that whether it was the Locofocos or the regular Democrats in Tammany, the only thing that changed for the work-ers was "a change of masters."

Given the short tenure of the Working Men's Party and the Locofocos, Walsh was skeptical of attempts to create an independent labor party, believing that third parties in American politics are doomed to failure. "The idea is the production of a weak and silly brain. Such things may be produced by local grievances—but they can exist [only] for a moment and never can extend far," he said referring to the Working Men's Party. Instead, New York's laborers, by their sheer strength of numbers, could take political power on Election Day through a Democratic Party purged of the "rich and idle dandies," Walsh said. In fact, the Democratic Party owed its success to the working-class voter who "battled faithfully" for its Jacksonian principles.

While the Working Men's Party and the Locofoco faction posed little threat to the major parties, the political clubhouses that followed in the 1840s appeared more menacing. Their members included a volatile mix of radicals and young foot soldiers recruited from the gangs of the poorest wards. The tactics of Walsh's Spartan Band were considered beyond the pale by even the most democratic of the Jacksonians. Editor William Leggett was a champion of the Locofocos, but he feared the anti-Democratic Party mob. "No one can tell where or when the flood of popular fury will subside," Leggett wrote after the election-day disturbances of 1834. The *New York Herald* called the Spartans the strongest and "most troubling" opposition to the Democratic Party, but admitted that while they are "wild and foolish, they have more moral and political integrity than the old rogues" of Tammany.[20]

Walsh and fellow-Spartan Edward Strahan, who edited the *Progressive Democrat*, made it clear that they, unlike the Locofocos, were not about to be co-opted or bought by Tammany's old rogues, "but will be free and independent." George Henry Evans urged the city's industrial workers to get involved in the political struggles of the day but reject the regular Democratic Party organization until it was run by the workers. "Every working man should be a politician," he said.

As Walsh proclaimed on the banner of the *Subterranean*, the Bowery Boy was "independent in everything—neutral in nothing." This dogged independence in politics, as well as in manners, was the pride of the Bowery Boys, who might "quarrel among themselves, yet let an enemy appear or let a friend be threatened, and they are devotion itself," as working-class journalist George Foster observed.[21]

Eventually, however, the political clubhouses realized they could not topple the old rogues entrenched at Tammany, and the old rogues needed the working-class vote to remain in power. The result, by the late 1840s, was accommodation. Moreover, the violent rivalries among the clubhouse factions and their poor skills as political actors tended to doom any chance they had of organizing as a real force for change. In the final analysis, The Spartans were more Bowery Boy gang members than serious revolutionaries. While clubhouse leaders employed the rhetoric of revolution when they wanted to appeal to the b'hoys in the streets, Slamm's Locofocos, Rynders's Empire Club, and Walsh's Spartans fell in line with the mainstream Democrats when it suited their political ambitions.

Whether working within the Democratic Party or battling against it, the Bowery Boys appealed to masses of workers who were denied formal political power. To recruit young men to their ranks and consolidate their hold on neighborhood politics, Walsh, Slamm, and Rynders tapped the informal power structures of the streets, including saloons, gun clubs, and volunteer fire brigades.

The weakness of government institutions, including the Common Council and the police, provided the Bowery Boys a wide political space to operate. New York City, at the time, was not governed; it existed, writes Jerome Mushkat in his modern history of Tammany Hall. Diarist Philip Hone described a city "infested by gangs ... brought up in the taverns, educated at the polls of elections and following the fire engines as a profession."

It would be inaccurate to make a clear distinction between gang member, saloonkeeper, politician, firefighter, and labor organizer. A Bowery Boy was often a mix of these, using one of the typically working-class roles to strengthen the other. The gangs of New York also evolved out of some of the tougher trades of the city—trades that attracted free-spirited men with little patience for middle-class affectations and conventions.

The butcher, with bloodstained apron and a strong sense of fraternity, was one such trade that was bound to the identity of the Bowery Boy. The butcher of the New York slaughterhouse was a bona fide urban cowboy, "a class of men whose influence in sound democratic principles are second to none." Two prominent Bowery Boys were closely identified with the slaughterhouse; Bill Harrington, a Centre Market butcher and semiprofessional boxer, was also a ward-level leader of the Whigs. And in the middle 1850s, Butcher Bill Poole emerged as an immensely popular working-class figure.[22]

Saloons were a convenient gathering place for politically active men, especially those like the Spartans who were locked out of regular Democratic Party meeting halls. Significantly, the saloonkeeper had a standing in the neighborhood that put him at the center of political and social life on the lower east side. With plenty of friends among the all-male electorate, saloonkeepers could rally regular customers on Election Day, deploying them to whatever polling place needed a few extra voters. The proprietor who got the vote out could be rewarded with political office; that, in turn, provided him the opportunity to dispense patronage jobs and solidify a loyal political base on the neighborhood level. Said one historian of Tammany Hall, this chain of events was a "circle of circumstances that was almost unbreakable." With the Spartan Association headquartered at Manus Kelly's saloon in the Sixth Ward Hotel, it was no wonder Mike Walsh called the saloons "the homes and nurseries of democracy." Referring to the often grim and despairing life in working-class neighborhoods, Walsh remarked that the saloons served a real need for the factory workers "who have scarcely room enough to turn around in, [and] seek excitement in public places."

Generally, the consumption and sale of alcohol was an important facet of the social life and economy of antebellum New York. By the 1820s, alcohol was sold in the backrooms of the increasing number of neighborhood greengroceries. Like the saloons, the greengroceries also became a center of neighborhood gang and political activity. In some cases the greengrocer could be counted on for a quick loan or to provide a place for the unemployed to gather on a Monday morning as employers scouted for idle hands to put in a day's work. In Mike Walsh's Sixth Ward, there were 204 groceries and 169 licensed taverns by 1850, serving a population of about 24,000.[23]

Gang members who enlisted in the service of political clubhouses also joined the city's volunteer fire companies. These fire brigades, each with their own distinctive traditions, insignia, and membership, served as a proving ground for demonstrating masculine bravado, courage, fighting skills, and leadership. Drawing from both the middle and working classes, the volunteer firemen numbered close to 4,000 by the middle 1850s. For the most part, the Bowery Boys, including Walsh's Spartans, were connected with Howard Engine Company No. 34.

The fire companies, which organized their own target and gun clubs, also took on a paramilitary cast. Fire brigades gave the Bowery Boys and other New York gangs an organizational structure, internal discipline, and equipment essential to the safety and security of the city. By the 1840s, New Yorkers were accustomed to watching armed Bowery Boys marching in the numerous firemen's parades that usually doubled as political rallies.

Sean Wilentz notes that the firemen's politicization was a reaction to failed attempts by city leaders to tame the volunteers. As early as the 1820s, the public questioned the desirability of a volunteer force that was too loosely controlled by city authorities and increasingly manipulated for political purposes. Of particular concern were the so-called runners: adolescent volunteers with plenty of time to loiter around the firehouse, steal what they could at the scene of a fire, or engage in pitched battles with rival companies.

The Common Council regarded the runners as a public nuisance and in 1824, warned fire brigades to eliminate the runner or risk losing their equipment. The council was ignored, and relations between the volunteer firemen and the city only deteriorated. Firefighters countered that without runners, two-thirds of the overburdened firehouses would be paralyzed. Fire companies typically used the runners to help drag heavy equipment to the scene of the fire. In fact, firefighters said most runners quickly learned the ropes well enough to become full-fledged firefighters.

In 1834, the council again attempted to control runners by excluding them from the firehouses except in the case of an alarm. Firemen interpreted the council's attempts at curtailing the runners as a direct attack on their autonomy. By this time, the fire brigades were emerging as a political force in the city and, in a demonstration of their contempt for the council's edicts, firemen rioted in August 1835 as a fire blazed. The fire brigades were, as Philip Hone observed, so powerful "that they appear to consider themselves above the law."[24]

It was the devastating Christmas fire of 1835 that brought the fire brigades to the center of New York's chaotic political stage. Destroying more than 650 structures and resulting in a staggering $25 million in losses, the fire of 1835 was unprecedented, even in a city that had suffered its share of fires. The blaze started on December 16 in a Pearl Street warehouse when stove coals ignited a leaky gas pipe. The force of the explosion literally tore through the roof. With temperatures that night plunging to well below zero, hydrants—and even the East River—froze. For their part, firefighters were fatigued and demoralized. They had fought two fires the night before and were, as usual, shorthanded. While the city population had grown from about 166,000 in 1825 to 270,000 in 1835, the number of firemen for that period increased by only 285 to a total of 1,500. It was not nearly enough manpower for a city at that time plagued with between 150 and 250 fires a year.

The firefighters said the failure to contain the downtown blaze, including a late decision to dynamite buildings in the path of the flames, was the fault of the Common Council. The council, on the other hand, laid the blame on the popular chief engineer, James Gulick. Aldermen who had been trying to curtail the firefighters' fiercely protected independence saw an opportunity to finally take control of the volunteer brigades. With this political collision, New York firemen found strength as a voting bloc.

The council's case against Gulick and the fire brigades was strengthened after Alderman Samuel Purdy was attacked by members of Engine Company No. 10 on the night of January 1, 1836. An assault on a city alderman now demonstrated that the city and the fire brigades were approaching open warfare. To make matters worse, Gulick, while not condoning the attack, refused to cooperate with the council's official investigation.

On May 4, 1836, the council, in a secret session of its fire and water committee, sacked Gulick. Firefighters responded by going on strike the next day, in the middle of another downtown fire. Within months, more than 800 firefighters out of the 1,500-man force turned in their badges rather than serve under the new chief engineer, John Riker. The number of fires in New York grew through 1836, and cases of sabotaged equipment were reported. A fire on September 27, 1836, resulted in a pitched battle between firefighters serving under Riker and those loyal to Gulick, now organized as the Resigned Firemen's Association.

That same year, Gulick ran for city register on the Whig ticket, and with firemen voting as a bloc for the first time, Gulick won with a commanding 19,443 votes, beating the Tammany rival by more than 6,000 votes. Gulick's wide margin of victory reflected the fact that firefighters crossed party lines to vote for their leader. The firefighters now had the city's attention as they marched through the streets like a conquering army in a mile-long torchlight parade to celebrate their victory at the polls.[25]

Emboldened, the firemen in 1837 organized to elect a Whig Common Council and mayor. Their success was helped by the Democratic Party split that year between Tammany regulars and the Locofocos. The new mayor, Aaron Clark, was particularly popular with the firemen because he had called for an open session when the council voted on Gulick's ouster. Under the Whigs, the chief engineer received a pay raise, and the volunteer brigades retained their coveted autonomy. The Common Council did try to cut down on rowdy behavior by dividing the city into five fire districts, an act that reduced the number of brigades rushing through the streets to fires far from the firehouse.

With the return of the Democrats to city hall in 1839, the power struggle continued. Mayor Isaac L. Varian, a fireman himself, ousted the chief engineer and stacked the Board of Foreman and Assistants with Tammany men by creating twenty new hose companies. The phony fire brigades, which did not possess so much as a bucket among them, were dubbed June Bugs. Blatantly political, the move backfired. Tammany retreated, and the June Bugs were dissolved. Firefighters remained politicized through the 1840s, split among Tammany Democrats, Whigs, and insurgent clubhouses. It was not until 1865 that an apolitical professional force was finally created.

The brigades, with their quasi-military hierarchy, uniforms, and esprit de corps, gave young factory workers a model of organization and a vehicle to express themselves politically at parades and rallies. The increasing involvement of the firefighters in the social and political struggles of the city's industrial laborers lies, in part, in the shifting class composition of the volunteer brigades through the antebellum years.

JUNE BUGS SQUIRTING

As New York's volunteer fire department became highly politicized, Tammany's attempt to create brigades of loyal Democrats, dubbed June Bugs, could only backfire. (Courtesy of the Library of Congress)

The city's population explosion demanded a larger pool of young men from different classes to staff the firehouses; between 1836 and 1854 the number of firefighters more than doubled from 1,500 to close to 4,000. The ranks of the fire brigades, dominated by merchants and artisans in the first decades of the nineteenth century, gave way to greater participation by factory workers and immigrants.

Firemen coming from the poorer segments of society were less zealous in protecting the property of the upper classes, and on occasion their rowdiness spilled over into looting at the scene of a fire. In a letter to the *New York Herald*, one fireman expressed the sentiment of many middle class New Yorkers who had earlier joined the fire companies and were now leaving "disgusted . . . with the political influence [that] keeps the disorderly characters from being expelled." Newspapers editorialized that for the most part the fire department "is disgraced by its connection with . . . the most disreputable characters," and some firemen called for the establishment of an internal police force, a measure adopted by Baltimore.[26]

Working-class political factions were well represented in the ranks of this new generation of volunteer firemen. Firefighters expressed the same anti-Tammany feelings that motivated the lower east side clubhouses whose members saw an arrogant Democratic Party leadership at odds with the strengthening industrial proletariat. Common Council meetings could be packed with club-wielding firemen showing their support for one alderman or another. The Democratic *New York Evening Post* accused aldermen of "perpetually tampering with the fire companies" in an effort to politicize them. As the historian of antebellum New York Edward Spann has noted, the man who could organize even a small bloc of voters from a couple of fire brigades could control politics in the ward. New York fireman Augustine Costello described firefighters who "could extinguish the political ambition of the most popular citizen as readily as they could put out the light of a blazing tar barrel."

Costello cautioned that it was only a matter of time before the firefighters would "control a political party or a political party will control them." With Mike Walsh's Bowery Boys in mind, chief engineer Alfred Carson warned in a report to the Common Council that the city could be held captive by a few demagogues ruling through fire companies and their well-armed gun clubs. He also claimed that as many as half the fires in the city were the result of arson.[27]

Carson convinced the council to confine fire companies to newly created fire districts that helped keep rival companies safely apart and also to make it illegal for runners to wear insignia. But Carson was largely ignored by aldermen beholden to firefighters and gangs for political support. In fact, some aldermen attempted, but failed, to oust Carson for his frank assessment.

Carson's subsequent reports to the Council in 1851 and 1852 again warned that through affiliated target and gun clubs, the fire brigades were a potential revolutionary force. The names of some of these target clubs, such as the Gulick Guards, indicated the politicized nature of the fire brigades and their affinity with the antebellum gang culture.

In 1843, the militancy of the fire brigades so concerned the city that the Common Council was forced to expel the Black Joke Engine Company from the department. Black Joke was led by Bowery Boy Malachi Fallon, a Walsh rival and Tammany partisan. His firehouse was stocked with an arsenal of muskets, pistols, and even a small cannon loaded with metal slugs and chains. Fallon was typical of the way gang leaders intersected with the politics of the city. He was a saloon owner; commander of the uniformed and well-armed gun club, the Black Joke Volunteers; and a warden of the Tombs jail where he often released partisans for service on Election Day.[28]

Bowery Boys like Fallon and Walsh were skilled at using the firehouses to build their political clubs with well-organized structures including officers, easy access to printing, and a network on the streets that could rally its minions when needed.

Typical of the aggressive style of politics arising from the volunteer fire brigades and neighborhood gangs was a large-scale downtown parade organized by the Bowery Boys in 1839, during the darkest days of a devastating economic downturn. Calling themselves "hard-fisted freemen" and patriots in the tradition of Thomas Paine, they spoke in the tough-talking language of the lower east side, promising to "flog the enemy with a long pole—a strong pole." Riding on horseback, Bowery Boy leaders, followed by fire brigades with their distinctive insignia, urged laborers to "awaken every patriot, every good friend of liberty ... for the coming election."

It wasn't only feelings of patriotism that brought the firefighters and Bowery Boys into the streets. These were groups distinguished by their antagonism to the middle and upper classes or, as they preferred, "the aristocracy." The revolution in France that deposed Charles X in 1830 was honored by a firemen's parade led by Gulick as grand marshal. A resolution celebrated "the triumphant and glorious contest for liberty and the overthrow of tyranny in France."[29]

To many New Yorkers, the city was fast becoming divided between the laboring class and the aristocracy; the respectable classes and the dangerous classes. New Yorkers saw a city where politics was distinguished by neighborhood demagogues who employed gangs in the battle for power; and where the government was either too weak or too corrupt to impose any order.

Reformers, such as Charles Loring Brace, predicted the revolutionary potential of this "dangerous class" represented by squabbling political clubhouses operating out of saloons. The city's street culture was for Brace an inchoate society, but he warned fellow New Yorkers that when the "multitude of boys swarming now in every alley come to know their [political] power and use it" they will unleash a war of classes and "leave this city in ashes."[30]

The opening shots of this class war came with a souring economy after 1837, and by 1849, as the city faced armed insurrection in the Astor Theater riot, New Yorkers were convinced that the European revolutions of 1848 were sweeping across the Atlantic. At the center of this revolutionary activity were Mike Walsh's Bowery Boys.

chapter 2

The Bowery Boys: Radical in Everything

The aristocracy, whether American or European, was at the heart of the Bowery Boys' discontent. Like Mike Walsh, Walt Whitman questioned the authority of any political party and embraced the romance of revolution. In his poem "Resurgemus," Whitman expresses his enthusiasm for the European uprisings of 1848.

> Not a grave of those slaughtered ones,
>
> But is growing its seed of freedom,
>
> In its turn to bear seed.
>
> Which the winds carry afar and resow,
>
> And the rains nourish

For Whitman, there was a poetics of class resentment. "I see an aristocrat / I see a smoucher grabbing the good dishes exclusively to himself and grinning at the starvation of others as if it were funny, / I gaze on the greedy hog."

Walsh echoed the poet's sentiment in his collection of speeches. "There cannot be anything peculiarly honorable in wealth though it certainly does enable fellows ... to gratify ... their dirty animal appetites." Walsh referred to his Bowery Boys as "young men who are dependent solely on the labor of their own hands.... They are radical in everything."[1]

Historian Sean Wilentz describes Walsh as "alone among the prominent New York politicians of the mid-1840s to speak in an unvarnished language

of class conflict, thrusting the labor theory of value into his listeners' faces."
George Henry Evans, who joined Walsh's Spartans in the struggle to organize a citywide labor union and press for land reform, said that while this
country's boundless frontier was a safety valve that could protect it from
convulsions like Europe's, revolution was still a last resort for American
workers destined to wrest power from the propertied classes.

In the final analysis, the Spartans were effective in articulating a protest
to the emerging capitalist order, yet they were too unstable to aspire to a
revolutionary movement. The Spartan Band remained, through its short
life, a ragtag street gang, which Walsh, in typical bluster, called "the Goth
and Vandal eruption of the shirtless and unwashed democracy."

The roots of the Bowery Boys' rebellion were in the Industrial Revolution, which transformed the American urban workplace and contributed to
the widening gulf between classes. Starting in the 1820s, economic and
political power was increasingly concentrated in the hands of the commercial and merchant elite: those who were investing in the new economy of
an industrializing America.

Historian Edward Pessen's data on antebellum wealth describes a rising
commercial class, which by 1845 represented 4 percent of the total population but controlled 80 percent of the city's wealth. In a city of almost
630,000 in 1855, only about 15,000, or under 3 percent, were landowners.
While there were only 102 New Yorkers with personal property assessed
at over $20,000 in 1820, there were almost 1,000 with wealth valued at
more than $100,000 by 1845. New York was becoming a city of
millionaires—twenty-one of them by 1845. Sean Wilentz calls these
changing patterns of wealth in New York between 1820 and 1840 a "steady
redistribution to the top, a phenomenon common to all expanding
commercial capitals."[2]

In America's commercial capital, the wealthy may have abandoned politics at the ward level, but they still held on to the mayor's office, the leadership of city departments, and federal patronage positions, as well as boards
of banks, insurance companies, and corporations seeking city contracts. As
directors of New York's banks, wealthy families controlled access to credit
and rates through the banks' discount committees. As owners of most of
the city's lots and real estate, they also determined the price of housing.
Reflecting the sentiments of working-class New York, faced with low
wages and steadily rising prices, Walsh told his Bowery Boys, "The more
wealth is concentrated in the hands of the few, the more miserable must be
the many."[3]

John Jacob Astor and Philip Hone were typical of the new rich. Hone
was a prominent merchant who invested in large-scale industrial ventures
such as textiles, coal mines, railroads, canals, and banks. Astor made his fortune

in real estate, investing about $2 million in Manhattan property; after the panic of 1837 Astor was quick to take advantage of the plunge in prices. By the time of his death in 1848, the Astor landholdings were worth $20 million and were yielding more than $200,000 annually in rent. Echoing the sentiments of many New Yorkers before and since, Astor said, "Could I begin life again, knowing what I now know, and had money to invest, I would buy every foot of land on the island of Manhattan."[4]

Fueling this new economy was a transportation and technological revolution that was quickly industrializing American production. Steam-driven machinery and innovations in transportation, such as the Erie Canal and the railroads, opened new markets and energized competition in the first half of the nineteenth century.

Completed in 1825, the Erie Canal connected the Great Lakes and the American Midwest to the New York port. Before the canal, it took twenty days to move cargo from Buffalo to New York City at a cost of $100 a ton. The canal reduced these figures to just eight days at a cost of $15 to $25 a ton. Railroads, which also opened markets in the Midwest to New York manufacturers, almost tripled in track miles between 1840 and 1849. The invention of the sewing machine, first patented in 1842, brought mass production to the clothing industry. As a result, the value of clothing sold wholesale in New York climbed from $2.5 million to $20 million between 1841 and 1853.

This high-charged prosperity in all sectors of manufacturing demanded changes in the method of production; the days of the small master craftsman supplying the demand for manufactured goods were coming to an end. Only those manufacturers with large-scale production could meet the burgeoning demand and effectively compete; in other words, those with access to capital, credit, and a large, cheap labor pool.

In 1840, an American manufacturer employing a dozen workers was considered large, but by 1855, about 70 percent of the manufacturing labor force worked for companies with more than twenty-five employees. In 1847, *The Voice of Industry* noted the societal changes, editorializing that "the mammoth establishments ... send their [products] to distant parts of the country and reduce smaller capitalists, ... constantly killing out their rivals."[5]

The new large-scale manufacturing put a premium on specialization and division of labor in place of artisanship. Employers hired fewer skilled journeymen in favor of production lines staffed by unskilled workers, who were paid at piece rates that could barely feed a family. Evans looked to his native England and warned workers in New York that they could expect a small number of capitalists to exploit the labor of hundreds; "the capitalist can pay any price he wants."

In the printing trades, for example, skilled pressmen were thrown out of work with the introduction of steam-powered presses worked by partially trained journeymen and child apprentices. A printer by trade, Evans said the swelling number of child laborers in the workforce was not only pushing wages down, but also contributing to the gang culture of the streets. Walsh, throughout his career, took up the cause of child labor, and as state assemblyman in 1847, he launched an investigation of child labor in New York factories. He proposed to at least limit their hours and set a minimum age that a child could be employed. Walsh's fellow legislators rejected the measure by a vote of seventy-one to thirty-seven.

With the advent of factory production came a drop in wages and the standard of living in practically every sector of manufacturing. Aside from the changes in production, New York workers also lost significant ground in a devastating economic downturn, the panic of 1837. In just a few months after the start of the panic, thousands were thrown out of work; in all, a third of the city's working population was unemployed by 1839.

Wages plummeted suddenly, falling by 30 to 50 percent between 1839 and 1843; and wages remained depressed through the 1840s, even as businesses recovered. For example, the pay of journeymen hatters fell from an average of $48 a month to $32 between 1835 and 1845. In the unskilled trades and in the textile sweatshops, wages fell to under $30 a month, not even subsistence for many families.[6]

Factory production meant not only a decline in wages but also a diminished status for the urban worker. Without access to capital and credit to compete effectively, the journeyman's once sure path to opening his own shop as a master craftsman was cut short. For historians of Jacksonian America, the change was far from just a matter of economics—it was a change in temper and ideals as workers lost upward mobility and independence. In many cases, the master craftsman was separated from the production process as he hired foremen to supervise. As a result, relations between employer and laborer became far more impersonal.

Propertyless working-class families in New York who found their incomes declining through the 1840s also faced unscrupulous employers and landlords, who drove them deeper into poverty. Some employers paid their workers with depreciated notes bought on a kind of open currency market, spurring Walsh, Evans, and other reformers to demand that workers be paid only with specie. Generally, the cost of living increased sharply by as much as 50 percent between 1843 and 1850, and as Manhattan land values rose, so did rents. Landlords were brutal in their treatment of tenants, sometimes demanding six months' rent in advance. In 1848 tenants demanded the New York State Legislature set a ceiling on landlord profits from rent and end the practice of ejecting one tenant in order to rent to another at a higher rate.

Taking up the case of powerless tenants, the Bowery Boy said that downtown landlords were raising rents so high that three or four working-class families were forced to share a single home. Referring to 1845, Walsh said "heartless and insatiable" landlords raised rents in most parts of the city by ten percent. "Some of them [landlords] allege that [raising rents] is owing to the great increase in taxes, thereby admitting the great truth ... all taxes are in reality paid exclusively by those who labor."

Some New Yorkers, fearing the idle poor, called for sweeping up the unemployed and putting them to work building sewers and other public works. Horace Greeley lamented that New York was "a city without order or organization in its police, without the means of removing the noxious refuse, without restraint on the noise and misbehavior of the rowdies."[7]

Class resentment and the consequent "misbehavior of the rowdies" occasionally erupted into full-scale warfare, as working-class families struggled to survive in the years after the panic. Pushed to the edge of starvation, young men took to the streets in violent protest in the unusually cold winter of 1837. As the price of food and coal escalated sharply, rumors circulated that merchants were hoarding stocks to keep prices artificially high. The price of flour climbed from $7 a barrel in the fall of 1836 to close to $12 by February 1837. Consequently, bread was suddenly out of reach to the poorest families. A rally at City Hall Park on February 13 drew more than 5,000, including members of working-class anti-Tammany factions and their gangs. John Windt, later a leader of the Spartan Association, and Alexander Ming Jr. of the Locofoco faction, told the crowd that barrels of flour were hoarded at Eli Hart and Company near Courtlandt Street.

Once there, the mob proceeded to throw as many as 500 barrels of flour and several hundred bushels of wheat onto the streets below, which became knee-deep in flour in some places. It took two National Guard companies to finally break up the crowd. Another merchant, S. H. Herrick and Company on Water Street, was also plundered. Ming was hailed as a hero on the streets, but his actions resulted in dismissal from his post at the customs house, which he held for six years. Ming was reinstated after convincing friends in Washington that he was not responsible for extremists who went on a rampage.[8]

For young American-born workers struggling to survive the transition from small-scale artisan manufacturing to a system of factories and sweated trades, ethnic and class loyalties often competed. In some cases, the divide between Protestants and Catholics proved stronger; in other cases, class antagonisms prevailed, with Catholics and Protestants putting their animosity aside to attack what they viewed as the moneyed aristocracy. Walsh,

Evans, and the Bowery Boys of the Spartan Band were less inclined than other New York gangs and clubhouses, which were fiercely anti-Catholic, to blame cheap immigrant labor for the unemployment and decline in wages following the panic of 1837.

John Commerford, president of the New York City General Trades' Union, became a close ally of the Spartans, and like Walsh, Commerford addressed both the American artisan mechanic and the proletarianized immigrant worker by phrasing economic issues in the language of class conflict. Commerford said native-born workers, who had become wage laborers in sweatshops by the mid-1830s, were just as exploited as newly arrived Irish and Germans. For Commerford, all were the victims of an impersonal capitalism, mass production, and especially, employers keen to replace higher-paid American journeymen with immigrant labor.

One Bowery Boy whose virulent anti-Catholicism stood in contrast to the more class-conscious Spartans was Ned Buntline. Born Edward Z. C. Judson, he adopted Buntline as a pen name; his 1848 novel, *The Mysteries and Miseries of New York*, detailed the grinding poverty of the city's working class. In his newspaper, *Buntline's Own*, he promised to expose the exploitation of sewing girls toiling in sweatshops by printing the names of every shop that paid wages as low as six cents a shirt. Sympathetic to exploited sewing girls, Buntline nevertheless was aligned with anti-Catholic political movements such as the American Republican Party in the 1840s, and he was a founder in 1853 of the ultraxenophobic Know Nothings.

To Buntline, artisan workers were being stripped of their livelihood and their dignity by greedy capitalists in league with Catholic immigrants intent on tearing down America's republican institutions. Like many higher-paid native-born butchers, printers, and carpenters who followed the American Republicans, Buntline believed the solution was to resist industrialization and keep unskilled immigrant laborers off U.S. shores.

Buntline and Walsh did stand on the same side of the barricades during the anti-English Astor Theater riots of 1849, but they failed to strike a lasting alliance. Walsh called Buntline's anti-Catholicism "the most illiberal branch of stupidity." Halting immigration, said Walsh, was "a ridiculous panacea of these poor deluded political quacks." Working-class advocates who opposed the nativist impulse recognized that much of the immigrant labor was engaged in digging ditches or working on canal projects that did not displace skilled journeymen. Referring to the American Republicans, Walsh said, "they stupidly lay all the blame on immigrants for low wages and high rents."[9]

Buntline was allied with Isaiah Rynders, whose Empire Club fought the Spartans for turf in the Sixth and Fourteenth wards. Rynders, who owned several saloons, first came to New York in the mid-1830s, after a brief career as a gambler, cook, and knife fighter along the Mississippi River. He also worked on Hudson River lumber boats and served as captain of a sloop, keeping the title of captain through his political career. Rynders later renamed his faction Americus to reflect its anti-Irish character.

Rynders, like Walsh, had a gift for theatrics that appealed to his mostly young followers. In one instance he wept publicly after receiving a lock of Andrew Jackson's hair from a Tennessee politician who had been made an honorary member of the Empire Club. Like Walsh, Rynders used his Empire Club as a base to launch a Democratic Party insurgency. Unlike Walsh, however, a practical Rynders quickly compromised with the party in power.

He was admitted into the ranks of Tammany insiders for bringing out the vote for James Polk during the presidential election of 1844. Polk's victory over Henry Clay in New York, and consequently the nation, was attributed to the Empire Club, which paraded its ranks through the streets under the slogan "The Unterrified Democracy Is Coming." In fact, the Empire Club marched in dozens of political rallies and certainly stuffed plenty of ballot boxes on Election Day on Polk's behalf. With no shortage of humor, Rynders's men disrupted a rally for Clay a week before the election by hurling lumps of clay at the Whigs.

Transforming street politics into street theater, Rynders delivered an Election Day speech on horseback outside the window of New York lawyer Benjamin Butler, who had nominated Polk during the Democratic convention. Rewarded with membership on the Tammany general committee in 1844, Rynders was also appointed in 1857 as U.S. marshal of the southern district of New York. Even as Rynders aspired to a role in national politics, he was still a ward-level demagogue prone to taking his disagreements to the streets. In one confrontation with city Whigs, members of his Empire Club assaulted, among others, the son of Alexander Hamilton.

After Polk's victory, some Democrats warned the new president to distance himself from the "rough, unpolished, ill-bred and ignorant ruffian." Henry Osborn, a Democratic officeholder from Troy, New York, told Polk that even as Rynders "solicits from you some appointment as a reward for his faithful services to the party," the Empire Club would only disgrace the Democrats. "Such a creature, so steeped in crime and infamy, was used by the democracy of the city of New York.... [He is] a bully to a brothel and black leg in every sense of the word."

In another instance of Rynders's impolitic behavior, the Empire Club plotted to assassinate utopian socialist and *New York Evening Post* editor Parke Godwin, after he denounced Rynders and Tammany in an editorial. Walsh intervened on Godwin's behalf, challenging Rynders to a knife fight in a locked room, which the leader of the Empire Club prudently declined.

Proven a coward by his neighborhood rival, Rynders withdrew his threats against Godwin.

Rivalries between these political factions often had less to do with differences in ideology than with personalities and battles for local power. Walsh's antipathy to Rynders, of course, influenced his public pronouncements regarding President Polk, who he called "a calculating politician with a thousand fold more ambition than honesty." Walsh particularly assailed the president for favoring a temporary alliance with the Empire Club over the Spartans. And in rejecting Rynders's (as well as Buntline's) anti-Catholicism, Walsh was acting partly out of a rank opportunism and partly from conviction—though with Walsh, it is difficult to see where one ends and the other begins.[10]

Born in Youghal, Ireland, in the county of Cork on May 4, 1810, Walsh arrived as a small child in New York, where his father acquired a mahogany yard and a furniture store. Neither Walsh nor his father, a graduate of Trinity College in Dublin, ever became U.S. citizens, a factor that made Walsh the only noncitizen ever elected to Congress. That revelation by Democratic Party rival John Kelly led to the end of the Bowery Boy's political career in 1854.

Although Protestant, Walsh's sentiments were closer to his impoverished Catholic countrymen than to either the British aristocrat or the American capitalist, both of whom he despised. Walsh's Sixth Ward was also overwhelmingly Irish immigrant, and he was quick to realize that any promising political movement in New York could not ignore the burgeoning numbers and rising power of the Irish Catholics and Germans arriving at America's shores through the Port of New York.

New York factories that supplied wider national markets were employing immigrants right off the ships. Even furniture making, which still could boast artisan shops owned by American natives and German immigrants, became a sweated contract trade as newly arrived Germans were recruited the moment they stepped on dry land to work for as little as $30 a year and free board. As a result, journeymen employed by the larger furniture makers had their wages reduced from $15 a week in 1836 to as low as $8 a week by 1846.

Walsh sympathized with the immigrant searching for a decent life in America, putting the blame for ethnic tensions and deteriorating working conditions on manipulative capitalists. Employers, said Walsh, went right up to the docks and sought the newly arrived who "know nothing of the state of the trade, prices, regulations, etc. and become willing victims to anyone who offers them immediate and permanent employment." During his term in the state legislature, this Protestant Bowery Boy came to the defense of Irish families brutalized during the passage across the Atlantic, and he proposed a bill to enforce a code of conduct on American vessels transporting European immigrants.[11]

Vessels loaded with men and women searching for the promise of America kept on coming during the antebellum years in numbers that had a definite impact on economic and social relations. In just the seven years between 1847 and 1854, 1.8 million immigrants passed through the Port of New York. Of course, not all stayed in New York, but the city became the center of the Hibernian diaspora in America, accounting for 12 to 13 percent of all Irish in the United States during the 1850s.

The result was a dramatic shift in the balance between the native-born and immigrant populations in just a decade. In 1845, New York's population was 371,000, of which 128,000, or about 36 percent, was foreign born. Ten years later, New York's total population rose to 630,000 and of that number 325,000, or 52 percent, were of foreign birth. The highest concentrations of the New York Irish were in Manhattan's poorer wards; Walsh's Sixth Ward was 70 percent foreign born by 1855. And Walsh took up the cause of the Irish diaspora; the starvation that forced so many to leave their country. He asked why as much as $40,000 collected for famine relief was not reaching Ireland: "Who are the contemptible asses who have management of the business?"[12]

A primitive racism played a part in the attitudes of the native born toward the Irish. In his extensive diaries, George Templeton Strong dehumanizes the Irish as "sons of toil with prehensile paws" and a physique suited for menial labor. In addition, the immigrant was characterized as a criminal element. Of the 27,000 criminal convictions throughout the United States in 1850, more than half were against foreign born. Whether harassment played a part in the number of convictions or not, this was a potent weapon in the hands of men like Philip Hone who referred to the Irish "as strangers among us," and who questioned their commitment to democratic principles even as they "decide the elections of the city of New York." Walsh said men like Hone and Buntline were unable to see that immigrants escaping harsh times in their native lands "possess a great advantage over American-born citizens and this may be attributed to their very frequent prosperity in business."[13]

Crowded into the poorest wards, the Irish occupied the worst lodgings and took the least desirable jobs, with many of the artisan trades closed off to them by the overwhelmingly native-born master craftsmen.

In the summer of 1843 the issue of business licenses emerged on the ethnic fault line when native-born butchers and other merchants, angry at Tammany for awarding licenses to Catholics, called for a new political party independent of Democrats and Whigs; the American Republicans were born. Charging that Tammany was buying Irish Catholic votes with business permits, the butchers and other tradesmen who joined the American Republicans pushed for a program to limit immigrants' economic opportunities. They were equally hostile to the Germans, claiming that German greengrocers were "taking nearly every good corner formerly occupied by Americans."

Although many young men who identified themselves as Bowery Boys joined the American Republicans, Walsh's Spartans rejected their appeal to bigotry. The Spartans opposed not only the restrictions against Catholics, but saw licensing in general as a brake on individual rights. In 1841, when three unlicensed butchers faced jail for selling meat on their own premises, Walsh and fellow-Spartan John Windt came to their defense and convinced the jury to acquit. It was a noteworthy accomplishment, Walsh said, to break up "the meat monopoly."[14]

Aside from business licenses, temperance became another issue that incited Catholic-Protestant discord in New York. Temperance measures, including pledges administered by Protestant missionaries, were supported by reformers, who saw sobriety as a necessary measure to make good citizens out of all Americans. Catholics viewed temperance as another volley in the Protestant culture war against immigrants.

As Mike Walsh drew support from proletarianized Irish laborers, he made it clear that temperance and other laws that regulated behavior were no cure for the class divisions that were widening in New York during the economic downturn of the early and middle 1840s. He described one temperance meeting as "an attempt to coerce people into drinking cold water and eating gingerbread in endeavoring to gain political power." Describing the speaker as "an ignorant blockhead," Walsh said he "felt a strong inclination to administer a kick or two."

Above all, it was the battle over schools that most clearly reflected the religious divide and demonstrated the growing strength of the Catholic newcomer in New York. The conflict over schools also awoke Tammany to the dire necessity of abandoning the nativists and exploiting the immigrant vote. In 1840, Bishop John Hughes, the leader of the city's Catholics, appealed to the Common Council to provide financial support for the struggling Catholic schools. While there was a system of free schools administered under the Public School Society, Catholics felt they were excluded by a curriculum that vigorously preached the prevailing Protestant doctrine. Working-class radicals like George Henry Evans character-ized the Public School Society as a "secret engine of bigotry and aristocracy." Although an atheist, Evans sympathized with Catholic opposition to the domination of Protestant theology in the public schools; what he preferred was a complete separation of church and state: "schools common to all ... disconnected from religious or irreligious influence."[15]

The Democratic-controlled council, first trying to ignore an issue that would split Tammany into nativist and pro-immigrant factions, rejected Hughes's appeal. Hughes then turned to Governor William Seward, who also had to step lightly in a Whig Party with far more nativist sentiment than the Democrats. Even Seward's modest proposals to remove anti-Catholic bias from the classroom were resisted by city and state Whigs.

Dissatisfied with both parties, it was time for Hughes to flex the political muscle of the Catholic voter. In the autumn 1841 campaign for state and federal offices, the city's Whigs nominated a nativist slate. Tammany Hall nativists and even some moderates, angry that Hughes had appealed to the Whig governor, simply ignored the school issue.

Hughes saw his opportunity to mount a challenge to Tammany by quickly forming a third party, the Carroll Hall ticket. Those Democrats also endorsed by the Carroll Hall party won. But the three candidates running exclusively in the Carroll Hall column, including Mike Walsh, went down to defeat. Evans, writing in the November 1841 issue of *The Radical*, said Walsh's defeat only proved to him that "the great body of the Irish are really and truly Democratic."

In running on the Carroll Hall ticket, Walsh was using the school issue and the Catholic vote to advance his career. He knew that for someone outside the Tammany power structure, political power would come by harnessing the vote of the Catholic newcomers. Already denied a place in the Tammany column that year, Walsh eagerly joined Carroll Hall as a candidate for U.S. Congress and although he lost, he siphoned enough votes from the Democrat to hand the Whigs a victory.

The Democratic Party learned a valuable lesson about ethnic politics in New York. Tammany Hall recognized the threat the Spartan Association, Carroll Hall, and other insurgencies could pose if they cornered the immigrant vote. The Democratic Party was quick to push its nativist wing aside, and with Tammany support, a new law was passed in 1842 that extended New York State's educational system to the city with an elected Board of Education. Under the law, each ward had representation on the board, and that meant active Catholic participation.

Both regular Democrats and insurgents like Walsh were certainly opportunistic in their defense of the immigrant voter. Fragile loyalties and the constantly shifting mood in the streets often governed relations between gangs, party factions, and ethnic groups. Hesitant to act in the early years of the Irish migration, Tammany started to make admittedly self-serving overtures to the immigrant in 1827 by establishing a naturalization bureau to speed up the process of citizenship. The impetus was a set of changes to the state constitution, beginning in 1821, that granted the vote to every white male over twenty-one years of age. By the 1840s, the Irish qualified to vote in numbers that could make a difference. Between 1841 and 1844 the Democrats naturalized 11,000 immigrants; in return, Tammany was rewarded with loyal voters grateful for the chance to become American citizens.

Walsh's Spartan Band could on one day battle Catholic rivals, like the pro-Tammany Faugh O'Bhallas, and on the next, advance the Catholic cause in the schools. However, in adopting George Henry Evans's land-reform platform, the Spartans were able to put the immigrant at the center of their vision of a new social order on the American frontier. "The exclusion of foreigners," Evans insisted, "is not the answer." Instead, he would settle industrial workers from America's cities in carefully planned communities on free lands at the frontier. Evans called the Irish "brave and enterprising" in fleeing poverty and persecution in their native land, and he said they were simply seeking the same dream of American citizenship as any Protestant immigrant.

Settling industrial workers in the West was appealing to the multitudes crowded into New York tenements and factories, but Walsh said Irish immigrants did not have to move far from the city to become farmers and self-sufficient artisans of a well-organized suburban community; he thought Staten Island could be just such a haven for new Americans. No doubt, he was looking forward to using his Staten Island homesteaders as a ready force of ballot box stuffers to be ferried to the city on Election Day. Walsh even proposed that ships bringing immigrants to New York's port pay the city a tax of one or two dollars for each passenger; money that would go towards building Staten Island's model commune of farms, light industry, and spacious homes. Any surplus would be used to pay an immigrant's way to lands further west in Wisconsin, Michigan, or Iowa.[16]

New York's fracture along ethnic and cultural lines at times erupted into violent street clashes, engulfing large parts of the city and requiring the intervention of the military. The worst of these confrontations occurred in 1849—the culmination of steadily rising anger and widening societal divisions. In most cases, if not all, the combatants were young men in their teens and twenties—men who were likely affiliated with a gang, a volunteer fire brigade, and a political faction.

One of the earliest larger-scale battles between gangs of New York Catholics and Protestants took place in June 1835 and involved more than 500 people, almost all of whom were under age twenty-one. It started with an attack by a Protestant gang, the American Guards, on the Catholic O'Connell Guards. Although the police were able to separate the warring parties, and U.S. troops were put on alert, the Bowery Boys renewed the fight by attacking the Green Dragon Tavern, owned by an Englishman who allegedly failed to show respect to a Bowery Boy firefighter. These

Bowery Boys, predecessors to Walsh's Spartans, then attacked a nearby Irish tavern resulting in more fighting and the ransacking of Irish homes and businesses. George Henry Evans, in an appeal to class solidarity, called on his Protestant coreligionists to cease their attacks. Just days after the riots, Evans characterized the Irish as "hard working, valuable people driven by oppression from their homes."

On New Year's Eve 1839, Bowery Boys and German immigrants clashed, resulting in the shooting death of a twenty-two-year-old Bowery Boy leader named John Armstrong. For a city deeply divided between ethnicity and class, New York was frighteningly well armed; immigrant groups, trade unions, and fire companies routinely marched in downtown parades with uniforms, muskets, and even light artillery.

New York City's various ethnic groups sought dignity, cohesion, and prestige by organizing into paramilitary target clubs and militia units. Many of these militia companies were later incorporated into the New York State Militia. Robert Ernst in his *Immigrant Life in New York City*, noted that Irish, German, French, and even Italian and Jewish military companies were formed through the 1840s and 1850s because of the unwillingness, before the Civil War, of the state militia to admit immigrants.

Mike Walsh admiringly described one such target club as the group returned to the city from its annual excursion on Long Island. "With over sixty muskets [they] made a most magnificent display. . . . The company is entirely composed of industrious mechanics most of whom are employed in the ship yards." For middle-class New Yorkers, these armed units carried real and perceived political weight in a city of election-day violence and proletarian rebels. Since many of these units were Catholic, the city's Protestants contended they were part of a papal army in America.

Partly as a reaction, native-born Protestants organized themselves in gun clubs and armed units, some sponsored by volunteer fire brigades or trades, as was the case with the Tompkins Butcher Association Guard. Again, demonstrating a high level of organization and internal discipline, many of these units wore uniforms and glazed caps, and were well prepared to be incorporated into New York State Militia regiments during the Civil War. A city this well armed and polarized was fertile ground for neighborhood demagogues, who soon found they could further their political careers by manipulating gangs and firefighters' organizations. The fire company, target club, and gang all gave their members a sense of identity and solidified their political and class loyalties.[17]

It was the anti-British Astor Theater riot of 1849 that crystallized the dangers inherent in a city of politicized gangs and fire brigades. Hearing Mike Walsh compare the National Guard to the repressive army of the Russian Czar, New York's "respectable classes" could only wonder if the

THE AMERICAN FIREMAN.
Always Ready.

The volunteer fire brigades were proving grounds for political leadership on the neighborhood level in antebellum New York. (Courtesy of the Library of Congress)

Astor Theater riot was a sign that the European revolutions of 1848 were sweeping across the Atlantic. The incident also underscored the danger of alliances between Protestant Bowery Boys and Irish Catholic immigrants. The Irish could be counted on to pelt an English actor with rotten vegetables, while nativist Bowery Boys were motivated by their strident defense of a genuine working-class American culture. Generally, both groups were anxious to rattle the sensibilities of the middle and upper classes.

However, it would be misleading to overstate the strength of this somewhat temporary concord between Protestant and Catholic gangs. In the Astor Theater riot they found common cause, but gang conflicts based on sectarian rivalries in the 1850s demonstrated that any alliance between young Catholic and Protestant workers in antebellum New York was fragile indeed.

The Astor Theater was built by the city elite and opened on November 22, 1847. The theater's construction was financed by New York's wealthy patrons of the arts, including the theater's namesake, John Jacob Astor, who was instrumental in developing much of the surrounding real estate. Mid-nineteenth-century New Yorkers embraced theater, but theatergoers were divided along class lines, with some theaters, like the Chatham and Lafayette, catering to the poor with entertainment that was closer to circus acts. The Park and Astor appealed to wealthier audiences with European dramatic performances. This cultural divide arising in the 1830s only served to sharpen the class distinctions in New York. Those differences were most keenly felt in the part of the city where the fighting occurred—the border between the overflowing tenements of the lower east side and more prosperous neighborhoods.

While the city elite imitated the styles of the European aristocracy and favored British actors, working-class audiences preferred American entertainers. To many Americans, Britain was still a menacing world power—remembered for the War of 1812. Americans also held the British responsible for calling in high debts after the panic of 1837. As early as 1825 this anti-British sentiment spilled onto the stage, when New Yorkers barred British actor Edmund Kean for not showing the proper respect to a Boston audience. In 1831, the English actor Joshua Anderson was chased from the stage of the Bowery Theater in two separate brawls complete with rotten fruit and bricks. The management of the Bowery Theater had to demonstrate its patriotism by covering the theater in red, white, and blue bunting. And in July 1834, a crowd numbering more than 500 stormed the Bowery Theater to protest the English-born stage manager William Farren, who had denigrated American tastes and manners.[18]

For an American actor, success on the New York stage could depend on whether he was one of the b'hoys, and it was not unusual for the Bowery Boys to urge their members to head to the theater and cheer one of their own. The lightning rod for the Astor Theater riot was the American actor Edwin Forrest, known as the Great American Tragedian. Forrest, who started his career at the Bowery Theater, could boast true working-class credentials, and he was a friend of radical causes including the Locofoco faction of the Democratic Party. In 1835, Forrest unsuccessfully sought the Democratic Party nomination for a congressional seat, and he was among those New Yorkers in 1842 who joined Mike Walsh in vocal support of Thomas W. Dorr's claim to lead Rhode Island on behalf of propertyless workers.

The merchant and political elite of the city naturally painted Forrest as a dangerous revolutionary. On May 8, 1849, a day after the first Astor Theater disturbance, Philip Hone entered into his diary a description of Forrest as a "vulgar, arrogant loafer with a pack of kindred rowdies at his heels.... The respectful part of our citizens will never consent to be put down by a mob raised to serve the purpose of such a fellow as Forrest."[19]

Forrest conducted a very public and nasty rivalry with the British actor William Macready, especially after Forrest was heckled and driven from the stage during his engagement at the Princess Theatre in London. His appearance was particularly galling to Macready because even he had not performed there. Forrest accused Macready of organizing the opposition to his performance, and Macready struck back with a libel suit. Audiences on both sides of the Atlantic were spoiling for a fight. They got their chance when Macready was to perform as Macbeth at the Astor Theater on May 7, 1849. To make matters worse, Forrest was playing the same role at the same time at the Broadway Theater.

On the evening of May 7, an angry crowd of mostly young men, some of them well-organized members of the Spartan Association, Rynders's Empire Club, and Buntline's Bowery Boy gang, gathered in front of the theater. When the doors opened, they rushed inside. Armed with eggs, vegetables, and stones they waited for Macready to appear and immediately started their attack, driving him from the stage and out a back door. The city's mainstream press put the blame for the assault on Bowery Boys agitated by class hatred and spurred on by demagogues. As one observer of the Astor Theater events wrote, for these men, "it was the rich against the poor, the aristocracy against the people."[20]

Emboldened by their successful assault against British culture, members of Rynders's gang the next day attacked the offices of the American Anti-Slavery Society. White working-class factions, like the Empire Club and Spartans, had little respect for middle-class abolitionists who would elevate the black man to free labor. White workers, already reeling from chronic unemployment and degraded wages, saw free blacks as another source of cheap labor for northern capitalists. For the gangs of New York, a volley against one class enemy was sufficient spark to attack another.

The city's cultural elite, including Washington Irving, Herman Melville, and Horace Greeley, were not surrendering to the masses, and appealed to

Mr. Edwin Forrest as Richard III

A friend of radical causes and the Bowery Boys, Edwin Forrest played Macbeth the night working-class youth took to his defense against British actor William Macready at the Astor Theater. (Courtesy of the Library of Congress)

Mayor Caleb Woodhull to protect the theater with National Guard troops for Macready's planned return on May 10.

The working-class opposition to Macready was well prepared. On the morning of May 10, lower Manhattan was plastered with large handbills signed by Buntline's ad hoc American Committee, urging the youth of the city to mobilize. A Bowery Boy network on the streets and in the saloons and firehouses, as well as access to printing presses, were instrumental in rallying thousands of young men. Typically, the broadsides made their appeal to class and culture:

> Workingmen! Shall Americans or English Rule in this City?
>
> The crew of the British steamer has threatened all Americans who shall dare to offer their opinions this night at the English aristocratic opera house.
>
> We advocate no violence, but a free expression of opinion to all public men!
>
> Workingmen! Freemen! Stand Up to Your Lawful Rights

Woodhull, the Whig mayor who had been on the job for just two days, convened an emergency meeting of his advisors early on the tenth. They agreed to call out the National Guard only if the city's police force of just over 1,000 men was overwhelmed. Just before six o'clock on the evening of the tenth, about 325 police arrived and, of that number, 200 were stationed in different parts of the theater. Others were stationed at vantage points near and across from the theater. While the police were taking their positions, 200 National Guardsmen were deployed on neighboring streets.

Indicative of the well-organized opposition, young men throughout the day bought up tickets for the performance, intent on repeating their attack inside the theater. By the time the doors opened at seven o'clock, the number of tickets sold exceeded the theater's capacity of 1,800. Outside, the streets were packed solid with men and boys as young as thirteen and fourteen, ready for a confrontation.

It did not take long before an outbreak of chaotic fighting; the police scattered, and the National Guard marched into battle against a mob estimated at more than 5,000. Again, Macready fled out a back door in disguise as rioters smashed through barricades and converged on the theater with paving stones and bricks. Small fires were set around the theater, in some cases by Bowery Boy firemen. In the melee, rioters attempted to grab rifles out of the hands of soldiers. First, the National Guard fired warning shots over the heads of the crowd but finally fired directly into the mass of people, the first time in U.S. history that soldiers shot point blank at American civilians.

The National Guard even deployed small field artillery as it marched in two columns from the front of the theater, with one pushing the rioters back on the Bowery and the other advancing against a crowd on Broadway. The wounded and dead were laid out on the billiard tables of the nearby Vauxhall Gardens, and some were treated at a neighborhood pharmacy. In the end, twenty-three were killed and more than one hundred wounded, including many innocent bystanders.[21]

Although Buntline was among the dozens arrested earlier, he was able to conduct the battle from his jail cell, ordering extra copies of his newspaper to be printed on May 11 and another poster calling the young toughs of the city to keep up the fight with the words, "Americans! Arouse! The Great Crisis Has Come! Decide Now Whether English Aristocrats And Foreign Rule Shall Triumph."

On May 11, anarchy triumphed. Rumors circulated that an attempt to overthrow the city government was planned with the help of armed gangs on their way from Philadelphia. The city confiscated weapons from neighborhood gun shops and stored them at the arsenal. Finally, mayor Woodhull declared martial law, but this did not deter opposition leaders from organizing a protest rally that evening.

By six o'clock, a crowd numbering in the thousands had gathered at City Hall Park. The meeting got off to a tragic start when a jerry-rigged platform loaded with people collapsed killing a small boy. But the meeting continued with most of the speakers representing various insurgent political factions. Their rhetoric combined issues of class and culture.

Bowery Boy leader Edward Strahan called the military "the right arm of despotism carrying out a wonton, unprovoked and murderous outrage." Rynders, who said he had appealed to the mayor to cancel Macready's performance, accused the city of "trying to please the aristocracy at the expense of the lives of [innocent] citizens ... to [use the army to] revenge the aristocrats against the working classes."

Mike Walsh predicted that the Astor Theater riot and the shooting of unarmed Americans would trigger a revolutionary "reorganization of the masses." Walsh compared the actions of the mayor with the repressive Czar Nicholas I, "who holds the lives of the people in little better estimation than that of dogs, [but] has always required three rounds of blank cartridges to be fired by the troops before they fire with ball upon the people."

Characteristic of Walsh's brand of radicalism, he accused the city of deploying "these gingerbread soldiers ... to trample the poor man under foot," and he asked whether the National Guardsmen that defended New York's political and mercantile elite also fought in the war against Mexico, or was it fought only with the sons of the poor? Walsh attempted to address the needs of those caught in the crossfire without regard to who was to blame for the violence. "Who will take care of the families they have made desolate—will Macready, will Forrest, will Woodhull?"[22]

The Bowery Boy's incendiary words incited some to try another assault, this time with intent to destroy the theater, but the crowd, smaller than the night before, was easily repulsed by National Guard troops still in control of the lower part of the city.

There were skirmishes with police and troops throughout the evening of the eleventh, as some tried to erect barricades or throw bricks from the rooftops. This fighting subsided when rioters learned that the National Guard would again fire on disturbers of the peace. Those who had supported Macready's return to the stage, and even those who were simply perceived as well-to-do, felt threatened enough to take up arms to protect their homes.

On the morning of the twelfth, the city was relatively calm although rumors persisted that a revolutionary army from Philadelphia, led by a man only known as the Panther, was on its way to renew the battle. There were also rumors that Macready, now in Boston, had been assassinated. Others whispered that Rynders had called out his gang for target practice and that a gun dealer had offered 2,000 weapons to help with the insurrection. With a city on edge, the Astor Theater remained under police guard, and with the help of a heavy rain, peace was finally restored.[23]

By May 14, the National Guard had withdrawn its forces, and on the fifteenth, there were funerals throughout the day for those killed. On September 12, 1849, ten rioters were put on trial, and all were sentenced to terms ranging from one month to one year. Buntline, identified as a ringleader, received the maximum of one year in jail and a $250 fine. When he was released from Blackwell's Island, Buntline was escorted back to the city by his unrepentant Bowery Boys, complete with an open carriage drawn by six white horses and a brass band.

Although it reopened on September 24, 1849, the Astor Theater itself never really recovered, and closed permanently in 1852. In 1854, the building was bought by the Mercantile Library Association and transformed into the Clinton Hall Library with 43,000 volumes and a book exchange that later became the largest bookseller in the city.

The press viewed the Astor Theater riot less as an expression of anti-British sentiment than as a struggle between competing classes; or as *The Home Journal* phrased it, the battle for the Astor Theater was between "the B'hoys of New York and the Upper Ten." The Whig press, in particular, feared that had the mayor not reopened the theater on May 10, "he would have declared that the laws of the city and personal right of very citizen must bow to the will of an infuriated mob."[24]

New Yorkers saw skillful demagogues such as Walsh and Buntline behind the scenes using the city's gangs and alienated youth as a force to intimidate the political and cultural establishment. There was an undercurrent of

Disorder in antebellum New York usually involved rival gangs for control of the streets, and, as in the Bowery Boy riot of 1857, the sides often split between Protestant native-born and Catholic immigrants. (Courtesy of the Library of Congress)

violent dissent roiling from the city's laborers that when tapped "breaks forth like an uncapped hydrant."

A decade later, in the summer of 1857, when Bowery Boys and rival gangs clashed in several days of violence that was largely over control of the streets, New York's merchants and middle class feared these young men would soon cease their internal struggles, unite, and turn their full attention to the class enemy. It was only a matter of time before the gangs, finished with fighting among themselves, would soon "pass the word, plunder the rich! and Stewarts or Tiffanys may be laid open for the mob."[25]

Reformers, shocked at the bloodshed they saw in the streets of New York in the 1840s and through the 1850s, called for rapid social and economic changes. As one observer of the Astor Theater riot concluded, "Society by an unjust distribution of the avails of industry enables a few men to become rich and consigns a great mass to hopeless poverty with all its degradations and deprivations. . . . Thousands of poor people know that they are robbed and plundered every day. . . . [The] mob is but a symptom of our social condition." Without addressing the inequality of society, the sacking of the Astor Theater would just be the first step toward full-scale insurrection by the "dangerous classes" armed with the same revolutionary socialism that threatened Europe. As early as 1837, diarist George Templeton Strong cautioned, "People talk ominously about revolutions on this side of the Atlantic."[26]

Even as some contemporaries warned that America's experiment in democracy itself was endangered by class war, historian David Grimsted makes a distinction between the revolutionary violence of Europe in 1848, which aimed at the destruction of the existing political order, and Jacksonian insurrection, which consisted largely of short-lived uprisings of people angry at one particular insult or injustice.

American urban disorder was usually directed against a particular incident, as in the case of a July 1834 assault against a shoe store after a woman was arrested for shoplifting. Two hundred rioters vandalized the shop, watched by as many as 2,000 spectators, many of them sympathetic. Grimsted maintains that American democracy was well suited to absorb these small outbursts of discontent, a sentiment that was reflected by the *New York Times* after extensive gang warfare in the summer of 1857. Disorder in America is local in nature and devoid of ideological significance, said the *Times*, while "in France they herald revolution." The solution: "close the grog shops on Sunday."[27]

While these American expressions of anger lacked the ideological content of European socialism, they were no less revolutionary in their aims to strike a blow at the class enemy. In one sense, the disorder of the Jackson age was tacitly encouraged by the temper of the times; the misplaced feeling of some that Jackson's ascendancy was license to take democracy into the streets.

Walsh's attack on the aristocracy of wealth and privilege was not limited to John Jacob Astor's theater or the exclusive club at Tammany Hall. For a brief moment, Walsh roused his Bowery Boys, clearly in the spirit of Jacksonian democracy, to storm the gates of property holders in Rhode Island in an episode in American history that proved more farce than socialist revolution.

chapter 3

On to Providence, B'hoys

Turmoil in Rhode Island in the spring and summer of 1842 took the Bowery Boys out of the limited milieu of New York City politics and thrust them into the center of a national controversy that to some looked like the opening shots of a revolution. The Dorr rebellion started as a peaceful and wholly justified attempt to open the right to vote in Rhode Island beyond landholders. It escalated into a chaotic confrontation among its eccentric namesake, Thomas W. Dorr, the government of Rhode Island, and President John Tyler. At one point, Rhode Island had two rival state governments competing for the loyalty of the populace.

The battle lines were largely ideological, with preeminent conservatives like Daniel Webster opposing New England socialists and Mike Walsh's Spartan Band. In an editorial, the conservative *Providence Daily Journal* knew how to rally the gentry as the controversy started heating up. The Dorr rebellion, the newspaper said, is a conflict that "proposes to realize here in Rhode Island the horrors of the French Revolution."[1]

Far from a Jacobin reign of terror, the Dorr rebellion failed to incite Rhode Island to revolution, and the Bowery Boys were sent packing right behind the remnants of Thomas Dorr's movement. However, Dorr's cause of expanded suffrage and greater political power for the burgeoning manufacturing towns of the state eventually was successful.

The stirrings of working-class discontent in Rhode Island were evident in the early 1830s when nonlandholders began to demand the vote. The state charter, adopted in 1663, and subsequent acts of the legislature granted the vote to white males with $134 in real property, which effectively excluded the large number of workers beginning to crowd into manufacturing towns like Providence, Bristol, and Warren during the nineteenth century.

Elected to the State House of Representatives in 1834 as a Whig, Thomas Dorr sought a centrist path to wresting political power from the landed gentry to which he and many of his reform-minded followers were members. A graduate of Phillips Exeter Academy and Harvard, Dorr was a reformer and vocal abolitionist in the best tradition of American middle-class liberalism. Among his achievements in the legislature was a bill, which became law, in favor of poor debtors.

In the same year Dorr was sent to the state house, he helped organize the Rhode Island Constitutional Party. While it adopted a moderate approach, the Constitutional Party was still viewed by landholders as a threatening revolutionary force. The conservatives argued that only those who owned a stake in the community, the landholders, could be entrusted with the vote. William G. Goddard, a lawyer and newspaper editor who taught moral philosophy at Brown University, framed the argument most succinctly: "Those who own the country, ought to govern the country."[2]

Confronted with strident opposition in the legislature to extending voting rights, Dorr proposed a compromise to give the vote to all adult males with a minimum of $250 worth of property—any property. After only three years, the Constitutional Party disintegrated, and Dorr was defeated for a seat to the U.S. Congress in 1837.

As the decade of the 1840s opened, pressure from the growing number of industrial workers in the state again forced the suffrage issue. By 1840, the population of Providence had increased to 23,172 from just under 16,000 in 1825. Estimates of white adult males excluded from the ballot by the property qualification vary, but it is generally agreed that by 1840 it was about 60 percent statewide. These demographic changes not only lent support to the suffrage cause, but added fuel to the related issue of legislative apportionment; the 1663 Charter was as inflexible on reapportionment as it was on the vote. Though Providence contained more than a sixth of Rhode Island's population and contributed about two-thirds of all taxes paid to the state in the mid-1830s, the city elected only a twentieth of the members of the state's House of Representatives.[3]

In March 1840, Dorr was among the founders of the Rhode Island Suffrage Association, clearly a more aggressive but still politically centrist group arising out of the failed Constitutional Party. The Suffrage Association called for replacing the colonial-era charter with a new constitution that would extend the franchise to "the mechanics and merchants, workingmen and others—who own no land." By the autumn of 1840, the Suffrage Association had dispatched speakers and agitators to tour the state and establish local chapters. It

Thomas Wilson Dorr demanded voting rights for the propertyless in Rhode Island, but his attempt in 1842 to set up a rival government with him as People's Governor only ended in disaster. (Courtesy of the Library of Congress)

also printed its own newspaper, the *New Age*. Dorr kept the Suffrage Association independent of the major political parties, but it did gain support from Democrats eager to enfranchise new voters who would turn the tide of Whig ascendancy in Washington.

Support for the Rhode Island cause also began building among the radical political factions of New York in 1840, when the First Reform Society of New York City circulated an "Address to the Citizens of Rhode Island who are denied the Right of Suffrage." The circular urged the propertyless and sympathetic landholders to call a convention and write a new constitution. The so-called New York Circular gave Dorr added incentive to build his Rhode Island Suffrage Association.

The first order of business for the Suffrage Association, again attempting to work within the political system, was to appeal to the Rhode Island legislature to call a constitutional convention. Digging in their heels, members of the legislature proposed a constitutional convention that would ignore the suffrage issue and advance a watered-down measure on apportionment. The legislature's tactics were enough to bring about 3,000 citizens of Providence out into the streets for a mass meeting in front of the state house on April 17, 1841. Marchers, who wore badges stamped with the words "I am an American Citizen," paraded the streets with banners that proclaimed "Worth Makes the Man, but Sand and Gravel Make the Voter" and "Virtue, Patriotism and Intelligence Versus $134 Worth of Dirt." Through the spring and summer of 1841, the disenfranchised, aided by a now well-organized Suffrage Association, staged mass meetings in towns across the state, with one in Newport in May and a second rally in Providence in July.[4]

While centrists tried to keep control of the organization, there were those calling for open revolution. Historians of the Dorr rebellion have referred to the spring of 1841 as a turning point, when many in the suffrage movement seriously began planning an uprising. Behind this transformation was a conviction of having exhausted all regular and peaceful political channels.

The Dorr rebellion also turned into a debate over the right to change the constitution through popular action by sidestepping the state legislature; the Suffrage Association called for a People's Convention to draft a new state constitution. Ignoring the fact that the vote was still restricted, the People's Constitution was ratified by the general public in a December 1841 plebiscite. Dorr's case was strengthened given that a majority of the state's 8,000 qualified landholders also cast their ballots for the new constitution. Predictably, support for the People's Constitution was strongest in the industrial and commercial centers. The new constitution granted the vote to every white, male citizen over the age of twenty-one who had resided in the state one year, and for six months in the ward or town where he would vote. A residency requirement was the answer to those critics who feared that expanding the right to vote would put power into the hands of transients and others who did not have a real stake in the community.

The legislature lost little time in condemning the new constitution, declaring it illegal. Suffrage opponents called a grand jury chaired by Rhode Island chief justice Job Durfee, who ruled that any constitutional changes within a state must be approved through the existing state legislature. President Tyler's Secretary of State Daniel Webster characterized Dorr's interpretation of government as "a sort of South American liberty" with governments falling at the whim of popular revolt. "What is this but anarchy?" Webster asked. "A liberty supported by arms today, crushed by arms tomorrow. Is that our liberty?"[5]

Conservative opponents were also quick to charge that suffragists solicited the vote from minors, foreigners, and prisoners convicted of robbery and manslaughter. A prominent suffrage opponent, Elisha Potter, said his investigation in Newport found a "long list of names of foreigners, persons who put in two votes ... and even of persons who had no existence at all" including one comically-named Peter Squirt.[6] The People's Constitution, the conservatives said, would put the political power of Providence, "not in the aristocracy of intellect or morals, or property but in the aristocracy of the dram shop, the brothel and the gutter; not in the ruffle-shirt gentry but in the gentry who have no shirts at all."[7]

This aversion to a government by the lower classes was magnified by what Rhode Islanders saw in New York City, where laborers, Irish immigrants, and neighborhood strongmen transformed every election into a minor revolution fought literally from ward to ward, street to street. Citing Mike Walsh's candidacy on the Catholic Carroll Hall ticket in 1841, conservatives in Providence warned that "in New York the foreign population rules the city.... In the last election they rallied [for] candidates pledged to vote for foreign interests and in opposition to the interests of native citizens." Rhode Islanders also took guidance from noted New York jurist chancellor James Kent, who said population growth in New York, especially among the Irish and poor, "is enough to startle and awake those who are pursuing ... universal suffrage." Kent predicted that New York would soon join the ranks of poor, overcrowded European cities where the workers are prone to insurrection.[8]

The possibility that New York's shirtless democrats and their Bowery Boy foot soldiers might come to Rhode Island to fight for Dorr's rebellion raised the alarm of "foreign" invasion and plunder. Some feared a pogrom led by Walsh's Spartan Band, prepared "to butcher the citizens and violate the chastity of the daughters of Rhode Island." As one frightened Rhode Islander asked, "Shall the best blood of the state be placed against the scum of New York?" The Boston press warned of New York gangs intent on "overthrowing the government and erecting on its ruins a mobocracy."[9]

Not all outside agitators were from New York; some followed the foremost socialists of New England, Orestes Brownson and Seth Luther. After Dorr's failed attempt to seize power in Providence in May 1842, one resident of the city was heard to mutter, "Brownson is at the bottom of this movement—they are only carrying out his doctrines."

Brownson, a leading abolitionist, addressed a meeting of Rhode Island suffragists in 1841 at Dorr's invitation. When Dorr was installed as People's Governor, Brownson approved, but he turned his back on Dorrism as he abandoned his earlier calls for socialist revolution in favor of a mystical Catholicism. Seth Luther, a Providence carpenter, also saw suffrage in the context of the wider class issues and remained faithful to Dorr to the very end. Not only was the property qualification a form of taxation without representation, Luther said it rigged the justice system against the working class because only landholders and their eldest sons could serve on juries.

By April 1842, the Suffrage Association was confident of the next logical step—a People's Government to be headed by the man who was clearly the movement's leader; Thomas Wilson Dorr was inaugurated People's Governor on May 3. Thousands, some of whom were armed for a fight, attended the ceremonies in Providence. In response, landholders and political leaders in the legislature rallied their own coalition, the Law and Order Party, under Rhode Island's elected Governor Samuel Ward King.

King enacted laws to severely punish anyone carrying out the duties of the People's Government, with some facing charges of treason and threat of life imprisonment. In addition, Governor King appealed to Washington for military aid and sent several emissaries to President Tyler, a man thrust into the presidency and reluctant to wage a civil war in New England. Tyler said that while he wanted to see a political settlement, he would be duty-bound to intervene only if revolt actually threatened to topple the state government.

To Governor King and the legislature, it seemed that the rabble had staged a coup that was both communist and Catholic. The hidden hand of Rome was never far from the surface of the debate. "Every Roman Catholic Irishman is a Dorrite," was the sentiment of the Protestant elite. In hearings on Capitol Hill after the Dorr rebellion had been crushed, one Congressman referred to "foreign intervention" from Catholic Ireland in the internal affairs of Rhode Island. Dorr's adversaries charged that 2,000 votes for the People's Constitution were from outside the state and as many as 500 votes came from "the shores of Ireland." The approximately 2,500 Irish immigrants in the state in 1842, with more drawn by the growing manufacturing sector, were viewed as a serious threat to Providence's Protestant power structure. "These are the men who will hold the rod of political power over our native citizens," predicted the *Providence Daily Journal*.[10]

As Thomas Dorr declared himself governor and assembled his shadow government, conservatives warned ominously that Dorr would hand the state over to "an aristocracy of the worst kind—with a small knot of demagogues for its head and a large number of foreigners for its tail." They feared that demagogues like Mike Walsh, backed by neighborhood gangs, socialists, and Irish Catholics, were already organizing in the saloons and firehouses of Manhattan.[11]

New York Democrats, whether inside Tammany or not, regarded Dorr as a true representative of Jacksonian ideals. With Dorr boldly issuing decrees as governor, his friends in New York prepared a petition circulated through the city calling on Congress to impeach President Tyler for threatening to use force against the People's Government. New York was not the only city where pro-Dorr rallies and petitions were organized. Philadelphia and Boston had their own very visible demonstrations of support, but it was in New York that the promise of armed partisans ready to meet the U.S. Army on the battlefield buoyed Dorr's spirits. On May 13 and 14, Dorr stopped in New York on his way back from an unsuccessful appeal to President Tyler in Washington. In boisterous displays of bravado from the Spartan Band and other working-class clubs, Dorr was encouraged to carry on, even as his closest advisers were telling him it was a lost cause. As contemporary observers and later historians of the rebellion noted, Dorr went to Washington a reformer and liberal. He returned to Providence via New York on May 16 a fanatic, pleased when one New Yorker assured him that if "John Tyler attempts to carry into execution the threats" of intervention, New Yorkers by the hundreds would "stand with you."[12]

Historian Arthur Mowry, writing 50 years after the events, notes that after leaving Washington, Dorr was still open to a negotiated settlement through the White House. Had Dorr bypassed New York on his return from Washington, "the civil war which broke out on May 17 would have been entirely averted." As Philip Hone recorded, Dorr "came to New York a lamb and was sent to Providence a lion by the Tammany sympathizers."[13]

Dorr displayed his characteristic naivety in believing that a handful of Bowery Boy street fighters could bring his government to legitimate power. In fact, the People's Government was already collapsing quickly around him. Soon after Dorr's inauguration, the movement split over whether to immediately seize state property. The new People's Legislature convened for two days in a Providence foundry but, heeding its moderates, failed to immediately take possession of the state house with its records and other sources of political authority. Dorr later conceded that "it was a mistake not to take state property after the inauguration," but that he was "prompted by a desire to act moderately and avoid an unnecessary confrontation.... Decisive action like this was deemed premature and I yielded to the wishes of my [more cautious] associates."[14]

As the People's Government weakened, Governor King prepared to break the insurrection by calling for federal assistance, forming special police companies in Providence, and amending the Riot Act to eliminate the required hour's delay between its reading and the use of force. Desperate, Dorr appealed to the Bowery Boys for help. During his tour of New York on May 13 and 14, Dorr had met with leading radicals including Walsh, union organizer C. C. Cambreleng, and the Locofocos Levi Slamm and Alexander Ming Jr. On his arrival to the city, Dorr and his New York partisans convened at a downtown hotel, where the Rhode Island contingent set up a temporary headquarters. Here, Dorr received the first real promise that Bowery Boys and labor activists would be willing to return to Providence and fight U.S. soldiers for the cause of expanded suffrage.

On the night of May 13, Dorr was accompanied by a thoroughly devoted contingent of the Spartan Band for an evening of revelry at the Bowery Theater. The spectacle of a man proclaiming to be Rhode Island's governor being treated like royalty by "Spartans, vagabonds and the scum of the Earth" was too much for the respectable classes in both New York and Providence. All sense of decency was cast aside, they said, as Dorr strode into the theater with Walsh's armed bodyguards.[15]

The enlistment at this time of the experienced New York street fighter Alexander Ming Jr. to the Dorr cause again raised the anxiety level among the Providence elite. Ming, a colonel with the Thirteenth Regiment in New York, and Lieutenant Colonel Abraham Crasto with the 236th Regiment, told Dorr they would accompany him back to Rhode Island with several hundred fighters, dubbed Minutemen, as his armed escort. A force to be reckoned with in the rough street politics of the 1830s and 1840s, Ming was a founder of the Locofoco faction when it split from the regular Democratic Party in 1835, and he was their unsuccessful candidate for mayor the following year. But it was during the downtown riot over the price of flour in 1837 that Ming earned his reputation as a dangerous revolutionary.

Dorr, energized by wild rumors that he could raise an army of up to 5,000 New York volunteers, addressed an enthusiastic crowd at Tammany Hall; hundreds gathered in the streets for a rally, complete with a brass band, artillery pieces, and red-shirted volunteer firemen marching in military formation. Boarding a carriage with Levi Slamm, Dorr was escorted to the docks for his steamboat ride back home. Slamm outdid his cohort Ming and promised a contingent of 1,000 men and a chartered steamboat to carry his expeditionary force from the streets of New York to Providence in the event they were needed to take on the U.S. government. Dorr's New York allies predicted a backlash in their favor in the event Rhode Islanders were confronted by "troops of the union called out to support an aristocratic form of government against the will of the people."[16]

The parades and receptions must have been overwhelming to Dorr, who perceived a mass movement capable of redeeming his government and repulsing even the U.S. Army. The conservative *New York Courier and Enquirer* more accurately described the rally as a "broad burlesque" and a "grotesque display," referring to the lower-class dress and accoutrements of the Bowery Boys and other street fighters. The *New York Herald* labeled

Dorr a "rootbeer revolutionist," and called the New York rally "ridiculous, preposterous and silly, . . . orchestrated by that clique that tried to govern the Democratic Party here as they would govern a school of children." In Boston, Dorr's supporters also rallied on State Street and proclaimed that Bostonians were "unwilling [to see] their fellow citizens of Rhode Island murdered by the hired soldiery of the United States."[17]

During that critical week in New York, President Tyler did make some attempt to head off a conflict, sending Webster to the city to meet secretly with representatives of both sides. Dorr's second in command, Duttee J. Pearce, proposed that the People's Government step down while a case was made before the U.S. Supreme Court. Riding high from his reception in New York, Dorr rejected all proposals for negotiation or compromise. Tyler lamented that Dorr's New York performance was so "extravagant as almost to extinguish the last hope of a peaceable result."

While Dorr declined Slamm's and Ming's offers to return to Providence with a small army, he was clearly counting on popular support if the federal government intervened. In fact, Dorr told the New York volunteers that he would rely on them only as a last resort and that he didn't see the immediate need to take people from their homes and businesses. "I [would] invoke your aid and that of your associates in arms [only in] an unequal contest [with government soldiers]."[18]

On May 16, Dorr returned to Rhode Island emboldened by the "people of New York that have extended the hand of a generous fraternity." Hailed as a working class hero, he rode to Providence from the port at Stonington in an open carriage drawn by four white horses. Once in the city, he was accompanied by about 1,200 partisans, of which about 300 were armed; some were as young as sixteen. The procession slowly moved down the streets to his headquarters where, in a dramatic gesture, Dorr brandished a sword handed to him at the dock in New York—a sword, he said, that once belonged to an Indian fighter in Florida. "It has been already dyed in blood and, if necessary, would again be in blood should the suffrage cause demand it," Dorr declared; some doubted the sword had ever seen anything more exciting than a dress uniform.[19]

Governor King, not amused by the street theater in New York or the literal saber rattling in Providence, was taking no chances. Federal reinforcements at Fort Adams could be in Providence only hours after an uprising, and muskets already had been delivered to the state militia from the fort. The governor immediately arrested as many conspirators as he could, and he reorganized militia companies, filling them with new but well-trained recruits.

Dorr was unshaken, deluded by dreams of a mass uprising. "If federal troops shall be set in motion by whatever direction against the people of this state, I shall call for aid . . . from the city of New York and . . . other places.... The contest will then become national and our state the battle-ground of American freedom." It was this kind of inflammatory language that cost Dorr the little sympathy he had in Congress and rapidly drove moderates from the movement.

Dorr was looking more and more like a potential dictator. With rumors of imminent invasion from the Bowery Boys, many businessmen began to shut down their shops and head for safety. Rhode Islanders also had a warning for Mike Walsh and Alexander Ming: If they intend to sustain their hero "upon a bloody throne" by venturing into the state, they won't leave alive.[20]

On May 18, the day after his return to Providence, Dorr made good on his promise to take up arms against the state—an attack on the arsenal at two o'clock in the morning that was a fiasco from start to finish. With about 250 men and two artillery pieces, Dorr's forces set out to occupy the two-story brick building. Dorr gave the order to fire, but the cannon only flashed harmlessly. Some blamed the particularly foggy and wet conditions; others suspected sabotage. Nonetheless the arsenal was well defended by militia and volunteers loyal to Governor King.

The failed assault shattered what was already a fragile movement. By eight o'clock that morning, Dorr had learned that his government had fallen apart, with most key members resigning. With the moderates quitting, Dorr could only count on about sixty core organizers. Men like Pearce and Burrington Anthony, who had accompanied Dorr to Washington to make the case to President Tyler, abandoned their leader. Even as Dorr planned the attack on the arsenal, Anthony was trying to persuade as many as he could that it was too extreme an action and would sink the movement.

It took some time to convince Dorr, even after the failure of the arsenal attack, to give it up. Dorr instructed his People's Colonel Henry D'Wolf to hold a position at Woonsocket and prepare for another assault, but the orders were ignored. On May 19, Dorr fled the state to avoid capture, while his most extreme followers retreated, waiting for their next chance to strike.[21]

As Dorr's cause in Rhode Island was collapsing, the Bowery Boys appeared to be just getting started. On the eve of the arsenal attack, another rally was held in New York's City Hall Park, drawing several thousand people. It was this sizeable gathering of pro-Dorr forces in New York on May 17 that seemingly transformed the Rhode Island cause into a mass movement, but as subsequent events show, this was an illusion. Organizers of the New York rally included Democratic Party insurgencies and club-houses, such as the Spartan Band, which needed a potent political crisis outside the city to divert attention away from the violent election-day riot only a month earlier. The city was on edge, as voting results were still contested in Walsh's Sixth Ward.

Some New Yorkers went so far as to suggest that Dorr was simply a puppet in the hands of the Spartan Band, which urged him on in order to raise a distraction from their own attempt in April to hijack the Democratic Party. As the Washington correspondent for the *New York Tribune* concluded, "The Jacobins who have usurped the government of [New York] are aiding and abetting the usurpation [of government] in Rhode Island."[22]

The downtown rally was a free-for-all, with plenty of musket rounds fired into the air. The speakers' platform featured the top figures of New York's labor movement, including C. C. Cambreleng and Ely Moore. The celebrated actor Edwin Forrest, locus of the Astor Theater riot, sent a message of support. Several hundred children from lower Manhattan orphanages were enlisted in the parade, and even convicts from Blackwell's Island were given a day's pass from sympathetic prison officials. It was not the first time prisoners were let out of their cells for political purposes. Prisoners, of course, stuffed ballot boxes on Election Day, but now the presence of convicted criminals on the streets in a mass political rally was a serious concern to New Yorkers who appealed for law and order. There were rumors of secret caches of weapons hidden throughout the city, ready for an army of up to 700 to fight in Rhode Island or renew the Spartans' battle for power in the Sixth Ward.

Even as late as May 20, with Dorr in hiding and the People's Government folded, Slamm and Walsh made a direct appeal for support. Men were to be organized into companies, dubbed Patriot Volunteers, ready to march at a moment's notice against federal troops. Sympathizers made their voices heard in Boston as well, even as news spread about the botched arsenal attack. As many as 5,000 gathered on State Street on the evening of May 18 for a rally that was described as the "most enthusiastic ever."[23]

Loud outdoor rallies and musket fire on the lower east side were not enough to save Thomas Wilson Dorr; Governor King had him on the run. Indicted for treason and with a $1,000 bounty on his head, Dorr first fled to Connecticut. From there it was back to New York, sometime around May 23, under the protection of the Bowery Boys. What Dorr found in New York, when he arrived in a well-guarded private carriage, was a small but dedicated group, filled mostly from the ranks of Levi Slamm's Locofocos and Walsh's Spartans. They believed they could stage a coup in Providence or at least make enough noise to intimidate Governor King into making a concession. The governor and President Tyler remained unsure of their next move, hoping that Dorr and the Bowery Boys were either bluffing or too small a force to cause much trouble. There was enough uncertainty, however, for Tyler to put the U.S. Army at Newport on alert.

New York Democrats were split, with the Spartan Band on one side and on the other, the more pragmatic majority, who realized the game was over. Dorr certainly was advised by the Democratic establishment in New York and elsewhere to negotiate. Jacksonian Thomas Hart Benton told Dorr, "This is not the age, nor the country in which to settle political questions by the sword." A sympathetic New Hampshire senator, Levi Woodbury, pleaded, "Keep calm, cool, yet resolute. Shun violence, insubordination and civil war—but move forward."

Even the flag of support that flew over Tammany Hall was lowered as Dorr was spirited from one Bowery Boy safe house to another for several weeks to elude bounty hunters searching New York streets for the fugitive governor. In one instance, his pursuers got close to their target only to be seized by bodyguards. One was captured, roughed up and released. After that, the Bowery Boys never let the People's Governor out of their sight.[24]

With Dorr back in New York, the rumor mill was again pumping out stories of an impending armed force from New York and Boston. Reports circulated that Slamm was spotted throughout the state. The political boss of Coney Island pledged an unlikely contingent of 3,000 and was prepared to keep Dorr safe on the south Brooklyn retreat. Governor King and other defenders of the government worried that substantial aid and a few muskets from New York might lift the sagging spirits of the movement and reunite its disparate elements. Such a turn of events would close the door to any political settlement; "If Slamm, Bang and company, and other high-minded gentlemen from New York will stay at home we will have quiet," said one contemporary observer.[25]

The quiet was broken and the worst fears of conservative Rhode Islanders were aroused with an act of terrorism attributed to a Bowery Boy street fighter who tried to derail the Stonington Railroad. His object was to take lives, placing an obstruction on the rail in time for a passenger train. Luckily a freight train arrived first and discovered the attempted sabotage. The man, only identified as Smith, was taken into custody and sentenced to three years in the penitentiary.[26]

By early June, the remnants of Dorr's movement were regrouping at a makeshift fort near the town of Chepachet, close to the Connecticut border. Dorr stayed in New York until he felt secure enough to make what he thought would be a triumphant return to the encampment. At this time, a small number of Dorr followers began training at Woonsocket, and bands of armed men sprang up in Providence, North Providence, Cumberland, and Glocester. Artillery pieces and cannon were stolen from ships and wharves and spirited to secret locations.

There were conjectures that Dorr's defenders would approach 2,000 with the promised aid from Slamm, Ming, and the Spartan Band, and that these forces were prepared to occupy Providence. That was enough to convince the governor to appeal again to President Tyler for federal assistance, as well as mobilize the entire state militia. Governor King increased around-the-clock patrols of Providence, stationed troops at various points along the state's border, and had currency in Providence banks sent to Boston for safekeeping.

On June 21, Dorr left New York, this time accompanied by about twenty Bowery Boys at his side. It is likely that Walsh and the Spartan Band were not counting on a military victory, but were more interested in proving that they, not the Tammany Democrats, were the genuine defenders of liberty. Traveling aboard the steamboat *New Haven*, they arrived first at Norwich, Connecticut. There Dorr was met by friends who planned a strategy to hold their ground at a fort they had built on Acote's Hill near Chepachet. When Dorr arrived on June 25, he found a crude encampment with no amenities, not even water. On June 26, as Governor King declared martial law, there was a force at Chepachet with estimates varying as widely as 250 to 800.

News came to Chepachet that government troops were advancing on the fortification. Brown College was turned into a barracks to house some

Thomas Wilson Dorr naively hoped that Mike Walsh's Spartan Band would save his People's Government in Rhode Island. Instead, Dorr's last stand at Acote's Hill was more farce than revolution. (Courtesy of the Library of Congress)

of the 3,000 to 4,000 troops that took control of Providence. No person was allowed to enter or leave the city without a permit, and the offices of the pro-Dorr *Providence Express* were occupied. About 500 muskets were sent to Governor King's forces from the sympathetic governor of Massachusetts. Finally realizing his time was up, Dorr sent a notice of surrender on June 27 to the *Providence Express*. Dorr, deluded to the very end, thought that thousands of New Yorkers were on the way but just didn't get to Chepachet on time.

Despite the surrender, Governor King's forces moved in the next morning, stormed the mainly undefended fort, and took 100 prisoners. None of Walsh's or Slamm's men were captured. Slamm was reportedly spotted at Woonsocket in the days preceding the collapse and was at Acote's Hill, getting out just in time to evade capture. Seth Luther spent the night hiding in a barn but was arrested the next day. Luther was jailed in Newport, escaped by setting fire to his cell, but was quickly hunted down and recaptured.

Martial law lasted for several weeks into July, with hundreds of arrests and houses searched for revolutionaries. Tensions ran high, and on the night of July 28, troops dispersed an unruly crowd in Pawtucket with volleys of gunfire over their heads.

The victors were less than kind to the vanquished. As a result of martial law, as many as 300 to 400 people were imprisoned without formal charges. One New York lawyer who offered his services to the accused was run out of town. The one hundred or so prisoners rounded up at Acote's Hill and vicinity were tied together with large bed cords and marched on foot for sixteen miles to Providence. Stragglers were pricked with bayonets to keep them moving. Once on the streets of Providence, they were paraded through a gauntlet of angry citizens.[27]

In March 1843, Dorr's partisans petitioned the governor for release from prison in exchange for a loyalty oath, and by the end of the month, Luther and company were out of jail. That prompted the *Providence Journal* to jibe that "Luther, the illustrious Seth Luther, is again at large! Tremble yea malicious and cowardly ... ironfooted oppressors of the people, tremble! Lo, the champion of freedom, the jail-burner is among you." This odd character of New England radicalism spent the next three years traveling the country mostly on foot, warning of the dangers of the moneyed aristocracy, until he was committed to an insane asylum in 1846.

The failure of Dorr's movement did not necessarily mean a complete failure for Rhode Island suffragists. A constitution drafted in the fall of 1842 was a step forward—the vote was extended to most native-born Americans who could pay a newly instituted $1.00 poll tax.

Through the summer of 1844, Walsh and George Henry Evans agitated to free Dorr from jail. Underlying their calls for Dorr's freedom were threats; "let Dorr be liberated peaceably if he can and forcibly if he must," Evans wrote in the *Working Man's Advocate*. In September, Walsh, fellow-Spartan John Windt, and Evans set sail for Rhode Island to join a mass rally in Providence. The Bowery Boy was warned to stay home, but once again defied the Rhode Island governor.[28]

Recognizing his popularity behind bars, Governor King finally released Dorr in 1845. Dorr and many veterans of his movement joined Walsh and Evans in the National Reform Association, which saw cheap western land as a perfect opportunity to free workers from the low-paying factories in the large northeastern cities. By 1851, three years before his death, Dorr was fully rehabilitated by the state.

In the final analysis, both Governor King and the People's Governor Thomas Dorr were equally naive to assume that the Spartan Band or Slamm's Locofocos were skilled enough as revolutionaries to stage a European-style uprising in New England. For Governor King it meant overreaction and a siege mentality that lasted long after the danger had passed.

Some saw Dorr as a latter-day Napoleon intent on establishing a dictatorship, backed by New England socialists and New York Bowery Boys. But whether Dorr had any Napoleonic fantasies (and he likely did not), he had convinced himself, to the exclusion of all other opinion, that he enjoyed wide popular appeal. Dorr speculated that Rhode Island's small size and relative insignificance discouraged the support he felt was his due. He also wondered if the People's Government could have gained Tyler's approval if they had promised him their endorsement in the upcoming presidential election, or whether Governor King had won over Tyler with vows to back him for a second term.

The People's Governor also pinned his hopes for change on men like Walsh, who had neither the ability nor the will to carry their ideas further than the street brawl. Dorr believed that an invasion of federal troops "would light the torch of civil war throughout the length and breadth of the country." Thomas Dorr and the Bowery Boy were perfect allies, each comically boastful and genuinely intent on remaking the world for the common man.

As late as 1845, before Dorr's final release, Walsh was again threatening to bring his Bowery Boys back to Rhode Island for "a day of retribution.... Recollect 500 democrats from this city alone can soon make Providence as level and desolate as ancient Jerusalem was [made] by the Romans." For the leader of the Bowery Boys, well-worded bluster was just part of doing business in the chaotic politics of New York City.[29]

chapter 4

Workies, Locofocos, and the Subterranean Masses

In his tribute to New York's optimism, intellectual vibrancy, and the city's rise as a manufacturing colossus in the years before the Civil War, Walt Whitman praised the working class: "In all of them burns, almost with a fierceness, the divine fire which more or less during all ages, has only waited a chance to leap forth and confound the calculations of tyrants, hunkers and all their tribe. At this moment New York is the most radical city in America."

New York was indeed a center of radical thinking, a refuge for bohemians and socialists of every conceivable sect. It was a time, writes labor historian John Commons, of "unbounded loquacity ... [a] golden age of the talk-fest ... the hot-air period of American history." The three decades before the Civil War saw the birth of working-class political factions that were distinctly American, as well as the emergence of utopian socialists with ideas imported from France, and German disciples of Karl Marx. Antebellum New York also witnessed a trade-union movement whose fortunes rose and fell between the panic of 1837 and the depression that ensued after 1855.[1]

New York's street gangs and Mike Walsh's Bowery Boys were part of this disparate working-class culture. They articulated some of the vital issues of the period—from the ten-hour working day to universal education to the land reform movement that was the driving force behind Abraham Lincoln's Homestead Act of 1862. New voices of protest and socialism, such as George Henry Evans's, looked to the Bowery Boys as potent allies in their appeals to the city's industrial proletariat.

The roots of the Bowery Boys' radicalism are found in two earlier movements that attempted to restore workers' dignity in a dehumanizing capitalism. The Working Men's Party of 1829 and the Locofoco faction that emerged six years later represented the earliest challenges to the Democratic Party from the left, but both were short-lived and easily reabsorbed by the Party of Jackson. While clearly addressing the concerns of the laboring classes, these factions were middle class in composition, with most leaders migrating, when it was expedient to do so, into the Tammany power structure. Neither socialist nor wholly conservative, the Working Men's Party and the Locofocos sought to democratize capitalism.

The Working Men's Party grew out of a spontaneous labor protest in the spring of 1829, when employers tried to increase the working day from ten to eleven hours without compensation. The economy was suffering from a recession, and the city's manufacturers sought to make up for losses that winter. On April 28, 1829, employers retreated from their demands when faced with thousands of laborers assembled in the streets of lower Manhattan. Out of that show of force the Working Men, dubbed Workies, were born, and in October 1829, they nominated a slate of eleven candidates for office. Tammany was largely successful in beating back the challenge, but the Workies did put one of their own, a journeyman carpenter, in the state senate. They also captured about a third of the votes in the city, an impressive showing for a first electoral contest.[2]

Tammany now realized that the constituency that put Andrew Jackson in the White House could turn to a third party if the Democrats were not responsive to labor's grievances and continued to exclude laborers from its leadership. But Tammany's worries were brief, as the Working Men's Party quickly split into irreconcilable factions leading to its collapse.

In other cities Working Men's parties were established with much the same pattern of initial electoral success followed by division and dissolution. A Philadelphia Working Men's Party was already under way in 1828, and similar parties sprang up in cities across New York State, New England, Delaware, and Ohio. Sympathetic newspapers were started in some of the southern states, including Charleston, South Carolina, and Tuscaloosa, Alabama.[3]

In the New York Working Men's Party, an extreme left coalesced around Thomas Skidmore, with a strictly communist program to confiscate and equally divide land, and even personal wealth, among all adults over age twenty-one. Skidmore was also an inventor and visionary who urged New York's governor to build a massive telescope to search for life on the moon. Unlike other reformers of his time, Skidmore advocated a truly revolutionary program that called for class war on an international scale. A century before the Bolshevik Revolution, Skidmore envisioned workers' states in which industry would be nationalized. Like Marx and

New York's Democratic Party was constantly challenged by factions, like the Locofocos, that demanded a fairer capitalism and a more inclusive politics. (Courtesy of the Library of Congress)

later Russian communists, Skidmore advocated the masses taking power and the means of production into their own hands. "Let the [workers] appropriate the cotton factories, the woolen factories, the iron foundries... houses, churches, ships, fields of agriculture." Anticipating the Marxist worldview, Skidmore saw a future in which the state would lose its relevance, and people from one nation could just as easily reside in another by simply swapping their equal share of property.[4]

While Skidmore advocated an entirely new order in American society, centrists who preferred a reformed capitalism followed George Henry Evans into the majority faction. In December 1829, Evans's moderate course prevailed, and Skidmore left the Working Men, reconstituting his extremist core into a Poor Men's Party—a failure at birth. At this time Evans formulated an ideological position that Walsh's Spartan Band later expressed in the 1840s. At the foundation of this ideology was the notion that answers to the working-class question would be American in content and achieved preferably through the ballot, not the barricades of revolutionary Europe. Evans also proposed the distinctly American idea that relief for the industrial workers in the cities of the eastern seaboard was to be found in settling the western frontier.

A leading intellectual of the Jacksonian Left, George Henry Evans saw an unbounded American frontier as the answer to overcrowded cities, low wages, and poverty. Western lands would provide a haven for factory workers, both native-born and immigrant. (Courtesy of the Library of Congress)

In his retrospective on the Working Men's Party written a decade later, Evans said that Skidmore's extremism raised concerns that the Working Men were intent on dismantling society altogether. The question of confiscating property sidetracked the Working Men, Evans said. Unlike Skidmore, Evans was not opposed to wealth, provided that it is earned without the unfair advantage of government favoritism and monopoly.

Evans also feared that Skidmore's strident anticlericalism would hurt the Working Men's cause, which was foremost about wages and labor conditions. Yet a strain of anticlericalism, including a demand to tax church property, ran high among the young men who called themselves Bowery Boys. Walsh, in a statement of principles of his Spartan Association, called for abolishing "any law that either establishes or restricts religion" including laws that closed the saloons on Sundays. Even as Evans championed a strict separation of church and state and called for eliminating chaplains in the state legislatures, he worried that these issues would "[throw] a firebrand into the people's ranks," distracting attention from more immediate economic concerns.[5]

Although courting the Catholic immigrant to his Spartan Band, Walsh kept up his attack on the clergy through the 1840s, referring to the struggle against "the monied and ecclesiastical tyranny over the ruins of this glorious republic." In one of his short stories, "The Victim of Hypocrisy," published by his Spartan followers, Walsh depicts revivalist preachers as fast-talking seducers of innocent girls and performers of drug-induced abortions on their unfortunate parishioners. Walsh also uses the story to expose the double standard of a nineteenth-century moral code "that disgraces the woman for her mistakes before society," while the man's actions are viewed as "a little excusable folly of youth."

The Bowery Boys saw widening class divisions in all aspects of social life, with wealthy congregations that "[build] new grand edifices and manufacture ministers by wholesale." Walsh took particular aim at the aristocratic Trinity Church, saying that the church's claims that it was responsible for $2 million in charitable donations was a "deliberate lie by the old shysters." Founded in 1697, Trinity Parish was a significant landholder in the city, with assets estimated to be more than $6 million. With Philip Hone and John Jacob Astor among the parishioners, this cornerstone of American Episcopalianism was an easy target for the Bowery Boys.[6]

Walsh said that Trinity spent more on its wealthy uptown parishioners than the poorer Episcopalian churches in the lower wards, and he proposed confiscating church property for use by the poor. When some of Trinity's real estate holdings came under question, and titles were challenged in the courts, Walsh scaled Trinity's fences to protest land in New York that he claimed had become an "exclusive and privileged preserve from which the laboring class was excluded." In 1846, Reverend Stephen Olin, the president of Wesleyan University, concurred with the sentiments of the Bowery Boys, complaining that the wealthy were busy building cathedrals in America's cities while ignoring the needs of the poor.[7]

The privileges of the uptown clergy were a volatile side issue, but education was a central concern. Evans's Working Men and later, the Spartan Association, made equal access to education central to their reform programs. Early on, the Working Men's Party advocated a measure that would have separated children from their families, sending them to government-run boarding schools. Evans retreated from this more extreme proposal to favor free tax-supported schools for all, a cause the Bowery Boys embraced zealously. "Who objects to a tax for the support of education?" Evans asked. "The rich man ... because ignorance is his harvest field." From his time as a Spartan Band outsider to his tenure in the state legislature, Walsh consistently advanced the notion that education was the best way for laborers and immigrants to enter the American middle class; the educational advantages of the upper classes perpetuated the master/servant relationship between the employer and the employed, he said.

Walsh echoed the Working Men's credo when he declared that all children should be given the opportunity to attend a university to "elevate the sons of toil to their true position in society." He urged the educated sons of the middle class to open their doors to workers, saying that Columbia College alone could accommodate "all who require a collegiate education in the city of New York without receiving a cent from the public treasury."[8]

Other planks in the Working Men platform included opposition to imprisonment for debt and compulsory militia service. Working Men also demanded a mechanics' lien law that entitled employees to make claims against bankrupt companies to recover back wages, a measure especially important to the building trades.

Debtors' prison was identified by the Working Men as a harsh punishment that fell almost exclusively on the poor. In 1829, as many as 75,000 persons in the United States were imprisoned for debt. "It makes poverty a crime," said Walsh who reasoned that the threat of debtors' prison tempts the poor into criminal behavior. Why owe $25, Walsh asked, when the same penalty is applied for stealing the sum? The New York State Legislature abolished imprisonment for debt by 1832, and in another decade it was abolished in most states, but through the 1840s, Walsh continued to press for easing the laws on debt collection.[9]

Militia service was another "grievous burden" felt by the working class. Compulsory militia training could take a worker away from his trade for up to three days, depriving him of the meager salary needed to care for a family. Working-class advocates also noted that the wealthy were able to pay the $12 fine and avoid service.

Consistent with their opposition to hierarchy and any hints of aristocracy in American life, the Working Men were critical of the military, with some going so far as to call for abolishing the army and navy except in case of war. Evans and Walsh both favored cutting back the size of the military and using the money for the relief of the poor. Not necessarily opposed to American use of force, as in the case of the Bowery Boys' enthusiastic support for the Mexican War, Walsh viewed the military as yet another exclusive institution with an "anti-republican tendency."

He condemned West Point, saying the elite officers' school fostered aristocracy and an abuse of working-class recruits more suited to Europe than the United States. Most American soldiers were held under the will of "some contemptible epauletted pauper, educated perhaps at West Point, to be tied up and flogged," Walsh said. In the navy, conditions were barbarous, Walsh told the readers of the *Subterranean*, "with inhuman, wanton cruelties ... and the degrading use of the cat."[10]

The success of the Working Men in addressing vital laboring-class problems sealed its own fate as an independent party. The Democrats were astute enough to promptly latch on to many of these issues. During the elections of 1830, Tammany was able to divide and conquer, eliminating the Working Men from the field of New York politics: "worm[ing] themselves into the confidence of the Working Men ... [to] weaken their ranks," as Evans recounted later. Tammany won back journeymen votes, for example, by taking credit for the passage of the mechanics' lien law.[11]

Even as they were neutralized by Jackson's Democratic Party, the Workies awakened a class consciousness in the industrial laborer faced with decreasing wages and an impersonal system of factories and sweatshops. In his *Chants Democratic*, Sean Wilentz sees the Working Men as representing a significant juncture in American political history, where a left-wing insurgency arose through "cracks in the party system." It was the "first time," says Wilentz, that "New York craft workers organized across trade lines and looked beyond their immediate grievances to the deeper causes of social and political inequality." The Workies challenged those institutions, said Evans, that made "the wealthy more able to oppress, and the poor less able to resist."

Although the Working Men's Party failed to establish itself as a third force in American politics, it started Evans's career as a leading voice of the Left in New York and New England for two decades. Born in Hereford, England, in 1805 to a lower-middle-class family, Evans immigrated to New York at the age of fourteen with his father and brother. Settling in Manhattan about 1828, Evans learned the printing trade. With the formation of the

Working Men's Party, he established the newspaper he would publish periodically for two decades, the *Working Man's Advocate*.

Through its life, the newspaper would form alliances with other leftist papers, change mastheads, editorial offices, and shift its ideological focus from advocating state-supported education to an almost obsessive demand for free public lands in the West. Evans's publishing ventures were a continuous drain on his finances and health, usually forcing him to appeal to his friends for funds to carry on the fight. Another paper, *The Man*, was published from 1834 to 1835. By 1836, exhausted and broke, Evans had relocated to rural Granville, New Jersey, about twenty miles from New York. There, he published *The Radical* from 1841 until his return to New York in 1844, when he revived the *Working Man's Advocate* as the organ of his National Reform Association.

Evans's drive to draw New York's working-class youth to the panacea of land reform led him to a rocky alliance with Walsh's Bowery Boys. In 1844, Evans and Walsh merged the *Working Man's Advocate* with the *Subterranean* for three stormy months. Shortly thereafter, in 1845, Evans changed the name of the *Working Man's Advocate* to *Young America*, demonstrating his support for the doctrine of Manifest Destiny and the promise of the American frontier.

With the Working Men's Party spent after 1830, the ever-practical Evans, who boasted only two years earlier of his independence from the Democratic Party, threw his support behind Jackson's reelection in 1832, hoping to continue to nudge the Democrats to the left. As Evans told the Dedham Patriot in 1834, as long as Jackson was "tinctured with workeyism," workers' advocates would be supportive of the president.

Andrew Jackson's Democratic Party was fully aware of the Working Men's appeal; consequently, the Democrats became the party of free trade and cheap land. The Whigs, centered on Henry Clay's American System, courted the support of manufacturers on the eastern seaboard by advancing a protective tariff that kept factories full and wages low. The Democratic Party was a natural home for men like Evans who opposed Clay's conception of a government that takes an active role in promoting the interests of the capitalist through tariffs and a policy of internal improvements.

Also drawn to the Jackson party, Bowery Boys Mike Walsh and Edward Strahan aligned with free traders and viewed protection as government intrusion at the expense of labor. New York trade-union organizer C. C. Cambreleng urged the formation of grass-roots organizations to oppose tariffs and manufacturers who ruled "by controlling the laws and converting the measures of government into sources of profit for themselves." Whigs countered that tariffs kept domestically manufactured goods within reach of the working class. Moreover, by keeping American businesses competitive against their European rivals, jobs were plentiful. Walsh, however, told the *Subterranean*'s readers that "a tariff, no matter how framed, [is] a protection only to our oppressors."

The Bowery Boys and former Working Men also joined the Democrats in opposition to allocating government funds for internal improvements such as turnpikes and canals, which they said siphoned money from the treasury to benefit factory owners with western markets. Internal improvements, opponents claimed, inflamed sectional jealousies, consolidated greater power at the federal level, and empowered a Washington oligarchy of men with strong financial ties to railroads and other utilities. In opposing a government contract to build a transcontinental railroad, Walsh said such a project would "immediately enhance the value of the immense tracts of unoccupied land which unprincipled and grasping speculators have monopolized." It would, he predicted, "enslave the honest toiling mass of our people throughout the vast future."[12]

Although New York's working–class advocates naturally gravitated to the Democratic Party, they struggled long and hard for a seat at Tammany's table. In October 1834, Evans, Walsh, and labor activists like John Commerford rallied at Tammany Hall to demand a Workingmen's Committee in the Democratic Party to represent the interests of the city's laborers. When that effort failed, these same men tried to create a distinctly progressive wing, the Locofoco faction. As in the case of the Working Men, the Locofoco faction was weakened by disunity, inexperienced leadership, and a Democratic Party keen on co-opting its dissidents.[13]

The Locofocos were born literally in the dark when, in November 1835, these Democratic insurgents tried to hold a meeting at the Military and Civic Hotel to nominate a slate of Common Council candidates. Tammany regulars shut off the gas to the room, but the resourceful rebels finished the caucus by the light of their Locofoco matches. Officially known as the Equal Rights faction, the *Courier and Enquirer* coined the name Locofoco, and it stuck.

One prominent Locofoco who remained a fierce rival to the Spartans through the 1840s was Levi Slamm—locksmith and barroom brawler turned newspaper editor and union organizer. Like Walsh and Evans, Slamm was part of New York's bohemian subculture; his Locofocos were often referred to as "Slamm Bang & Company" by newspapers looking for a way to express the unpredictable nature of such groups on the fringe of New York society.

In both 1836 and 1837, Slamm was the Locofoco candidate for the state assembly, and as a labor leader, he represented the journeyman locksmiths in the General Trades' Union in 1835. In his newspapers *The New Era* and *The Plebian*, with the motto "Press Onward," Slamm advocated limited government and an end to charters and licenses to business.

The heart of the Locofoco ideology was the somewhat libertarian notion of limited government and a fairer capitalism that would give every worker the opportunity to become a businessman. When government awarded an exclusive contract for ferry service, or even issued business licenses, it amounted to government-sanctioned, or chartered, monopoly, the Locofocos argued. The result was a restraint on trade and dampened hopes for aspiring entrepreneurs. Critics of Tammany Hall, the Locofocos also denounced a corrupt system under which licenses and contracts were granted as political payback.

Locofocos, as well as Working Men, often traced their ideological roots to Thomas Jefferson's belief that government should offer no particular advantage to the business class. The Locofoco *New York Planet* referred to "the principles of radical democracy as taught by the immortal Jefferson. . . . Laws are passed by the score to sustain rotten monopolies with the money of the people. Laws are made exclusively for the benefit of capital and against labor."[14]

Typical of the government-licensed monopolies was the city's thirty-year franchise to the New York and Harlem Railroad Company in 1831 for exclusive rights to operate a rail from the Harlem River to Twenty-third Street, and later to Fourteenth Street. Another source of Locofoco indignation was the exclusive contract granted in 1811 to the Fulton Ferry for service between New York and Brooklyn; the Common Council had blocked any competition.

Although they agreed with the basic Locofoco principle that government-chartered monopolies were unfair, George Henry Evans and Mike Walsh both stayed at arm's length from the faction for reasons that had as much to do with political infighting as matters of ideology. Like the Locofocos, Walsh sympathized with the entrepreneur locked out of lucrative government contracts that favored large, politically connected businesses. These privileged contractors were also responsible for millions of dollars lost in corruption and kickbacks. Walsh certainly was in keeping with the temper of his constituency when he told them, "My war cry is and has been—down with all monopoly." Walsh took a typically Locofoco stance when he said a city contract for a rail line down Broadway would "give away the public streets to an incorporated monopoly of purse proud knaves." Walsh also questioned a stringent requirement for licensing pilot boats whose job was to navigate vessels through narrow straits and difficult waters. As a result of the rule, the state contract was limited to only about twenty operators. He labeled the state's preference a "disgraceful conspiracy among the old monopoly pilots against the rights of their younger and more deserving rivals." In addition, as Walsh tried to attract Irish immigrants to the Spartan Band, he made a typically Locofoco appeal against business licenses that were often used to restrict competition in certain trades to native-born Americans.[15]

For William Leggett, the Locofoco editor and political theorist, a thoroughly unregulated marketplace would provide the greatest opportunities for all. Walsh and Evans rejected this laissez-faire doctrine as extreme. Instead of eliminating government's role, some ex-Working Men and Walsh's Bowery Boys favored a positive, activist government that would promote fairness and level the playing field, a conception closer to nineteenth-century socialism. In sharp contrast to the Locofocos, Evans preferred government operation of critical services, like railroads, ferries, and canals, that would serve the public interest, "not a regiment of rich aristocrats."

In the case of ferries between Manhattan and Brooklyn, Evans doubted that either a single contractor or a totally free marketplace with multiple ferry operators would best serve the city. Reflecting his preference for a government solution, Evans proposed "that the ferries ought to be free and that the expense ought to be paid out of taxes levied on the property of both cities." Workers were being gouged by steadily rising fares as Brooklyn became a more attractive residential community, said Evans, robbing "the labor of many an honest mechanic who crosses the river for his employment."[16]

Uncompromising in his stance against government planning, Leggett said municipal-run ferries, as Evans proposed, chip away at private property rights. Tax-supported services, Leggett argued, also would benefit the user at the expense of those who do not use the service. Evans countered by saying, "Every taxpayer in New York does use the ferry—if not directly, then indirectly.... We have no doubt that the making of roads, streets, canals, ferries and bridges is one of the few powers that belongs to the public authorities."[17]

Calling for government to address political and economic inequality, Evans carried the concept of positive government several steps further during his crusade for free public lands. Evans would divide the frontier into townships consisting of small farms and planned communities. The township government would be, in Evans's words, "the agent of society," with the power to draw the lines and limits of private property. Public works would be managed by the government, not private contractors.

Evans aligned with the Locofocos and President Jackson in the battle against the godfather of all monopolies—the Bank of the United States. Chartered in 1816, the bank had grown by 1830 into a financial and political colossus with branches in twenty-nine cities. Functioning as both a central bank and a commercial bank, it had enormous reserves provided by the government. As a commercial bank, it accepted deposits and made loans to the public, handling 20 percent of the nation's loans and holding a third of the nation's total deposits and specie. Such a powerful monopoly could restrict access to capital and exert a competitive advantage over the state banks, which resented the control the central bank had on the economy.[18]

Between 1832 and 1836, Andrew Jackson and his allies on the Left, including the Locofocos, Evans, and trade unionists, joined the fight against rechartering the bank. Power, influence, and money had made the Bank of the United States into a potent political threat to the Jackson presidency. Jackson opponents like Henry Clay were reaping large consultant and legal fees from the bank. "Money is power and this tremendous monopoly has now entered the political field," Evans said, warning that the Bank "has the power to regulate and control nearly all the commercial operations in the country."

Although Evans fought alongside the president to slay the Bank of the United States, he also attacked Democratic Party insiders who were profiting from the subsequent upsurge of state bank charters in New York. These insiders were fast becoming the officers of banks that would benefit as federal deposits from the central bank were transferred to new charters. Evans warned that while "a single despot is a curse; a host of petty tyrants is often greater." He complained that wealth and political connections offered an unfair advantage in the securing of credit, circumstances that deprived many journeymen from starting their own businesses. "The banks," said Evans, "should facilitate industry ... but they are now partial and exclusive."[19]

Evans and the Locofocos also extended the banking fight to paper money and the practice of many employers of paying their workers with depreciated notes from insolvent banks, or even with counterfeit notes. Evans praised the state legislature in 1835 for prohibiting the circulation of notes under $5, but Evans and Walsh both looked forward to the day when paper money would be confined to business-to-business transactions.

Even as Slamm's Locofocos and Evans's Working Men remained on the edges of the Jackson party, they were an influential voice for labor inside and outside Democratic councils. Proudly keeping the Locofoco label after rejoining the Democratic Party, Slamm's followers embraced progressive causes at home and across the Atlantic. Slamm, for example, joined Mike Walsh in condemning appeals to anti-Catholic bigotry. "Hatred to foreigners is a foreign principle.... Nativism is an exotic plant not indigenous to a free soil," Slamm said. Despite a personal enmity between them, Walsh admitted he and Slamm shared a desire to topple New York's economic and political aristocracy. "We are all engaged in the same glorious cause—the elevation of the downtrodden masses," Walsh said.

That glorious cause also brought New York's left wing and Bowery Boys into contact with European socialists and revolutionary movements, reflecting a genuine internationalism among the working-class clubhouses. Slamm left the pages of his *Plebian* open to those who showed solidarity with European socialists—"intelligent men of the right kind." The British Chartists, socialist rebels against the inequities of the Industrial Revolution, provided some of the ideological foundation to the Spartan Association and Evans's land reformers.[20]

For his part, Evans included the Chartists and "communists of England, Ireland, France and Germany [among] the noble pioneers" of the land-reform movement. For their part, the main Chartist newspaper, *Northern Star*, published out of Leeds, often cited Evans on the condition of the American labor movement. In addition, veteran Chartist Thomas Ainge Devyr joined Evans and Walsh as they organized land reformers in 1844. In his *Young America*, Evans recognized the influence of the German communists coalescing around Karl Marx. "The ideas of the communists are just enough to take hold of the whole moral and intellectual energies of the Germans."

Sixth Ward workers raised money in support of the Polish uprising in 1831, and Evans blamed American capitalists, who supplied loans to Czar Nicholas I, for the Poles' defeat at the hands of the Russian army. In the years following the European uprisings of 1848, Walsh and other Bowery Boys rallied at the steps of Tammany Hall for Louis Kossuth and the Hungarian revolutionaries. Referring to the not-forgotten ardor of the French Revolution, Walsh said the "spirit of the age [is] a glorious leveling." And using language that bore striking similarities to Marx, Slamm recognized that the "history of the world is the history of a struggle of labor and capital."[21]

Yet for all the rhetoric and bravado of class warfare and internationalism, men like Slamm, Evans, and Walsh fell short of urging workers to take up arms. As insurgent Democrats at heart, they held out hope that reforms within the Democratic Party would eventually narrow class distinctions. Slamm himself cautioned, "No drastic revision of society should be attempted," referring to those who experimented with utopian socialism imported from Europe.

Despite the similarities in their views, Walsh saved his most bitter language for Slamm. For the leader of the Bowery Boys, principles often took a back seat to political infighting and personality conflicts. It is likely that Walsh's antipathy to the Locofocos was largely personal; particularly galling to the Bowery Boy was Slamm's decision to return to Tammany after 1837, and as a Tammany insider Slamm helped block Walsh's bid for the Democratic nomination to state office in 1841.

While appealing to the honest men who joined the Locofoco ranks, Walsh attacked the leaders who he accused of betraying their ideals for political and financial gain. Slamm, he said, lacked the courage or ability to take the Democratic Party out of the hands of the moneyed elite. Instead, he was bought out with Tammany bribes and lucrative patronage jobs for his lieutenants.

Walsh wondered how the *Plebian*, with only 300 subscribers, could stay in business. Selling political endorsements, the *Plebian* was rewarded with city printing contracts or cash payments, and some aldermen were indebted to Slamm for as much as $1,000 for getting out the vote on their behalf, Walsh charged. Here was a man, Walsh said in his characteristically stinging style, who was "too lazy to work for a living and too stupid to honestly acquire one by any other means." It was little wonder Slamm successfully sued Walsh for libel landing the Bowery Boy in jail on Blackwell's Island.

In the final analysis, the Locofocos posed the same threat to the Democratic Party as the earlier Working Men's Party and the later Spartan Band. Not strong enough to win on their own, the Locofocos were still able to drain sufficient votes from Tammany to hand the Whigs victories in municipal elections in 1837. In a bid for the mayoralty in 1837, the Locofoco candidate polled only 4,000 votes, but that was enough to split the Democratic vote and elect a Whig mayor. The Whigs were also helped that year by an anti-Tammany backlash following the dismissal of popular fire chief James Gulick.

While Slamm was lured back to Tammany, some conservative state Democratic leaders, such as Governor William Marcy, were reluctant to accommodate the Locofocos, fearing the Whigs would not only exploit the Locofoco designation, but go to great lengths to misrepresent the influence of the Left in the party. Tammany was fractured for years to come, as conservatives chafed at what they saw as pandering to Locofoco causes. Some conservatives bolted the Democratic Party and joined the Whigs—defections that pleased Locofocos, who could talk of rejoining a more ideologically pure Democratic Party.

The failure of both the Working Men's Party and the Locofocos to emerge as alternatives to the two-party system only strengthened the hands of political clubhouses like the Spartan Band, which tapped into the steadily rising discontent of Irish immigrants, unskilled laborers, and skilled workers who were losing ground to the factory system. Tammany, which had adopted many of the causes of the Working Men, was still too slow to respond to economic distress, and independent political action seemed futile. Evans said it was not enough for workingmen to become politicians; they failed because they could not unite in a common program that distinguished them from Tammany.

With the panic of 1837 and the hard times that followed well into the next decade, the response to low wages, high prices, and long hours could vary from union organizing to dabbling in utopian socialism to disorder in the streets. The Bowery Boys, under Mike Walsh, took all these paths, as they expressed the frustrations of an increasingly radicalized proletariat.

The conviction that labor and capital were irreconcilable in the industrializing economy crystallized for many by the middle 1830s, but there were rumblings from organized labor even in the first decades of the nineteenth century, as tradesmen, imbued with the spirit of Jefferson's republicanism, claimed that employers alone should not control wages. New York City's trade-union movement began largely in the city's benevolent organizations, which sought common ground between artisan master and employee; they paid accident, sickness, and death benefits or assisted journeymen on the way to opening their own shops.

Strikes were a rarity in the early 1800s, yet an 1808 strike by a union of shoemakers, the Journeymen's Cordwainers' Society, was a prelude to the steady deterioration of labor relations through the first half of the century. The shoemakers struck a prominent employer, Corwin and Aimes, that was subcontracting work to lower-wage nonunion journeymen. When other master shoemakers came to the aid of Corwin and Aimes, the workers called an unprecedented general strike. By the late 1820s and early 1830s strikes were becoming more frequent and the tactics more confrontational, as in the case of the weavers' strike of 1828 that saw attacks on unsympathetic journeymen.

By the early 1830s trade unions began to adopt a keener sense of class identity. A quicker pace in labor organizing, coupled with inflationary prices and a successful carpenters' strike, led to the establishment in 1833 of the General Trades' Union (GTU) of the City of New York. Composed of representatives of nine trades, the GTU was a catalyst to a rising tempo of walkouts until the panic of 1837 put an abrupt end to the GTU and labor activism. In its four years, the GTU represented up to two-thirds of the city's workers.

While GTU members retained their autonomy as craft unions, a citywide convention coordinated strikes and aid to strikers. Distinct from earlier artisan labor societies, the GTU kept out the master tradesmen, making it genuinely worker-controlled. Yet the GTU steered a moderate course, sticking mostly to wage issues and supporting a strike only after it was approved by the full convention. GTU president John Commerford cautioned his members not to rely on strikes and confrontation with employers as the only path to higher wages. Consistent with its centrism, the GTU upheld the right to private property and called for uniting employers and employees "for the mutual benefit of both."

The GTU and its successors resisted political alliances, but these unions did not avoid politics altogether. The GTU leadership, for example, spoke out against the use of prison labor that dumped cheap goods on the market.

Products of prison labor undercut the prices journeymen could offer by as much as 50 percent. Prison labor hit the building trades especially hard, and masons in New York refused to work with stone cut in the shops of Sing Sing prison.

Union pressure led to legislation in Albany in 1835 to limit the number of convicts to be employed in any one occupation and, in a move that seems counterintuitive today, the New York State Legislature also barred convicts from learning a trade. Bowery Boy and Spartan George Wilkes, while calling consistently for prison reform and humane treatment of men behind bars, was pleased when the Common Council defeated a measure that would have put prisoners on Blackwell's Island to work manufacturing saddles. "There are few among us who are not strongly desirous of seeing the criminal properly and beneficially employed, but a sense of justice is superior to a consideration of expediency," he said.

Despite these political concerns, the central issue of the GTU was wages; the four years of the GTU saw as many as 150 strikes and other walkouts for higher wages, as well as challenges in the courts to employers who branded the walkouts as conspiracies against free trade. In 1835 the New York State Supreme Court ruled in favor of employers in Geneva, New York, saying that a strike by journeyman shoemakers was a criminal conspiracy and that union pressure was injurious to trade. The rationale was that if Geneva employers were held to a higher union wage scale, they could be undercut by shoemakers in a neighboring town.

The court's ruling was a green light to manufacturers to fire strikers and raise the level of confrontation between master and journeyman. In February 1836, stevedores and other dockworkers struck for wages; the threat of a citywide strike and its impact on the city's economy so concerned Mayor Cornelius Lawrence that he called up the National Guard to force the dockworkers to back down. That only galvanized the GTU to threaten a general strike.

When journeyman tailors went out on strike the same year, they were arrested on conspiracy charges and fined heavily. In addition, Democratic Party leaders in the midst of fighting the Locofoco insurgency refused to let strike leaders meet at Tammany Hall. Organized labor counterattacked with a rally that drew thousands of workers to City Hall Park on June 13, 1836. A handbill distributed throughout the city reflected the mood of a rank and file growing far more militant than even the GTU leadership. Describing the court as a "tool of the aristocracy against the people," the workers' position was that "wage slaves of the north are now on a level with the slaves of the south."

Commenting on this awakening labor militancy in the late 1830s, Philip Hone reflected the opinion of many of the city's economic elite, who

Collaborator with Mike Walsh on the *Subterranean* and editor of the sensationalist *Police Gazette*, George Wilkes espoused progressive causes from prison reform, to opposition to the death penalty, to universal education. (Courtesy of the Library of Congress)

feared an alliance of Bowery Boys, immigrants, and labor activists: "The elements of disorder are at work; the bands of Irish and other foreigners, instigated by the mischievous councils of the trades' union and other combinations of discontented men, are acquiring strength and importance which will long be difficult to quell."[22]

Aside from the devastating panic of 1837, the GTU was severely weakened by political fractures. The main issue was collaboration with the

Democratic Party. Ely Moore, who served as the first GTU president, cast his lot with Tammany and was duly paid back with a seat in the U.S. Congress in 1834. Moore lost considerable credibility with union men when he was appointed to a New York state commission to investigate convict labor and sided with those who minimized the threat to journeymen workers. John Commerford, who succeeded Moore in 1835 until the GTU's demise in 1837, sought a more independent political position for labor.[23]

The GTU in New York was followed by similar large-scale trade unions in other cities. A General Trades' Union was founded in Philadelphia in 1834, and that same year delegates from these unions met in New York to organize the National Trades' Union (NTU), the first nationwide labor federation. Focused on raising wages, the NTU also attracted reformers who came out of the Working Men's Party and later gathered under Evans's and Walsh's National Land Reform banner. The NTU advocated free public lands to settlers in the West, improved conditions for workers in the garment trades, and abolition of child labor. Influenced by the progressive ideas of the Working Men, the NTU supported universal education and attacked what it called the "monopoly of knowledge." Ex-Working Men, Bowery Boys, and union men were united in their demand for libraries and well-qualified teachers in the city's poorer wards.

Unwieldy with competing interests and personalities, the NTU met again in New York in 1835 and Philadelphia in 1836 before disappearing in the aftermath of the panic. Commerford's dream of one fraternal union stretching from Maine to Florida evaporated with a worsening economy that put so many men out of work that those remaining lost all leverage they had with employers. Labor activism would not reemerge until the mid-1840s.[24]

Commerford, while not abandoning trade unionism altogether, aligned with Evans's land reformers and the Spartan Association. To Commerford, the fragile labor movement meant that the cure to industrial misery ultimately lay in the vast stretches of farmland to the west. Walsh and Commerford condemned speculators who kept up the price of land, putting it out of reach of urban laborers who yearned for refuge on the frontier.

With economic recovery starting slowly in the mid-1840s, the labor movement was revitalized; workers were back on the job but were still victims of wages that could hardly keep up with rising prices. In 1844, Evans asked why master tailors could not raise their journeymen's wages when business was improving at most tailor shops in the city; "some can't even earn seventy-five cents a day, and the women half that sum," he complained.[25]

In addition, by the mid-1840s, unions, which were concerned primarily with the plight of skilled workers, were superseded by new voices that addressed the increasing number of unskilled workers and immigrants.

These unskilled workers, almost 40 percent of the city's workforce by 1855, included the longshoremen, cartmen, coal heavers, lumberyard workers, quarrymen, pipe layers, railroad stable men, street pavers, and the ditch diggers who built Central Park. They were joined by the newly proletarianized tailors, shoemakers, printers, and textile workers in a more assertive labor movement.

As the number of unskilled workers grew, barriers within the labor movement between unskilled and skilled workers started to break down. In 1854, striking longshoremen were encouraged by shipwrights, who agreed to prevent their journeymen from working until the strike was settled. This new style of trade unionism was expressed by the National Typographical Society, which told its members in 1850 that "it is useless to disguise the fact that there exists a perpetual antagonism between Labor and Capital."

Through the 1850s, printers represented the more militant of the trades; Ely Moore, John Windt, Walsh, and Evans were printers by trade, as were many of the Locofocos. Although a locksmith, Slamm learned the printing business enough to put out two working-class newspapers. Contributing to the radicalization of the printing trade was the growth of the mass circulation newspaper as a political instrument; the number of American dailies grew from 50 in 1830 to 138 a decade later. Advances in technology also freed up printers like Walsh, Evans, and Slamm to focus less on the technical end of the business and more on using their papers to promote a political agenda.

Labor historian Richard Ely, who notes a similar trend in printers' unions in Europe, proposes that their activism may be related to the role the printer played as journalist and intellectual. Walsh saw a direct benefit to the Bowery Boys from advances in printing machinery that made possible a partisan press that "kindles into flames the dormant energy of the masses who demand that labor shall be respected." Bowery Boy George Wilkes told the readers of his *Police Gazette* that "the power of the press" lays before the public "what smug and snug officials are so anxious to withhold."[26]

Those same innovations in technology threw significant numbers of skilled pressmen out of work, replacing them with younger apprentices who were receptive to appeals from the Left. Technological advances and new machinery that revolutionized production in almost every trade contributed to the changing relationship between labor and capital. Yet for the Bowery Boys and their allies in the land-reform movement, technology was not necessarily the problem, and smashing the engines of progress was not the answer. In their 1844 land-reform manifesto, *A Report to the People of the United States*, Evans and Walsh refer to the "onward march of science and machinery," predicting that once society is reorganized with an American frontier open to the multitudes, "machinery, from the formidable rival, will sink into the obedient instrument of our will."[27]

They understood that the forces of the Industrial Revolution were irreversible, and that a Luddite response would be inconsistent with an American culture of progress. The most extreme member of the Working Men, Thomas Skidmore, was an inventor working on improvements in gunpowder manufacture, papermaking, and a metal casting process to mass-produce globes cheaply, believing that a sound knowledge of geography was essential to an educated working class. Skidmore's position, like Walsh's, was that technology could serve the good of society if it is in the hands of the workers themselves. The optimism that science and progress would eventually free mankind from the drudgery of factory labor was echoed by another early American socialist, William Heighton, who predicted that science "is destined to burst the chains of human oppression."

Commerford called mechanization "inevitable" and "destined to revolutionize the economy," disagreeing with those who wanted to deny patents to innovations that would put men out of work. "This [progress] cannot be avoided, as machinery does contribute to the wealth of the nation," he said. Instead, Commerford proposed a federal program that would train displaced workers for comparably paying jobs in the new industrial economy of the mid-nineteenth century.

Expressing the nationalism of the Young America movement, Walsh praised the abundance of open territory and the ingenuity of American technology that was spreading westward; iron and steam were shaping the continent for the benefit of all mankind, he said. Anticipating the American century, Walsh proudly concluded:

> We have the triumph of machinery most amply displayed.... Our ships are models of elegance unequalled for speed [and] bear in their capacious holds the excess of our produce to every portion of the globe.... In the United States machinery is of the most perfect construction and the most extensive application, increasing the power of the people to an extent that is incredible.[28]

Linking invention with his advocacy of free public lands, Walsh said that advances in railroads, shipping, and farming would allow American workers to more easily settle and exploit the frontier, draining population from the overcrowded cities of the Northeast.

As the labor movement saw signs of new life, Evans, Walsh, and Commerford took up the cause of land reform as the encompassing remedy. However, the land reformers had to compete for the workers' attention with those who wanted to keep the labor movement within the confines of the bread-and-butter issues of wages and hours. Evans regarded conflict with capital through strikes and union organizing futile in the long run. Workers, he said, should withdraw from the factory system—to find alternatives that would restore the ideals of the American Revolution.

chapter 5

Go West Young Proletary

I n February 1844, George Henry Evans returned to New York from
his farm in rural New Jersey with a solution to the labor crisis and a
plan bordering on obsession to sell it to the American people. For
Evans, free public lands in the American West, organized around carefully
planned suburban farming communities, would make every worker a
self-sufficient master of his own destiny. By drawing the oversupply of
labor from the cities, workers that remained in New York and other urban
centers would see their wages rise.

Although Evans wrote consistently in favor of free public lands through
the 1830s and early 1840s, he made it the centerpiece of the National Reform Association he founded and the revived *Working Man's Advocate*. Evans
was drawn back to the lower east side by a new sense of labor activism as
workers returned to their jobs. What they found upon returning to work
were wages that remained at subsistence level and factory conditions as bad
as they had been before the panic of 1837.

Evans said he observed far more paupers in the streets of New York than
previously. Prices for many basics rose as much as 30 percent between the
middle 1840s and early 1850s. Estimates that it took a weekly budget of
between $10.50 and $11.00 for a family of five to live in New York in
1851 were contrasted with salaries that barely kept up or fell short.

Single-mindedly, Evans began and ended every discussion of America's
problems—from slavery to war with Mexico to child labor—with the call
for free public lands to settlers. He sought allies literally on the street corners

of New York and in the utopian socialist communes of New England. In the poorer wards of New York, Evans enlisted the support of the Bowery Boys, who would be helpful in spreading the word deep into the city's working class culture. For the Spartan Association and other political clubs in the city, Evans's land-reform scheme had an irresistible appeal, and it brought the Bowery Boys into the center of a national debate on the conditions of the American working class.

The uniquely American promise of the open frontier as the answer to class conflict shaped not only American ideas of socialism, but defined a generation of antebellum radicals including Mike Walsh. The land reform movement also gave the Bowery Boy and his Spartans a patina of respectability and a national platform. Walsh pledged himself to the land reform position "to the exclusion of every other subject" and boasted that his Spartans were rallying to free public lands as early as 1841. Walsh, of course, was adept at using any issue as leverage in his battles with rival neighborhood factions. In this case, he told working-class youths that the Spartans, not Isaiah Rynders's Empire Club, were the true advocates of settling the poor and degraded factory workers on the virgin soil.[1]

Evans recognized the influence the Spartan Association wielded among the lowest rungs of the laboring class, calling the Spartans "a body of honest, hard working men in a political association." As an intellectual, Evans may have differed in temperament, but he praised Walsh as the "one man in this city, since 1835, [who] has ... the self-devotion to print the great truths that are to redeem the downtrodden masses." Evans came to Walsh's defense when the Bowery Boy was jailed for libel, saying Walsh was a political prisoner: "It was gross injustice." Robert Ernst, a historian of New York's Irish and German immigration, observes that "Evans, the more profound thinker, tried to win over Walsh, the better leader." Consequently Evans was not above playing to Walsh's monumental ego when trying to sway a packed meeting hall of shouting Bowery Boys to join the land-reform movement.[2]

During the fall of 1844, Evans and Walsh briefly merged their two newspapers. It was a poor match of strong personalities, and the papers went their separate ways after only three months. Charging that Evans had suppressed one of his editorials, Walsh withdrew from the partnership. More likely, the reason for the breakup was that Walsh's diatribes and vigorous self-promotion competed for space with Evans's land-reform cause. Walsh was too volatile for Evans, who wanted less sensationalism and more thoughtful discussion. Despite the publishing fiasco, the Bowery Boys remained as committed as ever to land reform, and joined Evans in the labor struggles of the early 1850s.

With the National Reform Association, Evans drew a core of energetic believers and, as in previous working-class insurgencies, much of the leadership came out of the printing trades. The group's first central committee included four printers; Walsh; Irish Chartist Thomas Ainge Devyr, who was editor of a small left-wing newspaper in the Williamsburgh area of Brooklyn; John Windt; and Kentucky-born Lewis Masquerier. Evans also found enthusiastic allies in labor organizer John Commerford and the German Marxist Hermann Kriege. The National Reformers attracted their share of veterans of the Working Men's Party and Locofoco faction, including James Pyne who was prominent in both movements.

In March 1844, the National Reform Association set up headquarters at the corner of Chatham and Mulberry streets, opening their doors to meetings every Thursday night. They also organized a speakers' bureau consisting of meetings staged by Walsh and Devyr in city parks to catch the attention of workers as they returned home in the evening. Between March and September 1844 they held as many as eighteen such street-corner rallies.

True to Walsh's strategy of organizing politically on the ward level, he and Evans built, in just a few months, a solid network of National Reform clubs

An eccentric visionary and partisan of Mike Walsh's Spartan Band, Lewis Masquerier urged Central Park architect Frederick Law Olmsted to turn 80 acres near New York into a model community powered by windmills. (Courtesy of the Library of Congress)

in most wards of the city. By September 1845, National Reform clubs were active in the Second, Tenth, Eleventh, Fourteenth, Sixteenth, and Seventeenth wards. In addition, there were land-reform groups in several states, including New Jersey, Pennsylvania, Ohio, and Massachusetts. Typically, speakers, like Commerford and Windt in one meeting in the Fourteenth Ward, called for settling native-born and Irish newcomers on western farms. "The American people are an emigrating people," said Commerford.[3]

Evans recruited workers who felt the effects of factory wages that had never recovered from the panic and the ensuing depression. In their July 6, 1844, statement of principles, *A Report to the People of the United States*, Evans, Walsh, Devyr, and Commerford made their case to New York's working class. Printing 20,000 copies, they invoked a patriotic message designed to attract those who viewed America as an exception to the monarchies of old Europe. The United States, they said, was distinguished by a constitution that was "so just and equal that it may well claim divine origin."

For Evans and Walsh, political power achieved through the vote would usher in a revolution without the uprisings that rocked Europe. The National Reformers called on members to stack Democratic Party caucuses in order to elect sympathetic candidates, and they petitioned Congress to enact a homestead law. In a handbill circulated throughout the city in 1846, Evans urged American workers to "Vote Yourself a Farm" by putting into office those who would endorse the National Reform platform.[4]

The National Reformers proposed a litmus test for any candidate, Democrat or Whig, seeking office on the local or national level. To win the reformers' endorsement on Election Day, candidates had to submit a written pledge to support free homesteads to settlers. Free land to settlers dominated the agenda, but the National Reformers also adopted much of the old Working Men's platform, including universal suffrage, free trade, the ten-hour day, and elimination of government charters and privileges to business.

Learning from the experience of the Working Men's Party, Evans and Walsh resisted the third-party route. Evans and Walsh were not willing to declare the National Reform Association a political party, holding out hope that they could get the Democratic Party to fully endorse their platform. In some cases, when neither the Whig nor the Democratic candidate would support free homesteads, the National Reformers reserved the right to run their own candidate. The wide appeal the land-reform program had, especially within the Democratic Party and among Whigs who later joined the Republicans, discouraged National Reformers from launching third-party candidacies. In 1846, for example, a combined slate of National Reformers and Regular Democrats included Walsh for State Assembly, Windt for State Senate, and Commerford for Congress.

While they attracted trade-union leaders to reach a wider working-class audience, National Reformers had little faith in strikes. With workers free to settle on public land, the need to strike for higher wages, which Devyr called "paltry ends," would disappear. Still, the National Reformers were able to enlist prominent labor leaders who said the lesson of the GTU and the panic of 1837 was that workers needed an alternative to simple trade unionism; Commerford was optimistic that free homesteads would become part of mainstream trade-union thinking.

The first issue of Evans's *Working Man's Advocate* on March 16,1844, devoted its front page to a diagram that held the key to universal happiness and prosperity. It was a square divided precisely into a grid of smaller squares, each representing plots in a planned model community. In the center was a space for public buildings, light manufacturing, and a park; four main roads radiated from the center to each of the corners.

While Evans and German émigré Hermann Kriege debated about the appropriate size of each farm, Evans thought individual grants of fifty to eighty acres would "give each American citizen twenty-one years of age [a] farm for life." Proposals to grant settlers larger farms, up to 160 acres, would physically isolate each homestead and weaken the structure of the larger township, Evans said.

Regardless, Evans estimated that it would be centuries before population on the public lands of the American West would shrink each homestead down to 10 acres, the least number of acres possible to support a family. By then, the world would have found a new panacea. "Have we not boundless territories of unsettled, almost unexplored lands?" Evans asked. Profoundly naive, Walsh also envisioned that as the country's population increased the land apportioned to each citizen would simply be adjusted. "This would be repeated at stated periods, at least every twenty-one years. As all settlers will be aware of the conditions at the outset they will have no cause to object to these subsequent divisions."[5]

Evans proposed that these "rural republican townships," which he called "permanent, well-organized and orderly," would be laid out by the federal or state government in one of the few functions of government above the local level. As self-contained suburban utopias, the communities would be responsible for their own courts, police, and care for the indigent. "The people of each township [would be] empowered to expel, by a vote at their annual town meeting, any settler who should neglect to cultivate the farm."

One of Evans's most enthusiastic disciples in the land reform-movement, Lewis Masquerier, presciently envisioned a system of windmills to generate energy on every homestead. In a letter to the architect of Central Park, Frederick Law Olmsted, Masquerier predicted that with sufficient wind power and urban planning, the future landscape of the country—and the world—would be "a rural city." He suggested Olmsted build such a model community on 80 acres near New York "to give instruction to the thousands who visit it. . . . It would [be] something like heaven on earth."[6]

At first, the townships would be located near enough to large cities so they could establish a healthy trade of agricultural produce with finished goods. As more communities were organized, they would form a network linked through trade and highways. Eventually, overcrowded cities would become obsolete, as the nation returned to the Jeffersonian idyll of the small farmer and artisan manufacturer. Evans revered Jefferson as the "rebel of rebels," who would have agreed that large cities only contributed to inequality and poverty, and that government works best on the local level. "I am of Jefferson's opinion that the great cities are great nuisances, and there ought to be a considerable vacant space between houses," Evans said.

Not surprisingly, the National Reformers designed their model communities around a similar idea that Jefferson devised to divide counties into smaller wards. Evans was likely influenced by Jefferson's notion that every American was entitled to at least fifty acres of soil. Bowery Boy Mike Walsh also cited the founding fathers, saying the "right of every man to own a proper share of the soil is a natural consequence of the doctrines of the American Revolution."

Both Jefferson's ward and Evans's township "would be a small republic within itself and every man would become an acting member of the government" through direct participation at meeting houses established at the center of each community. With government limited largely to direct citizen participation, Evans envisioned the disappearance of politics and officeholding. Without disputes over landholding, property lines, and rents, the number of laws and lawyers could be greatly reduced, Evans predicted. Like America's third president, Evans wanted a far more simplified code of laws that would come up for periodic review by an informed electorate.[7]

The underpinning of the National Reformers' ideology was an uncompromising opposition to the sale of land and a call to limit the amount of land one man could own. Land should be free, like air and water; only the purchase of improvements, such as a farmhouse, should be allowed. By making a distinction between land and property, Evans argued that his plan would simply guarantee any citizen the right to a homestead to occupy and cultivate; it would not mean Skidmore's program to seize farms to be divided among the masses. In addition, Evans called on Congress to pass a homestead exemption that would shield land from debt collection.

For the National Reformers, no other reorganization of society was needed to relieve the suffering of the multitudes. Writing in the *Subterranean*, Walsh said that the crime and poverty that plagues New York's poorer wards would disappear "if every person had an equal share of the soil. . . . Vice and immorality will disappear with the inequality of society."[8]

The National Reformers proposed, as a start, settling 10,000 New York workers at taxpayer expense to the western frontier. Evans estimated that at $200 per head, the cost would be cheaper in the long run than public assistance to the poor. Devyr calculated that for $15,000, most of Brooklyn's paupers could be settled on public land; a bargain compared with Brooklyn's $25,000 annual expenditures on the indigent, he said.

In addition, supply and demand would force wages up for those remaining in the cities, and as Devyr cheerfully predicted, "The country will get rich and the government will strengthen." Devyr also urged the National Reformers to set up their own workers' fund that would provide loans so those thrown out of work could travel to the West. The loans could be repaid with produce cultivated by the new farmer.[9]

Calculating every possible benefit from land reform, Evans proposed that it would bring peace between whites and Indians. Evans, who rejected the pervasive racism of the time, consistently criticized the "disgraceful and merciless" treatment of the American Indians at the hands of the U.S. government. Evans reasoned that with land distributed fairly and equitably, there would be no need to cheat the Indians out of their share and no need to conquer; a standing army would no longer be needed at the frontier. Land claims in Oregon were causing friction between whites and Indians, and "already they talk about exterminating the Indians," Evans wrote. North America was large enough for all if organized by the government into planned farming communities.[10]

The national Democratic Party, realizing the political rewards of adopting land reform, did propose measures to settle workers in the West. One was preemption, a system under which squatters were allowed to remain on the land if they paid a minimum price of $1.25 an acre when the land came up for public auction. No friend of the National Reformers, Henry Clay regarded even preemption as a cue for the rabble of the cities to occupy territory that could be far more productive if tended by middle-class farmers with the capital for improvements. On the other hand, Evans said preemption fell short of his singular demand for free land to settlers.

Some religious leaders in the poorest streets of New York saw the logic of Evans's argument, as they struggled with desperate poverty. Louis M. Pease, a Methodist missionary who established the Five Points House of Industry, was sending as many as sixty New Yorkers a week to public lands in the West at the height of the depression in 1855, and Horace Greeley told the city's unemployed that they could find a better life just two days' travel from the city. The Children's Aid Society enticed young gang members to give up the vices of pool hall and saloon to move west before they fell into a pattern of violence and criminal behavior. Charles Loring Brace, who founded the Children's Aid Society in 1853, reasoned that resourceful young men could as easily adapt to the hard life of the farm as to the far rougher city streets. "The streets of New York," Brace said, [produced] a "bright, sharp, bold [and] racy crowd of little fellows," but the streets were also a breeding ground for insurrection, he warned. The lower east side street gangs could vent their anger either at the ballot box or by raising the banner of communism. The solution, he said, was to send them packing to rural New York, Pennsylvania, and to the American West where they would make ideal pioneers.

Newspaper editor and Whig reformer Horace Greeley embraced French utopian socialism before aligning with George Henry Evans and his scheme to turn urban workers into self-sufficient farmers. (Courtesy of the Library of Congress)

While the National Reformers would set limits on the amount of land any one family could own or inherit, they remained committed to private property—an important distinction that put Evans and the Bowery Boys at odds with the followers of Charles Fourier's communal socialism. Imported from France, Fourierism was one of a number of experiments in utopian socialism finding a popular audience in the United States. Fourier's followers in the United States and the National Reformers vied for influence in the revived labor movement of the mid-1840s. Neither was successful in capturing the long-term attention of workers, who increasingly viewed both schemes as utopian fantasies.

The poorer wards of New York City were particularly susceptible to utopian sects after the panic of 1837 left thousands destitute. A devastating cholera epidemic in the early 1830s and the unrelenting poverty and filth also gave rise to a general feeling of hopelessness. It was an environment in New York and elsewhere in the country that saw not only attempts to build socialist communities, but also experiments with religious ideas beyond the mainstream Protestantism. Swedenborgians, with their notions of connecting with the spirit world, and Mormonism's search for an American Jerusalem took hold of the antebellum imagination.

Typical of the utopianism that swept through New York in the 1840s was the Millerite sect. Like modern cults that attract adherents with hopes of salvation from above, the Millerites promised believers that the end of the world was set for April 1843. Stores advertised white ascension robes for the expected journey to heavenly communities in the American West; believers sold their property and camped out in tents for days, awaiting the appointed hour. When the anticipated rapture passed without a crack of doom, the sect's founder, William Miller, set a new date of October 1844. These religious and utopian longings drew scorn from conservatives who lumped Fourierists, Mormons, Millerites, and National Reformers in the same camp of oddballs bent on overturning society. Referring to "charlatan philosophies," the *New York Herald* warned of a "terrible awakening" in New York's working-class neighborhoods.

No communal experiment was as successful in drawing converts as the Fourierists. Albert Brisbane, Fourier's zealous American disciple, convinced Whig reformer Horace Greeley to open up the pages of his *New York Tribune* to a weekly column in 1842 advocating and carefully explaining the basic tenets of Fourier's master plan to remake the world. In essence, Fourierism was based on the idea that a network of socialist communes could thrive and serve as a model to reorganize society. In each commune, property would be common and tasks rotated in order to share the most unpleasant chores among all participants. Working-class children would receive the kind of thorough education unavailable to them in the cities, and women would be elevated to a status equal to men. In Brisbane's utopia no one could earn more than ten or less than six cents an hour.

These communities were dubbed phalanxes and were to be built to exacting standards from Charles Fourier's design. At the center of the phalanx would be a massive building consisting of three wings, divided into apartments, communal kitchens, covered walkways, libraries, and classrooms. Carefully arranged orchards and gardens would ring the acreage. "The [phalanx] may be compared to a town under one roof," Brisbane told the *Tribune*'s readers. Brisbane estimated 300 as the optimum number of families per phalanx, but smaller ones could be established with fewer than one hundred families. Agriculture would dominate the phalanx's economy, but Brisbane also left room for light manufacturing.[11]

The son of a wealthy New York merchant, Brisbane, like many utopian dreamers, had the means to travel abroad and devote his energies to academic and romantic pursuits. He traveled to Berlin, attending Hegel's lectures at the university, and met Fourier in Paris in 1831. Abandoning the abstraction of Hegelian philosophy, Brisbane set sail for home with a lifelong commitment to build phalanxes across America. He formed a Fourier Society in New York in 1837 and in 1840, published his *Social Destiny of Man*, an exegesis of Fourier's works. Brisbane attracted the interest of the New England transcendentalists, and even American political leaders like John Calhoun, who worried that American workers were ripe for revolution unless removed from the crowded cities.

Between 1842 and 1846 as many as twenty-four phalanxes were founded with about 3,000 members, mostly skilled workers, intellectuals, and a few charlatans. Brisbane believed that eventually a network of phalanxes would erase political borders, leading to a global federation of two million phalanxes replacing governments and nations. Wildly unrealistic, Brisbane's vision of a new world order collided with the practical questions of financing these ventures. The capital needed to establish a viable phalanx approached several hundred thousand dollars, significant sums that had to be raised through wealthy subscribers.

Three phalanxes dominated the movement: the North American Phalanx in Monmouth County, New Jersey; the Wisconsin Phalanx; and Brook Farm in Massachusetts. These were the only phalanxes to survive more than three or four years. It was Brisbane's own North American Phalanx, operating from 1843 to 1855, that attracted the most attention as a model for future communities, and with Greeley's help, the commune was able to sustain itself and make a profit through farming.

Brook Farm, originally a colony of New England transcendentalists centered around the ideas of Ralph Waldo Emerson, adopted the Fourierist model in 1844. Members of Brook Farm were typical of the more skilled craftsmen who were attracted to Fourierism, but Brook Farm was plagued by mismanagement and financial problems. In 1846, fire destroyed parts of the community, and within a year the experiment was dissolved.

Although a competitor for the hearts and minds of the New York working class, Brisbane maintained good relations with the Spartan Association and National Reformers; Brisbane published a detailed explanation of Fourierism in Levi Slamm's *Plebian* and in the first issue of Walsh's *Subterranean* in July 1843.

Much of what Brisbane proposed, such as the abolition of armies, universal education, and the advancement of laboring men, appealed to the Bowery Boys. "The vast force of men and machines called armies and navies are engaged in producing nothing, or wait to be employed in the work of destruction," Brisbane wrote in the *Plebian*. But men like Slamm and Walsh stopped short of advocating a wholesale reorganization of society along Fourierist lines, saying that private property and capitalism could be reformed in a way that erased class distinctions. Fairer, more accessible capitalism and free land in the West would remake America, not French socialism.[12]

In fact, Evans and other critics were quick to point out that phalanxes usually started with crushing debt, leading to failure. Brisbane's logic that one common kitchen was more efficient than one hundred private kitchens did nothing to remove the stigma of communal property among Americans reared in a culture that exalted individualism. Even Robert Owen, whose New Harmony experiment in Indiana two decades earlier was a model for Fourierists, conceded that individualism and private property were concepts too ingrained in America to be supplanted by communitarian ideas. "On the whole, we regard Fourierism … to be an impracticality," Evans agreed. "The rich will not engage in it, and the poor can not." Evans said that under Fourier's plan, those with sufficient capital could purchase larger shares of the phalanx than other shareholders, creating a less-than-egalitarian class structure.

Brisbane, on the other hand, critiqued Walsh and Evans for relying on a political solution to the class inequities created by the industrializing economy, saying that "politicians are far from desiring to free the laborer from the evils he endures.... Look to yourselves, not to politicians." The Bowery Boy was not convinced, retaining his commitment to the ballot and his belief that governments and politicians would, partly out of self-interest, see the benefit in relocating the poor to the fertile public lands. For an equally uncompromising Brisbane, the differences between the National Reformers and the Fourierists were "fundamental and irreparable."[13]

Irreparable differences aside, these two groups often crossed over into each other's camp when it suited their purposes. Evans and Walsh, for example, saw the utility in leaving the door open to cooperation with the phalanx at Brook Farm; with it, they could gain a foothold in the reawak-ening New England labor movement. In the same vein, because New York was a center of the land-reform movement, Fourierists forged temporary alliances in order to advance their own cause in the city.

As they started to wane in influence in the late 1840s and 1850s, many of Brisbane's followers eventually joined the land reformers. Greeley, who had been seduced by Brisbane's promise of a perfect system that would raise the proletariat to the level of the Whig gentleman, threw his full support to the National Reformers. The Bowery Boys revelled in Greeley's turn-about. As the *Subterranean* phrased it, "Horace Greeley has become a thor-ough convert to Mike Walsh's well known doctrines which is a little strange when we consider the fact that Greeley has been until recently a most bitter opponent of Mike and his principles." Walsh said that calling Greeley "a Mike Walsh man" would be premature—the former disciple of Fourier's "paradoxical isms" was still "too timid, too fond of money to become a true disciple of mine." By 1862, six years after his death, Evans's goals were largely realized, not by the Democrats, but by the upstart Republican Party. Influenced by the National Reformers, Abraham Lincoln's Homestead Act gave 160 acres to anyone who would pay a $10 registration fee and pledge to cultivate the land for five years.

American Fourierists and other antebellum reformers debated on whether to call themselves socialists. Brook Farm's Charles Dana praised the class-conscious laborers of 1848 Paris, but for the most part, the Fourierists went no further. The Brook Farm intellectuals sought "a balance between [European] conservatives seeking constitutional monarchy and radicals seeking a leveling communism." Dana maintained that revolutions were useful only in the transition from monarchy to republic; Americans, with the freedom to es-tablish their own communities anywhere on the continent, could avoid Europe's uprisings.[14]

Karl Marx and Friedrich Engels labeled Fourierism socialist, but with the qualifier "utopian," a reference to its middle-class composition and obvious impracticality. In essence, Marx rejected both Fourierism and the National Reformers who attempted to craft a new society on the American soil. In the *Communist Manifesto*, Marx and Engels abandoned any hope in dreams of social utopias and "isolated phalansteres." Not all of Marx's disciples, however, adhered to the Communist orthodoxy. Some found common cause with the Bowery Boys and Evans's land reformers. Hermann Kriege, who sought a uniquely American path to communism, was an enthusiastic advocate of Evans's land-reform plan. As a result, Marx loudly branded Kriege a heretic and excommunicated him from the emerging Communist League in 1846. Afterwards, Kriege found a new home at Tammany Hall.

A Westphalian journalist, Kriege came to New York in 1845 and established the *Deutsche Jung-Amerika Gemeinde*, or German Young-America Community, as well as the Social Reform Association, which he affiliated with the National Reformers. Kriege's newspaper, *Volks-Tribun*, was never on solid ground financially and lasted less than two years. Evans himself made a strong appeal for German support, viewing the Germans as a rising political force and receptive to unconventional ideas. Kriege favored alliances with New York's subterranean socialists and veterans of the Working Men's Party, which he and Marx both praised as a class-conscious political movement. Hosting a large variety of public events in the German community, Kriege's Social Reform Association grew to more than a thousand members and became the leading political club for German New Yorkers.

Kriege hewed closely to the contours of the National Reformers' ideology, warning land speculators, "hands off our land," and branding Fourierism as muddle-headed. Referring to Fourier's middle-class disciples in the United States, Kriege said, "No wonder then that this system finds its most active adherents among the Whigs, merchants and capitalists." Typically, a meeting of German socialists in 1845 pledged "to recognize the National Reformers [as] our fellow laborers in the cause of progress, as the advocates of the cause of the oppressed children of industry."[15]

Marx and Engels sharply rebuked Kriege for affiliating with the National Reformers. In their May 11, 1846, *Circular Against Kriege*, Marx and Engels charged that Kriege was leading German communists in New York down a noncommunist path, weakening the movement in America; "compromising in the highest degree to the communist party both in Europe and America." It was not that Marx entirely rejected the National Reformers. Marx saw the necessity of working with democratic movements as a step toward communism and called the National Reformers "historically justified." He predicted that "as a product of the proletarian movement [they] will inevitably press on to communism." Writing in the *Deutsche-Brusseler Zeitung* in November 1847, Marx claimed that "just as in England the workers form a political party under the name of the Chartists, so do the workers in North America under the name of the National Reformers."[16]

Engels, in his *Principles of Communism*, also acknowledged America's distinct political conditions and the usefulness of Evans's land reformers in the march toward communism. For Engels, building a communist movement in the United States demanded an opportunistic alliance with the National Reformers, whom he claimed were the best prepared to "turn the [American] constitution against the bourgeoisie and use it in the interest of the proletariat."[17]

Where Marx parted with Kriege was the latter's enthusiasm for the homestead movement as an alternative to the inevitable class struggle. For

Kriege, the notion of free homesteads no longer represented an interim stage for the American proletariat—it became an end in itself. The heart of Marx's objection was that Kriege put America outside the determinist paradigm. To Kriege, America, with its sturdy democracy and abundant resources, was an exception and poised to take a different path to development than Europe. This was a powerful challenge to Marx's conception of history.

Despite its abundance of land, America, said Marx, was not exceptional but subject to the same inexorable historical forces as Europe. Marx poked holes in the National Reform math that predicted a virtually inexhaustible supply of public land for American and immigrant farmer. National Reformers' estimates were fancifully optimistic, in some cases predicting a 400-year supply of accessible unspoiled farmland for anyone who wanted it. Closer to the truth than the land reformers, Marx said the American West would be well populated by the end of the nineteenth century, and since the promise of virgin soil would fuel European immigration, "Kriege's all eternity might well be foreclosed even earlier."

Countering Kriege's promise of unbounded frontiers and opportunities, Engels warned Germans coming to America not to be deluded into thinking that the sight of prosperous American farmers meant that communism in the New World was not inevitable. Referring in the *Circular* to Kriege's "childish pomposity," Marx also attacked his sentimentality, idealism, "flirtations with religion," and endorsement of private property rights. Turn everybody into a landowner? It's a wish, said Marx, "that is just as practicable and communist as that everybody should be turned into an emperor, king or Pope."

Marx and Engels mocked Kriege's optimism in a section of the *Circular* entitled "How communism became love sick." In a thoroughly condescending tone, they list Kriege's many references to love in the *Volks-Tribun*, such as "everything may be achieved by love." That was too much for the revolutionary Marx who commented, "Kriege is preaching in the name of communism the old fantasy of religion which is the direct antithesis of communism."[18]

Coming to Kriege's defense was Wilhelm Weitling, another German communist who broke with Marx and emigrated to New York. Weitling was alone in the Communist League to oppose Marx's *Circular Against Kriege*, saying that German communists in the United States must be free to adapt their ideas to America's exceptional social and political conditions. Weitling later joined the National Reformers and Spartans in the labor federations of the early 1850s.

With his expulsion from Marx's international movement, Kriege on July 4, 1846, removed the slogan "Up with the Workers, Down with Capital" from the masthead of his *Volks-Tribun* and categorically rejected revolutionary communism. In addition, Kriege not only maintained his unyielding support for the National Reformers, he joined Tammany Hall. "With our entire organization, we join the mass of the Democratic Party and we join its struggle … against the monopoly that controls the land."

Recognizing the growing political power of the German diaspora and the popularity of western homesteads, Tammany endorsed land reform in return for Kriege's promise to get out the German vote for the Democratic Party in the 1846 elections. "If Tammany Hall adopts our measures," vowed Kriege, "we shall take up a position on its left wing."

In aligning with the Democratic Party, Kriege said he took his cue from Mike Walsh, who traded his outsider status for a place inside Tammany that same year. In a rally of his German following just before the election, the veteran Marxist said that while Tammany wire pullers had earlier "dispersed among the people to shout down Mike Walsh," honest Democrats chose this "true representative of their rights, a man from their midst" to serve on the ticket.

Walsh pledged the Spartans to Tammany, telling his constituents in the Sixth Ward that he was satisfied the Democratic Party was "purged of its scoundrel leaders" and was prepared to seriously address land reform and other laboring-class issues. Of course, the self-serving Bowery Boy was keenly interested in the party's nomination for state office that year. Although elected to the state legislature on the Tammany ticket, he remained a less-than-cooperative gadfly for several more years to come.[19]

Kriege did travel to Berlin in 1848 to participate in the uprising but returned to the United States, which he regarded until his death as humanity's greatest hope. In accordance with his wishes, Kriege was buried with an American flag draped across his chest.

Engels could only shake his head, confiding in August 1851 to the more orthodox communist Joseph Weydemeyer that once in New York his "greatest handicap will be that the useful Germans who are worth anything become easily Americanized" and seduced by the New World's "rapidly growing prosperity which makes bourgeois relations seem a *beau ideal* to them." Outside New York, a cultivated German would be lost, Engels warned. "Philadelphia and Boston are terrible provincial holes."[20]

Unlike Kriege and the German communists, Walsh and Evans could speak the language of class in a way that resonated far more deeply with native-born Americans still steeped in the ideals of the American Revolution and committed to a constitutional form of government. At the same time, the National Reformers could appeal to English-speaking Irish immigrants who, as largely unskilled laborers, were drawn by promises of farms far from the crowded cities.

Yet many New Yorkers saw the spectre of class war lurking beneath the National Reformers' moderate ideology. Mordecai Noah, who was on the receiving end of one of Walsh's anti-Semitic tirades, labeled the National Reformers "a sect to uphold the wildest and perhaps most laughable principles . . . a fantasy conceived only by half idiots." The conservative *New York Sun* warned that plans to divide land called to mind the excesses of the French Revolution with their "new and strange theories of government."[21]

With the revival of the labor movement in the middle 1840s, workers too began to view Evans's planned settlements on the frontier and Brisbane's phalanxes as a distraction and an escape. Bread-and-butter issues competed with these more esoteric manifestations of working-class discontent for supremacy in the new trade unions of the late 1840s and 1850s.

The rebirth of the antebellum labor movement started, in part, among the mill workers of Massachusetts. *The Voice of Industry* reported that while Massachusetts woolen mills were increasing output and showing a profit, workers' wages were reduced from $1 to 75 cents a day. In June 1844, skilled and unskilled workers throughout New England gathered at Fall River, Massachusetts, to address wages and to demand a ten-hour limit to the workday. Evans and Walsh approached the Fall River labor organizers with an invitation to unite, and while they were rebuffed at first, the National Reformers were given a seat at the table when they agreed with the mill workers that the ten-hour day was at the top of the agenda.

With a working day of twelve to thirteen hours in most eastern states, reformers struggled during the 1830s and 1840s to reduce the burden. They succeeded in 1840, when President Van Buren established a ten-hour day for federal government employees and contractors, but in order to regulate the hours in the private sector, it was necessary to appeal to the state legislatures. By 1847, New Hampshire was the first state to pass a ten-hour law.

Walsh enthusiastically championed the ten-hour movement because he saw it as a way to interest workers in a political solution to their economic distress. As Walsh explained, if workers would send their own to the legislatures, they could not only institutionalize a shorter workday, but also ensure free schools and other progressive measures.

Remembering the failure of the General Trades' Union to exert leverage against employers after the panic, the National Reformers remained skeptical of strikes and walkouts, but Walsh agreed to help build a union of Massachusetts mill workers and other sweated trades in the interest of creating a united front. On October 16, 1844, that united front took shape as 200 delegates of the New England Workingmen's Association (NEWA) met at Boston's Faneuil Hall with a dream of creating a national movement to raise the American worker from the misery of wage slavery. It was the "glorious commencement of a second revolution in this country; a peaceful revolution," they declared.

Among the delegates was a New York contingent that included Evans, Devyr, Walsh and his Spartan Band, as well as socialists from Brook Farm and even the somewhat eccentric vegetarian anarchists from the Skaneateles commune in western New York. Aside from petitioning state legislatures to set limits on hours of employment, the NEWA made a typically socialist appeal for greater control by the workers of the means of production—a "system in which every laborer has a direct personal interest in the fruits of his labor."[22]

Despite oratory that roused workers to their feet, Walsh could only persuade a few New York trade-union leaders to attend the Boston convention under the National Reform banner. The mill workers of the NEWA and a more militant generation of trade unionists in New York viewed land reform as just another response to the desperate conditions of the working class. The priority now was to address the immediate concerns of workers held virtually in bondage.

Once in New England, the New York Bowery Boy discovered firsthand the dismal conditions inside the Massachusetts mills. He heard compelling accounts of women, practically imprisoned, working thirteen-hour days and crowded into company barracks where the windows were often nailed shut. The conditions of the Lowell factory women were "far more oppressive than any Negro slavery in the south," Walsh said.

Walsh delivered passionate speeches to striking workers in Lowell and offered them the solidarity of the Spartan Band, much as he had Dorr's partisans in Rhode Island. The Bowery Boy was described by one sympathetic Boston newspaper as "the young champion of the New York Spartans," whose speeches at Faneuil Hall were "full of genuine pathos, correct knowledge and forcible description."[23]

Also visiting Brook Farm at that time, Walsh made a brief and purely tactical partnership with the Fourierists to gain more influence among the competing groups in the NEWA. Walsh's Bowery Boys had little in common with the skilled New England artisans and intellectuals who joined Brook Farm, but radicals of all stripes formed shaky alliances so their voices could be heard in the curious polyglot of the NEWA and subsequent labor federations.

This fragile compact of practical union organizers and assorted reformers, however, could not hold together. The NEWA convened again in Lowell in March 1845, this time with up to 2,000 delegates. As before, Evans, Walsh and a noisy cluster of Bowery Boys attempted to put their land reform program at the top of the agenda. But the NEWA was deteriorating quickly into factionalism. Labor delegates refused to recognize the Bowery Boys, and Fourierists from Brook Farm battled for control of the convention. Finally, the more moderate Brook Farm delegates prevailed, and one of their own, Lewis Ryckman, was elected president of the NEWA convention. A platform was adopted that included a strong Fourierist plank as well as purely trade-union resolutions such as the ten-hour day and opposition to prison labor.

Ryckman, of course, had his own unorthodox ideas for recreating society. He proposed a permanent Industrial Revolutionary Government that would replace the U.S. government and organize society on the basis of hundreds of phalanxes. Outlandish schemes prevailed, and consequently, a Boston meeting of the New England Workingmen in May 1845 that was supposed to be a call to action became a debating club for Evans's land reformers, Ryckman's Fourierists, and even the Skaneateles anarchists.

Proper Massachusetts reformers, shocked at the rough manners of the proletarian street fighters of the lower east side, complained to Greeley that Walsh's Spartan Association had called for "burn[ing] the Sunday School books which [were] poisoning the minds of the young." New Englanders "reared in Sabbath schools and churches" walked out as Bowery Boys linked "capitalists and priests [who] have joined hands to grind and oppress the laboring man." Walsh said he never lost his ardor for the New England mill workers and was encouraged by his supporters in Massachusetts to resume the struggle despite "unfounded accusations of rowdyism."[24]

The history of the short-lived labor federations of the mid-1840s and 1850s shows a movement that was hopelessly split among leaders, each with a passionate belief that he alone held the blueprint for a workers' paradise on the American landscape.

Unable to convince the New England Workingmen that they should dedicate themselves to land distribution in the West, Evans parted company with the NEWA and called a convention of his own in the summer of 1845. The final split between practical trade unionists and reformers came in September 1845, when union men finally ousted the Brook Farm delegation. With the Fourierists pushed out, the NEWA was now in trade-union hands and prepared to address the more immediate concerns of wages and working conditions.

As the 1850s opened, trade unions were pressing for decent wages and taking to the streets in large-scale strikes; carpenters, shoemakers, quarrymen, and tailors intensified the struggle against employers. As Dixon Ryan Fox notes in his study of labor's rise in New York, "workers bettered their condition when they ceased attempting to reconstruct society, and through their trade unions attended strictly to raising their own wages." Recognizing this change in thinking among union men, Evans and Walsh put aside their skepticism of strikes in order to better seek labor allies. Walsh denounced sweatshop labor and, like Ned Buntline, deplored the pitiful wages paid to women in the needle trades. He urged the government to reject any contract that paid substandard wages.

In the spring of 1850, New York's carpenters and tailors staged strikes that paralyzed and polarized the city. Reflecting their more militant and practical stance, the carpenters ignored pleas from Horace Greeley not to strike. Greeley's high-minded appeals for workers not to beg for concessions from employers, but to pool their capital and set up cooperative employee-owned joint stock companies, were ignored as middle-class claptrap.

The largest trade in the city, tailors were subject to some of the worst sweatshop conditions. The basis of the tailors' strike was the putting-out system in the ready-to-wear clothing trade. Clothing merchants were able to drive down wages by cutting cloth in their factories and then distributing the precut cloth to less-skilled tailors who stitched the seams at home. The system put skilled tailors into competition with semiskilled seamstresses.

On July 22, after a month of strikes and outdoor rallies, tailors and police clashed outside the offices of a company well known for substandard wages and union busting. Five days later, thousands of workingmen rallied at City Hall Park, and in August, more violence broke out between laborers and police. The summer's agitation left two dead and dozens arrested. To the conservative *New York Herald*, these battles with police were a "striking illustration of socialism and what it would bring."[25]

With the heightened labor agitation came renewed demands to unite New York's workers into a powerful, centralized labor federation. This new and short-lived attempt to unify the city's trade unions centered around the New York City Industrial Congress. Here, Mike Walsh found another forum to denounce wage slavery and the aristocracy of wealth, leading his Bowery Boys into the intensified labor struggles of the 1850s.

Founded in June 1850 with about fifty union locals under its umbrella, the New York City Industrial Congress put the unskilled laborer and immigrant at the center of union activity. Labor delegates assured the rank and file that the Industrial Congress would be a union federation not a discussion group; most workers in the Industrial Congress rejected politicians and utopian schemes, and concentrated their efforts on raising wages. Regardless, Walsh pushed an aggressive political agenda. Starting in the late 1840s, Walsh urged the trade unions to throw out politicians who colluded with employers in breaking strikes and "send to the legislature and every hall where laws are made or taxes are assessed the strong and sound sense of labor."

Not far from his confrontational Bowery Boy roots and clearly striking a chord with the new breed of socialists, Walsh cautioned that if legislation was not sufficient, revolution was possible—waging "eternal war with capital until it is made subordinate." Influenced by socialist thought on both sides of the Atlantic, Walsh also sought greater workplace democracy, saying, "Every worker who comes to a corporation should be a partner therein and not the slave of money."[26]

The Industrial Congress exhibited greater solidarity between unskilled Irish immigrants and skilled native-born workers than previous labor federations. Walsh helped organize Irish laborers from the poorer wards, including his own Sixth Ward, into union locals affiliated with the Industrial Congress. Unlike earlier attempts at union building, the Industrial Congress was also more heavily influenced by the German workers of the city. Veteran communist Wilhelm Weitling led the German Central Committee of the United Trades, which represented German-speaking workers in the Industrial Congress.

Anticipating Marx's advice to American communists, Walsh recognized the necessity of uniting America's English-speaking and German laborers in the face of their employers' strategy to divide and conquer the immigrant worker. The Bowery Boy told native-born workers not to fight the German laborer but to strike a blow against the employer who benefits from underpaying newly arrived immigrants. Twenty years later, Marx instructed Siegfried Meyer and August Vogt: "In America ... a coalition of the German workers with the Irish is the most important job you could start on at the present time."

New York's German community grew through the antebellum years, and by 1855, the Germans were already the majority of the city's tailors, cabinetmakers, and bakers. It was among these trades that some of the more militant elements of New York's working class emerged. As a result, the New York City Industrial Congress came to life as a combustible mix of union agitator, German communist, and political clubhouse. In the words of one New York Congressman, the Industrial Congress was an offspring "of the German school of socialism ... partly political, partly agrarian." New York conservatives like James Gordon Bennett warned that revived unionism, with its "vast importation of foreign socialists," would mean the death of America's political parties, and their replacement by "a new one, under the banner of socialism." This alliance could lead to insurrection, with armed Bowery Boys marching on Wall Street, Bennett predicted. To confirm his fears, Bennett had only to watch as Weitling joined the Bowery Boys in the July rally in City Hall Park in support of the striking tailors. The protest turned violent when some attacked employers and smashed shop windows.[27]

Weitling was part revolutionary and part utopian socialist. He even experimented with a model community, the short-lived Communia, Iowa, and proposed a U.S. Congress based on occupational representation rather than geographic. But he did not envision an accommodation with capital, and saw New York's shirtless democrats as a potential revolutionary force. "Everybody is ripe for communism, even the criminals," said Weitling in 1845. "Criminals are a product of the present order of society and under communism they would cease to be criminals."

The struggle to control New York's Industrial Congress began before its first meeting. Trade unionists led an unsuccessful fight to bar the National Reformers, Spartan Association, Fourierists, and assorted anarchists. The Industrial Congress became a forum for virtually every labor, land, sanitary, and political reform in vogue, says Iver Bernstein, historian of the antebellum labor movement. Some journeymen pressed for a resolution that any delegate to the Congress be a "practical laboring man." The representative of the silversmiths' union told delegates, "We will have no capitalists and no lawyers (we'll call you at your office as soon as we get a lawsuit)." As they had in the NEWA, Walsh and Evans, armed with their own strategy, attempted to divert workers in the Industrial Congress from the very immediate issues of strikes and wages.

As it became apparent that the National Reformers and Spartan Band were staging a coup by strong-arming delegates to pledge their support to them, some trade unions withdrew their representation. "The great error of the [Industrial Congress]," said Bennett referring to the Spartans among others, was that "it did not originate with the trades but with a knot of political tricksters."[28]

Evans, Walsh, and Chartist Thomas Devyr were clearly in charge of the Industrial Congress by autumn, and they used it to press their political demands on the national level—petitioning the U.S. Congress to pass a version of the Homestead Act. Devyr delivered an impassioned case for limiting landholdings to "destroy the commercial cannibalism that renders the various classes enemies of one another." Walsh and Devyr also proposed a system of city rent inspectors, who would be elected by popular vote in each ward with a mandate to organize rent strikes in dwellings they felt were no longer fit for human habitation.

In addition, the Spartan Band pushed the Industrial Congress to act as a power broker in city elections, to elect candidates who would endorse the land-reform platform. Walsh was busy packing Democratic Party caucuses, ward by ward, with workers from the Industrial Congress who declared their loyalty to the National Reform program. On Election Day 1850, Walsh had secured several wards with insurgent labor and land-reform tickets. Striking fear into Tammany regulars, he established neighborhood clubs, like the Sixth Ward Industrial Reformers, that joined the Spartans in mounting a new challenge to the Democratic Party.

With a thoroughly political agenda, the New York City Industrial Congress no longer represented the rank and file and was acting more as an arm of the National Reform Association and the Spartan Band than as a trade union. While some workers, like the saddlemakers, endorsed free homesteads, others, like the plasterers and machinists, were hostile to "political meetings" when they wanted to discuss wages and hours exclusively.

As the Spartan Band and the land reformers hijacked the city's trade unions, the ever-astute Democratic Party was quick to respond; Tammany was now faced with a potent labor movement manipulated by an explosive combination of communists and lower east side street gangs. On June 3, 1851, Tammany leaders invited delegates of the Industrial Congress to a mass meeting. Here the Democrats proposed to include workers' planks in the party's 1852 platform, hoping to neutralize this most threatening insurgency from the Far Left before the presidential election. Walsh, who had earlier made accommodations with Tammany when it suited his political ambitions, was convinced, and threw the full support of the Industrial Congress to the regular Democratic Party. He was amply rewarded with a nomination for U.S. Congress. To the trade unionists who sought higher wages and better working conditions, power replaced principle.

The *Herald*'s Bennett was not surprised by the Walsh-Tammany coup, predicting earlier that the "honest tradesman" would be duped by "sinister influences" and that the Industrial Congress would "fall into the hands of a few wire pullers [who would] sell the trades to the highest bidder." One union member complained of those who "use working men associations [as] mere tools for the furtherance of their personal interests."[29]

Meetings of workers through the 1850s were riven by debates on whether to admit the politically ambitious to their ranks or even into the proceedings. Many felt betrayed by the radical Bowery Boy, now turned Congressman. At a meeting of the New York machinists' union in April 1853, while Walsh was serving in Washington, one laborer appealed for political action on the part of the workers. He was answered with, "we don't want any politics." "This is a meeting of machinists; this aint a political meeting;" and "where is Mike Walsh? He's in Congress."[30]

Walsh defended his compromise with the very Democratic Party he had battled since the autumn of 1841, saying it was the culmination of a decade's work to purify Tammany of the men he labeled the idle dandies. In his typically boastful style, Walsh said he was determined to carry "free thought and action for the first time into that temple" called Tammany. Now Democratic Party insiders, the Spartans promised to replace the "pot house politicians" with "honesty and fair dealing" and make the ward-level Democratic Party committee the center of political action in the city. "Corruption in the city will not cease until the nominating powers are vested completely in the people," Walsh promised.[31]

There were attempts in 1853 to resurrect the General Trades' Union, but most individual trades, having learned from the disappointments of the Industrial Congress, sensed manipulative politicians behind the scenes. They also learned that as individual trade unions they could negotiate with employers just as well on their own, without a larger labor federation.

The Bowery Boys' coup was hollow, as trade unions abandoned the Industrial Congress, and the depression of 1855 all but doomed organized labor, just as the panic of 1837 had ended the General Trades' Union. With the onset of the depression, thousands of men lost their jobs, along with their leverage with employers facing bankruptcy. By midwinter of 1855, more than half of the nation's skilled laborers were out of work.

Walsh was now a Tammany leader, having handed the Industrial Congress and the land-reform movement over to the Democratic Party. With hard times through the middle 1850s, Bowery Boys, volunteer fire brigades, tavern owners, and other manifestations of working-class culture in New York made their alliances with the political party that could render real benefits at the street level: jobs, food baskets, and coal in the winter. Political power in the wards and the promise of patronage after every tumultuous election was something the trade unions, and certainly the utopian socialists, could never deliver.

chapter 6

The Bowery Boy
Goes to Washington

U npredictable, volatile, and with loyalties that shifted effortlessly, Mike Walsh and his Spartan Band were crashing Tammany's gate from below as early as 1846—the year Walsh was elected to the New York State Assembly on the Democratic Party ticket. His election was met with the wild factionalism and violence that characterized political life in antebellum New York. He told the faithful readers of his *Subterranean*, that the "leaders of Tammany Hall denounced us as destructive and used every means to crush me.... Instead of shrinking from the contest, we met them in Tammany Hall and elsewhere and triumphed over all their power and wealth." The Bowery Boy turned legislator proudly informed working-class New Yorkers, "The election of Mike Walsh has determined one fact: The people are stronger than parties."

Walsh listed the Spartan Association's accomplishments to voters, saying they broke up monopolies and gave less politically connected tradesmen an opportunity to make a living. "We prevented honest peddlers from being outlawed by rich storekeepers.... We brought the land question before the people; and alone we advocated the annexation of Texas long before Tammany."[1]

As he had in the past, Walsh waged political battle with rival gang leaders for a place inside the Democratic Party, and in this case, his partisans were successful in beating Isaiah Rynders's efforts to deny Walsh the nomination.

Walsh's victory in the general election was accomplished by blatant fraud at the polls. Tammany operatives, now in league with the Spartan Association, even opened the jail cells the night before Election Day and spirited about forty convicts across the river under the protection of bribed police and prison officials. As the polls opened, these convicts were prepared to vote "early and often," as Walsh was fond of saying.

In an odd twist to this election, Walsh claimed after his victory that his enemies attempted to poison him, but told the Spartans that he would take his seat in the Assembly even if he only "had a spoonful of breath left." Walsh arrived at Albany proclaiming his credentials as a bare-knuckles fighter for the proletariat: "I am the slave of no party, a follower of no political clique. I came here with my merits and demerits extensively canvassed. I am proud; the advocate of a houseless and shirtless democracy. I am here to obey no party drill or to submit to any political dictation."[2]

Despite this posturing, which played well with the voters back home on the lower east side, Walsh did represent a "political clique" vying for control of a Tammany Hall that was severely split over patronage, national politics, and above all, personalities. As historian of Tammany Hall Jerome Mushkat writes, during the latter half of the 1840s "there was really no Tammany Hall but only various splinter groups, each with partial legitimacy."[3]

Two major factions emerged out of New York's Democratic Party at this time; they were ostensibly divided over the issue of extending slavery into the territories. The Barnburner faction, adopting a Free-Soil plank, centered on former President Martin Van Buren. Barnburners supported the failed Wilmot Proviso, which would have given Congress the authority to prohibit the extension of slavery in the territories acquired from Mexico. The other major faction, the Hunkers, advocated a Texas annexation policy that put the matter of slavery in the hands of the local population.

Despising both the Free-Soil doctrine and Van Buren personally, Walsh aligned with the Hunkers. Uninterested in the moral arguments of abolitionists, Walsh favored Texas annexation and unimpeded westward expansion as a means to fulfill his vision of settling the industrial proletariat on the western frontier. Walsh and the Hunkers also maintained that Texas annexation and the consequent conquering of the rest of the continent was the only truly patriotic stand. Neither Barnburner nor Hunker could gain full control of Tammany, but Walsh's Spartan Band led the Hunkers' fight in the streets, breaking up Van Buren's Barnburner rallies. Horace Greeley feared these "hard drinking ruffians" were forcing the Democratic Party into a proslavery position.

In his *Tammany Hall*, Mushkat notes that matters of principle inevitably gave way to a "vicious, expedient battle for raw political power." To Walsh, the Van Burenites were hypocrites whose ideology only masked their hunger for power and their desire to "fasten upon the public carcass." Walsh admitted what was obvious to all Democrats—the schism was largely over political power, patronage, and personalities. "The fact is," he said, "there is not a particle of difference between the leaders of either faction."[4]

The New York Democrats' disarray led to a Whig resurgence. The Whigs saw victories in city elections in 1847, and the following year, as the Van Buren Barnburners cleaved further from the national Democratic Party into the Free-Soil Party, the Whigs scored another important series of electoral successes. They put Zachary Taylor in the White House and defeated the entire Tammany slate for Congress. Hunkers were dismayed that the Barnburners would sacrifice victory at the polls for free soil. "We find some men whose democracy is worn with a proviso," editorialized one newspaper sympathetic to the Hunker position. The Whigs now controlled the patronage prize, and Tammany was forced to seek an end to its internal warfare.[5]

By the spring of 1849, the Democratic factions were heading toward reunion on the state level, a concord that was derailed in the city by extremists on both sides, including Walsh's Hunkers. A proposed state convention in Syracuse was to forge a compromise, but the most extreme Hunkers, centered on Walsh, kept the Democrats in the city divided. Demanding more Hunkers on the state ticket, Walsh's men branded the state convention traitorous. The Whigs reaped the benefits of Tammany infighting by winning control of the city in elections that same year. The political factions also took on new names by 1849, with Walsh's uncompromising Hunkers now labeled Hard Shell Democrats and a coalition of Free-Soilers and moderate Hunkers referred to as Soft Shell Democrats.

As before, despite ideological differences, the real struggle between the factions came down to political power and winning the spoils of office. When asked about the difference between the leaders of the two factions, Walsh said with his characteristic wit that it just came down to one being an "honest man and the other a rogue." He explained further:

> The Barnburners are now what are called Softs and we are called Hards. The best illustration of anything hard is a diamond. We all know what soft means in morals. A man soft in morals is one open to any rascality. A Soft in politics is pretty much the same thing.... A Soft is simply an individual whose morals and politics are of the putty character.[6]

Elected to the New York State Assembly in 1846, 1847, and 1851, Walsh represented the Hunker position on national policy, but often turned his attention to the day-to-day problems that had held the attention of laboring-class advocates since George Henry Evans's Working Men's Party of 1829. Walsh introduced resolutions to shorten the working day and abolish child labor. Appointed to a special committee investigating abuses in the private sector, Walsh asked constituents to send him information on working conditions in their trade. With a seat on the assembly's Prisons Committee, Walsh also sought to limit competition to workingmen from cheap prison labor. "Every dollar earned in your state prisons is a dollar stolen out of the pocket of the unemployed laborer. It is bread taken from the throats of his starving children," said Walsh, who quickly earned a reputation in Albany for the dramatic turn of phrase and a knack for self–promotion.

Appealing to his core constituents, he told anyone who would listen that he came to Albany at great personal sacrifice, leaving his family and arriving with "scarcely money enough to get a shave." Fans back home could order a new daguerreotype of Walsh through the *Subterranean* for just twenty-five cents or read of the exploits of the Bowery Boy in Albany: "what is really going on among the big fish and little fish."[7]

Surely motivated by his untiring quest for publicity and his fear that certain newspapers were omitting his speeches, Walsh proposed an independent newspaper supported by a fifty-cent-a-week contribution from each legislator. This newspaper would publish speeches and proceedings verbatim, careful to include Walsh's every word.

Considering himself a guardian of the public trust, Walsh attacked wasteful spending that he said only went into the pockets of his fellow legislators and their preferred contractors. He latched on to the state printing contract as an example of this "system of robbery," with much of the printing as "wholly useless." Consequently, he called for the oversight of a state printing office. Familiar with the pay and working conditions in the printing trade, Walsh also proposed that in any government printing contract the printer be required to pay his workers the highest prevailing wages in the industry. "While we were taking care of the capitalist we should not lose sight of the interest of the workers, that they have fair wages for their labor," he said.[8]

Claiming to be disgusted by the wholesale corruption in the legislature and the "allure of wealth and power" that dominated political life, Walsh threatened to resign his seat only a few months into his first term. He charged that his fellow legislators changed their votes "like so may spaniel curs before the clerk has time to announce the result—and at the dictation of wire pullers." As usual, it didn't take much to change his mind. With his penchant for stretching the truth, Walsh said he was persuaded to stay by fellow legislators and "hundreds of citizens of Albany." As a state legislator he was, after all, serving the "holy cause of justice and humanity."

Walsh was not as generous in describing his colleagues in the state assembly, referring to them as the "dull clowns who whine" about the lack of amusement in the state capital, but who drink in "bacchanalian revels which doubtless cost the city treasury a pretty nice sum." With his long-time distrust of lawyers and middle-class reformers, he suggested that "convicts in accordance with their idleness and villainy" be trained as lawyers or clergy, and when a resolution was introduced to grant the use of the Assembly chamber to the State Agricultural Society, Walsh said it would be fine with him if the experience could persuade lawyers in the legislature to take up farming.[9]

Arguing that lawyers did not act in the best interests of working people, Walsh proposed plain-English laws for legal proceedings, "to abolish the senseless jargon ... the ridiculous Latin words that nobody understood." He said the only opponents would be lawyers who "mystify the law so that nobody could understand it and then charge to explain it." For example, he suggested the term "compulsory summons" instead of subpoena. When a legislative committee was proposed to simplify legal proceedings, Walsh insisted on the appointment of laborers. In the end, neither the committee on legal proceedings nor a plain-English law was approved by the New York legislature. It was defeated, said Walsh, "by shyster lawyers" protecting their "beastly occupation."[10]

A decade earlier, Evans had expressed his disdain for the legal profession, asking New Yorkers in 1834, "why do we allow them to cheat and fleece us?" Evans's Working Men's Party also advocated such progressive measures as a simplification of the legal code, and urged each state legislature to call an annual special session to "repeal, simplify and condense existing laws so as to fit them all into a child's spelling book." Echoing Thomas Jefferson, Evans said the laws of the state then should be distributed to every citizen, and ratified or rejected by the voters on Election Day.[11]

Walsh's interest in demystifying certain professions for the benefit of the less educated extended to medicine, as he sought to require makers of pharmaceuticals and remedies to accurately label their contents "in plain English." Likely one of the earliest attempts at truth in labeling, Walsh's bill addressed the problem of medical quackery that resulted in injury and in some cases fatal poisoning.

Directly influenced by the Working Men's ideology, Walsh tried to shift public spending priorities to the least advantaged while he served in the legislature, for example, demanding public assistance to destitute widows. In one case, Walsh opposed a $500 appropriation to the College of Physicians and Surgeons. Instead of a grant to the medical college, he preferred government spending on soup kitchens for the unemployed or to improve New York City's public schools, "bringing learning within the reach of every child." Walsh was a strong voice for free public education through the college level, saying "the children of the rich are sent to the best schools.... In the meantime the children of the workers are attaining the brief elements of knowledge." In language that anticipated the liberal ideas of the latter part of the century, Walsh said that money should also be spent to clothe and feed children "as a necessary inducement to attend school."[12]

Despite his attempts to represent the interests of New York City's laboring class, Walsh spent a considerable amount of time engaged in harmless buffoonery, waiting for the expected laugh from the assembly chamber. In the State Assembly and in Congress, he was the master of the one-liner and the annoying procedural objection, at times exasperating fellow legislators. When told in Congress that a bill he overlooked was published in the *Evening Star* he replied, "We are not all star gazers."

Elected in 1852 to the U.S. Congress as Tammany's candidate, Walsh brought this freewheeling and at times clownish style to Washington. He represented the Fourth Congressional District, which included the lower east side and his Sixth Ward stronghold. While Walsh was able to win the general election with 60 percent of the vote, his nomination was won in a brawl between his Hard Shell partisans and rival Soft Shells that left ten persons severely injured.

To his critics, Walsh's election was a fraud "from beginning to end; an unparalleled outrage." In that same year, Walsh attended the Democratic National Convention in Baltimore, reflecting his brief interlude of legitimacy within the Democratic Party. The Bowery Boy, like the majority of New York's labor radicals, was committed to Michigan Senator Lewis Cass for the nomination because of Cass's support for settling workers on western homesteads. The Democratic Party's labor wing also lent its support to Cass in 1848. Nominated for president, Cass lost to the hero of the Mexican War, Zachary Taylor. When Cass made a campaign stop at Tammany in 1852, Whigs saw it as pandering to the radical wing. "When General Cass says he wants free land for the landless, he stoops low for votes." Walsh even made Cass an honorary Tammany brave, but that was not enough to secure again the Democratic nomination, which went to Franklin Pierce.[13]

Walsh's flamboyance may have served him well in the Sixth Ward and even in Albany, but on the national scene he was ineffectual. Overall, New York City's delegation to the thirty-third Congress was more concerned about political battles at home than addressing issues of national importance. Walsh, partly from a sense of self-importance as the workingman's defender, did occasionally rise to the floor to advance the cause of greater economic and political democracy.

However, as in Albany, he was best remembered for a great many pointless procedural objections. When members of the House discussed a resolution calling on the Secretary of the Navy to provide Congress information on the construction and expense of government steamers, Walsh objected for no apparent reason, only angering the Speaker. As in

Michigan Senator Lewis Cass was the Bowery Boys' favorite for president. Mike Walsh even made Cass an honorary Tammany brave, but Cass went down to defeat against Zachary Taylor in 1848 and lost the Democratic nomination in 1852 to Franklin Pierce. (Courtesy of the Library of Congress)

Albany, Walsh poked fun at colleagues he felt were acting too aristocratic. He also expressed concern about certain questionable appropriations, such as salary increases to politically reliable bureaucrats. To make his point about pork-barrel legislation, Walsh asked for funds to build a lighthouse at Chittenango, New York. When he was challenged that Chittenango, near the Erie Canal, would not need a lighthouse, Walsh answered that "a lighthouse there is quite as democratic and quite as necessary as two-thirds of those log-rolling appropriations." In another discussion on appropriating a half-million dollars for continuing construction of water works for Washington DC and Georgetown, Walsh, with his typical sarcasm, asked, "Considering the generous and energetic character of the citizens of Washington ... would [it] be in order to introduce an amendment giving them coffee, tea, milk, sugar and whiskey for their water?"[14]

In more serious moments, Walsh advocated raising the pay of enlisted men in the army, and consistent with the Jacksonian Democrats' suspicion of tax-supported internal improvements in the West, opposed federal spending for a transcontinental railroad. "I will never vote to give a solitary inch of public domain to railroads or any other ... transparent humbug brought here for the purpose of robbing the people, and violating the constitution," he charged.

When Congress debated laws against the Mormon practice of polygamy in the Utah territory, Walsh defended the rights of the members of the religious sect who, except for taking multiple wives, were "as good citizens and as faithful to the Constitution ... as the citizens of any other state or territory." Walsh was prescient in anticipating the growing Mormon strength in the West. Although only a decade old, Mormons "are rapidly gaining in strength and numbers. They will soon become one of the most powerful sects ... in this country," he predicted.[15]

Walsh's career as a U.S representative from New York was doomed not only by his inability to function seriously on the national level, but his support for the lost cause of slavery. In 1854, Walsh voted for the Kansas-Nebraska Act—effectively opening the territories to slavery. Antagonism to abolition on the part of the Bowery Boys and antebellum labor radicals in New York seems incongruous in light of their strident demands for lifting the workingman out of poverty and powerlessness. Yet a convoluted argument that put a priority on abolishing northern wage slavery first, as well as a prevailing racism, put the Bowery Boys on the wrong side of history. As Arthur M. Schlesinger Jr. observed in his *Age of Jackson*, in refusing to oppose slavery, men like Walsh "were casting themselves adrift in national politics ... putting themselves outside the mainstream of democratic development."[16]

By allowing the territories to determine for themselves whether to permit slavery, the Kansas-Nebraska Act was a crucial piece of legislation leading to the Civil War. Sponsored by Senator Stephen A. Douglas, the Kansas-Nebraska Act ended thirty-four years of the Missouri Compromise, which had excluded slavery everywhere in the Louisiana Purchase north of Missouri's southern border, except for Missouri itself. Abolitionists saw the end of the Missouri Compromise as a signal to slaveholders to expand the "peculiar institution" westward. Of the seven Congressmen representing New York City in the thirty-third Congress—all Democrats—six of them voted for Kansas-Nebraska, including Walsh and William Tweed, the future Boss of Tammany. This was the case despite strong opposition from the city's major newspapers to opening the territories to slavery.

The *New York Times* urged voters to dump Walsh, Tweed, and the other "enemies of freedom" in the next election. In fact, of the six New York Congressmen who voted for Kansas-Nebraska, only Walsh ran again in 1854, and he was defeated. New Yorkers reelected John Wheeler, the sole member of the delegation who voted to retain the Missouri Compromise.

With the Kansas-Nebraska vote, the *New York Times* wrote the Bowery Boy's political obituary, saying, "He damaged his position when he first came to Washington by uniting with the Hard Shells in a merely fractious opposition. He has capped the climax of folly by a course which must close his political career in New York amid the disappointment of his friends and distrust of his constituency."

But did Walsh betray his constituency? He lost his bid for renomination narrowly, by eighteen votes out of more than 7,000 cast, when he faced Soft Shell Democrat John Kelly. Walsh carried the two wards that made up the core of his support, an indication that opposition to the Free-Soilers was greater among working-class voters than the *New York Times* appreciated. Walsh's defeat, as narrow as it was, likely had less to do with national politics than with the campaign skills of a man nicknamed "Honest John" Kelly.[17]

Some members of the New York delegation, including Walsh and Tweed, justified their vote to repeal the Missouri Compromise on constitutional grounds. They said the South was just as entitled as the North to settle the territories as they see fit. Constitutional considerations aside, New York City Democrats were more concerned that free blacks would represent another source of cheap labor to Northern capitalists; the system of wage slavery would only be strengthened with the end of chattel slavery. Walsh, who obviously never experienced slavery, made the argument that slaves were treated better than working men because the slaveholder had to protect his financial investment. "A man in the south gives $1,200 for a Negro he has to support. He has to feed him, he has to clothe him, he has to provide for him in old age, and to bury him when he is dead," Walsh explained.

Walsh viewed abolitionists as middle-class reformers, out of touch and unsympathetic with the urban proletariat in their own city. "There is as much slavery in the North as in the South," he said. And couching his sentiments against abolition in the typically crude racist language of the times, Walsh referred to "many men who have a particular feeling of veneration for the African race and it generally extends to the female portion of it. They have no love for white people."[18]

The labor organizers and Bowery Boys of the lower east side had expressed their nascent racism and hostility to abolition a decade before the Kansas-Nebraska vote when they rallied behind John C. Calhoun's 1844 presidential campaign. Even socialist intellectuals, such as Orestes Brownson and Theophilus Fisk, were wooed by Calhoun who, on the surface at least, could speak the language of the workingmen's advocates. Playing to the fears of urban factory workers, Calhoun warned that if freed, blacks would compete with white workers, driving their pitiful wages even lower.

Calhoun held out no hope that whites and blacks could ever coexist as free men; the races, he said, "cannot live together in peace or harmony except in their present relation." Calhoun raised fears of freed blacks

Mike Walsh's Bowery Boys joined the failed effort to put South Carolinian John Calhoun into the White House. Calhoun appealed to working-class voters who were fearful that emancipated slaves would become another source of cheap labor for northern capitalists. (Courtesy of the Library of Congress)

gaining political power and displacing native-born workers as well as Irish immigrants who were struggling for a place in the social pecking order in New York and other cities of the eastern seaboard. Boston abolitionist Wendell Phillips told the New York Anti-Slavery Society that "prejudice does not reside in any one class. There is prejudice against the Negro among the working class. Let the conscience of the North awaken a little."[19]

Isaiah Rynders, whose Empire Club took up the cause of the native-born worker, was fond of sending his young toughs to break up abolitionist meetings, occasionally requiring the attention of the city police. In one case, Rynders's men forced their way into an abolitionist meeting, and posing as a doctor, one of them lectured on the superiority of the white race.

Even veterans of European Marxism who settled in New York kept their distance from abolitionists. Hermann Kriege agreed with the Bowery Boys, arguing that free blacks would contribute to the existing oversupply of labor, forcing wages down further. "We will not better the position of our black brothers through abolition but will infinitely worsen the condition of our white brothers," he said.

Friedrich Engels, sounding like one of the b'hoys, also felt industrial workers were no better off than plantation slaves. "The slave is sold once and for all, the proletarian has to sell himself by the day. Being the property of one master ... the slave has a guaranteed subsistence." Walsh used the same logic when he said, "The only difference between the Negro slave in the South and the white wage slave of the North is that the wage worker has to beg for the privilege of becoming a slave. The one is the slave of the individual and the other is the slave of an inexorable class."

The more progressive George Henry Evans accepted the equality of the races, saying, "I should consider myself a disgrace by asserting that the Negro is not a man." But Evans's solution was to settle emancipated slaves west of the Mississippi, creating a separate African American homeland. "They have been violently deprived of their native home and the least that we ought to do is to give them another where they can dwell in peace," Evans said.[20]

As a working-class advocate foremost, Evans put aside the moral argument against slavery in favor of the purely economic case for first addressing the distress of northern wage laborers. "It is not difficult to foresee ... who would first suffer from want of employment and the reduction of wages consequent of competition" with emancipated slaves, Evans argued.

Of course, Evans claimed his National Reformers were the "true Free-Soil men" by opening the frontier to anyone willing to settle and cultivate the land. The Van Burenites, he said, were misusing the term "free soil" for political gain, focusing their energies solely on the extension of slavery into the territories. A genuine Free-Soiler, Evans explained, "cannot shut his eyes to the large portion of the white laboring population of the United States ... who consume a less proportion of the fruits of their industry than the colored slaves of the south."[21]

That line of thinking enraged abolitionist William Lloyd Garrison who took aim at Evans as a "professed reformer" who is either "grossly ignorant, or perversely knavish." Garrison asked, is it "worse to work for whom he pleases, when he pleases, and where he pleases, than to be compelled to toil under the lash of a slave driver?"[22]

Fear that freed slaves would flood northern factories to the benefit of rapacious employers was not the only issue that attracted New York radicals to the presidential ambitions of John Calhoun; they were also drawn to the South Carolinian's critique of Henry Clay's American System. Sounding like Slamm's Locofocos, Calhoun said, "The action of the government, the moment it steps beyond its constitutional limits, is to favor business at the expense of labor."

Consistent with Jacksonian ideals, Calhoun opposed Clay's advocacy of a central bank and federally funded internal improvements that Democrats said benefited one section of the country over another. In a letter courting the Democratic Party in New York in 1840, Calhoun asked,

> Shall we, after the great progress made, turn back to the Hamilton policy, reunite the government with the banks, create anew a national bank, build up another funding system, reenact a protective tariff, restore the misnamed American System with all its corrupting and dangerous consequences? Or shall we … restrict the government rigidly to the few great objects assigned to it; defense against danger from abroad; preservation of peace and tranquility at home; and a free and open commercial intercourse, within and without?[23]

In rallying insurgent Democrats against the Whig Party's brand of capitalism, Bowery Boy Edward Strahan warned the readers of his *Progressive Democrat* that public expenditures for internal improvements only serve to enrich land speculators. Southern planter and northern wage worker were also united by Calhoun's opposition to protective tariffs; both were suspicious of the new generation of large-scale manufacturers and a government that doled out favors to them at the expense of the farmer and the factory laborer.

Tariffs started as a device to raise national revenues, but by the Jackson years they were a vital means to protect domestic manufacturers from European competition. To Calhoun's supporters in New York, the tariff benefited northern industrialists exclusively, while hurting workers by raising the cost of imported goods. To southerners, the tariff was a burden that fell disproportionately on their region, as they paid higher prices for manufactured products. Tariffs were blamed for a slowdown in cotton exports to Europe and depressed prices, as planters had to sell their crops in an unprotected foreign market. Calhoun said tariffs relegated the agricultural south to a subordinate position; instead, he advocated free trade and the full participation of the United States in the trans-Atlantic economy.

Keenly aware, as early as 1828, of the emerging class structure that impoverished thousands of urban factory workers, Calhoun gloomily predicted in *Exposition and Protest*: "After we, the planters, are exhausted the contest will be between the capitalists and the [laborers]; for into these two classes it must ultimately divide society.... Wages must sink more rapidly than the prices of the necessities of life until the operatives will be reduced to the lowest point."

Firmly opposed to Martin Van Buren, Walsh organized his Bowery Boys for Calhoun in the summer of 1843. He enlisted his Spartan Band and labor allies like John Commerford, who was attracted to the free-trade cause. Levi Slamm endorsed Calhoun but, always hedging his bets, made a backroom deal with Tammany to get out the vote for Van Buren. It was a hodgepodge coalition, based more on a distaste for Van Buren and his wire pullers at Tammany than on any coherent strategy. It was a campaign of "uninformed talent and enthusiasm," Arthur Schlesinger Jr. writes, describing Calhoun's New Yorkers as "men acting as self-appointed champions of the bewildered masses." Yet the Calhoun movement in New York prompted one Maryland politician to appeal directly to the South Carolinian to bring his campaign north. "You may feel reluctant to travel through the northern states at this period, [but] you have very many and enthusiastic friends here and in the New England states, Pennsylvania, Michigan etc., who will give you a cordial welcome."

Packing neighborhood party caucuses with laborers pledged to Calhoun, Walsh was set on denying the Free-Soil Van Buren the support he needed at the state nominating convention in Syracuse. On the eve of the convention in August, Walsh called a rally of Calhoun supporters, Irish immigrant and native-born together, at City Hall Park. As the *New York Herald* observed, the factory laborers of the Calhoun camp "will form a solid phalanx to support their friends and measures backed by the b'hoys, subterraneans and radicals in general."

Loud outdoor demonstrations were not enough to defeat the Van Buren forces in the city, who won the votes to send their delegation to Syracuse. But even after New York Democrats made their choice, Walsh persisted in bringing his forces into the streets for Calhoun and against Van Buren. Calhoun was informed by one New Yorker "of the zeal that animates" the New York Calhoun committee. "They are not at all frightened by the proceedings of the Syracuse Convention. They have called another meeting this evening . . . not exactly a Calhoun meeting but of all opposed to the proceedings of the convention." That demonstration on September 14, 1843, drew more than 3,000.

Calhoun eventually withdrew his candidacy, saying that his supporters were robbed of their rights in the face of a nominating system that was controlled by professional office seekers and political managers, a reference to Tammany's well-organized Van Buren campaign. State conventions like the one in Syracuse, Calhoun said, put the political process "in the hands of a few who make politics a trade."

Years after Calhoun's run for the presidency, Walsh still referred to him as a man of "stern integrity who does not truckle to northern fanaticism." And Walsh still held out hope for the 1848 presidential race, telling the Eighth Ward Calhoun Association, "I will cling [to Calhoun's candidacy] as long as a gasp of breath remains in my body."

Evans, a more politically astute observer of national politics than Walsh, was not as easily wooed by Calhoun. Evans warned workingmen that if Calhoun would hold "the working classes of the South in perpetual slavery" how could white northern workingmen expect much better. Evans also suspected that Calhoun was waffling on internal improvements by turning the question into a national security issue when it suited him. Arguing that the Mississippi is America's inland sea, Calhoun said the land at its shores should be improved with federal funds; such improvements would fall within the constitutional powers of the government to provide for the national defense.[24]

Martin Van Buren's failure to clinch the nomination in 1844, which went to James Polk, was in large measure due to the issue of Texas annexation. Abolitionists and Free-Soilers, clustered around Van Buren, opposed annexation on the grounds that it would mean one or two more slave states. Independent since 1836, the Republic of Texas was settled by slaveholders, moving the cotton crop westward. Many Americans urged entry into the union early on, as the young republic struggled. Annexation meant war with Mexico, since Mexico never recognized Texan independence. Some even feared British intervention, as England worried about an expanding United States.

In New York City, the Texas question demonstrated just how out of touch the Tammany leadership was with the rank and file of the party in working-class lower Manhattan. For Walsh's Bowery Boys, war with Mexico was a test of patriotism, but above all, Texas annexation inspired a vision of an American West open to the crowded masses of the industrial Northeast. In the sweatshops of the lower east side, annexation was not a matter of slave versus free state—that issue was largely irrelevant. With territory to the Pacific, America is "preserve[ed] as an asylum for the oppressed of all nations," John Commerford said. Reflecting popular support for annexation, Levi Slamm told his followers, "We need Texas.... It would be advantageous to the United States both militarily and commercially."

Van Buren's principled Free-Soil position ended his chances for nomination and led the way for Polk, an enthusiastic supporter of bringing Texas into the union, even if it meant war. Rynders mobilized his Empire Club for Polk in the 1844 presidential race under the banner "the unterrified democracy," helping him carry the city and the state.

Some Democrats even charged that opposition to annexation was motivated less from the principle of free soil, than from strengthening capital at the expense of labor by keeping wages low in the overcrowded cities. As for the threat of foreign intervention, the Bowery Boys were unfazed—annex even if it means "war with Mexico, with England or the whole world," Walsh declared during an outdoor rally of the Spartan Band and labor activists at City Hall Park.[25]

Manifest Destiny, land for the growing American democracy, and separation of the New World from Europe with its aristocracies of wealth and privilege—these were the pillars of the Young America movement that Evans and Walsh embraced in their zeal for annexation. Evans, renaming his newspaper *Young America* in 1845, embraced John O'Sullivan's Manifest Destiny doctrine that saw Texas as one step in the inexorable triumph of the American idea.

Always in step with the passions of the Bowery Boys, Walt Whitman was moved by the romantic ideal of an America open to the Pacific. Whitman made it clear that the fight for Texas was "in the interest of mankind, that [American] power and territory should be extended—the farther, the better."

Walsh was characteristically impatient: "Go ahead Mr. Polk—two oceans united will have your name on the page of history." The opponents of annexation would only limit our greatness, O'Sullivan said, "checking the fulfillment of our manifest destiny to overspread the continent ... for the free development of our yearly multiplying millions." If Britain or France (or Catholic Mexico) objects, they are on the losing side of history, boasted the men who called themselves Young America. In one hundred years, O'Sullivan said presciently, "all the bayonets and cannon ... of Europe" will be no match for an America of "250 or 300 million ... destined to gather beneath the flutter of the stars and stripes" from the Atlantic to the Pacific. O'Sullivan rebutted Free-Soiler arguments that Texas annexation would mean more slave states. An open continent to the northwest would result in just as many free states, "to say nothing of those portions of Texas where slavery cannot spring or grow."[26]

With Polk in the White House, Texas was annexed in 1845 by joint congressional resolution, and in January 1846, Zachary Taylor led his troops to the Rio Grande. The Bowery Boys took up the unfailing banner of patriotism, with Walsh urging the War Department, "We go for this war, we go for whipping the Mexicans." The Bowery Boys responded with calls to raise regiments of volunteers from the streets of New York, as in one plea in the *Subterranean* in December 1846 that was to "rouse every man to a sense of duty." In fact, working-class recruitment in New York and other cities may have been a factor in reducing the incidences of urban disorder during the war years.

A decade later, Walsh again appealed to the nationalism of the Young America movement by encouraging the annexation of Cuba and war with Spain if necessary. In 1855, Walsh stood behind the failed attempt of General John A. Quitman to convince Franklin Pierce to liberate Cuba and annex the island. This freelance adventurism also had enthusiastic support and financial backing from southern slave owners who looked forward to another slave state in the union.

Quitman, who had served as governor of Mexico City during the American occupation in 1848, raised money and volunteers under his Order of the Lone Star, but he could not persuade the president, who was feeling the political backlash in the North from the Kansas-Nebraska Act. In a letter to Quitman in September 1854, Walsh urged the southern general to war: "Revolution and independence first, and annexation after, is the only possible way in which Cuba can be saved to the south."

True to the ideology of the Young America movement that envisioned an industrial and inherently superior United States spreading progress across the continent, Walsh called the Rio Grande a "line between penury and want on one side and wealth and abundance on the other." Mexico, he said, had not yet harnessed the power of steam and manufacturing that was remaking the United States into a modern power. In Mexico, Walsh said, "machinery is of the rudest kind" while north of the border "our farmers are using chemistry to unlock nature's storehouse." To the patriotic Bowery Boy, the difference between the two nations simply was that "Americans are intelligent, industrious and free."

It is the English-speaking world, said Walsh, that will carry the benefits of technical and social progress to the uncivilized parts of the globe. Expressing this nationalism in other areas, Walsh was a strong advocate of bringing European immigrants quickly into the mainstream of American life. For example, Walsh objected in 1852, when New York State printed a German-language edition of the governor's message to the legislature for the benefit of New York City's rapidly growing German community. Reflecting the view of America as melting pot, Walsh was eloquent about his adopted country. "It is the policy of this government to receive every race and class ... and blend them into one individual people ... to diffuse but one language and one Americanism." He said that by assimilating into a single American identity, all citizens could engage in "perfecting our free institutions."[27]

Both Philip Hone and George Templeton Strong record in their diaries the enthusiasm of the Bowery Boys for Texas annexation, as evidenced by their crashing of opponents' meetings. The Whig gentleman Hone, who feared a combination of war with Mexico and the threat of inflamed sectionalism, observed that during one public meeting, Walsh's "gang of ruffians, . . . prize fighters, and pardoned felons got possession of one corner of the room and interrupted with . . . 'hurrah for Texas,' 'for Calhoun' and vituperative epithets of British gold [and] Wall Street brokers."

For some Bowery Boys, settling the American West was more than the realization of democratic ideals or establishing a rural haven for factory hands. The promise of fortune, both political and monetary, attracted a few ambitious men from lower Manhattan westward to California in the late 1840s and early 1850s. Predictably, they brought with them their combative brand of electioneering and ideology of class warfare.

Following the California gold rush, "the red shirts of New York firemen and the rich brogues of the Bowery were seen and heard" in the streets of San Francisco, wrote Alvin Harlow in his *Old Bowery Days*. The style of the Bowery Boy firefighter certainly fit with that of the frontiersman. Both searched for adventure and wealth in a nation they considered unbounded in potential. Both glorified individualism, personal courage, and physical strength. Pioneer and New York b'hoy shared a disdain for puritanical reformers, with their temperance pledges and warnings about the vices of gambling and prostitution.

After release from jail for his role in the Astor Theater riot, Bowery Boy Ned Buntline headed West, stopping in St. Louis long enough to participate in an Election Day melee in 1852. The disturbance began when rumors spread that German immigrants supporting the Democratic Party had blocked Whigs from voting and tampered with ballot boxes. Buntline, leading the charge on horseback, mobilized the city's American-born to fight the Germans in the city. Further west, Buntline befriended Bill Cody, suggesting the stage name "Buffalo" and introduced the frontier legend to American audiences in his *New York Weekly*.

Three of the Spartan Band's leading street brawlers, David C. Broderick, George Wilkes and Yankee Sullivan, left New York for the lure of California gold. Of all the Bowery Boys, Broderick was one of the more politically ambitious. Bringing the rules of the Spartan Band to the Wild West, Broderick engineered his election to the U.S. Senate from California, even as his political machine in San Francisco was routed in a violent coup by the respectable classes.

Broderick was born in Washington DC, where his father, an Irish stonemason, contributed to the building of the U.S. Capitol Building. The family moved to New York, where young David became a part of the Bowery Boy subculture. Joining Howard Engine Company No. 34 and the Spartan Band, Broderick also opened a saloon in Greenwich Village he named the Subterranean, in honor of Walsh's newspaper. Consistent with the role of the saloonkeeper as a political force in antebellum New York, Broderick's Subterranean became a center for mobilizing the Spartans on

Bowery Boy David Broderick left the Lower East Side for California in search of political fortune. A tough Spartan Band street brawler, he fought off the San Francisco Committee of Vigilance to win a seat in the U.S. Senate. (Courtesy of the Library of Congress)

Election Day. As foreman of Engine Company No. 34, Broderick had a particularly nasty rivalry with Engine Company No. 27. In one fight during the summer of 1842, Broderick was severely beaten and his cap taken as a trophy. Broderick and Walsh counterattacked; in the ensuing fight Walsh had a few fingers broken and Broderick ran for his life.

Broderick saw Walsh's potential as a charismatic leader of the urban proletariat and even urged Walsh to commit suicide as an act of martyrdom, on the way to the jail at Blackwell's Island in November 1843. Broderick was among the Spartans who denounced the libel charges against Walsh as purely political and told Walsh that by suicide he "would stir up the vengeance of the populace upon their oppressors." Walsh had other plans and weakly staged an "attempted" suicide by drawing a pistol and pointing it to his chest. The gun was easily wrestled from his hands by his wife. Then, on the ferry, Walsh dove into the East River but was immediately fished out of the water. While Broderick lost some of his respect for the hero of the shirtless democrats, he organized a raucous reception for Walsh upon his release from jail, complete with a horse-drawn carriage parading the streets of lower Manhattan.

As an alderman for the Ninth Ward, Broderick distinguished himself in July 1846 by introducing legislation to reorganize and improve the efficiency of the city police. Most significantly, Broderick's police bill gave the police chief authority to shift officers from one ward to another, strengthening the force in parts of the city suffering from the worst crime.

Broderick made his first foray into national politics in 1846, able to garner the Democratic Party nomination for U.S. Congress, but Tammany soon discovered there was still too much Bowery Boy in Broderick for a place in the national party. In a stunt typical of the b'hoys, Broderick so enraged Democratic leaders they withdrew their support before Election Day. Broderick was invited to a reception honoring President Polk, but instead of taking his appointed position in the receiving line, Broderick intercepted Polk minutes earlier, escorting him ahead of his Tammany superiors. He may have gotten the President's ear, but Broderick lost the Democrats' confidence. Too ambitious for Tammany, Broderick set sail for San Francisco in 1849 in search of gold and power. He promised Walsh that he would triumphantly return to New York as a U.S. Senator.[28]

Once in San Francisco, Broderick set up a private mint with fellow Sixth Ward firefighter and alderman Frederick Kohler. They produced five-dollar and ten-dollar gold pieces in a perfectly legal enterprise, although Broderick likely weighed the gold with his thumb on the scale. Broderick profited enough to buy up some San Francisco real estate—seed money for his entrance into California politics.

Fellow Bowery Boy and Spartan George Wilkes also joined Broderick in San Francisco. In New York, Wilkes was for a time Walsh's partner and coeditor of the *Subterranean*. Wilkes went on to found the *Flash* and *Police Gazette*, popular scandal sheets. His bestselling expose of corruption in the Tombs prison in 1844 described politicians who used extortion and blackmail to "derive four-fifths of their income from female prostitution."

Arthur Schlesinger Jr., in his *Age of Jackson*, describes Wilkes as a "dissolute and ruthless scoundrel, a frequenter of brothels and publisher of obscene books." But Wilkes also was a shrewd political operative and street fighter; in San Francisco he took on the job of managing Broderick's 1856 campaign for the U.S. Senate.

As in New York, one sure path to political power in San Francisco was through the volunteer fire company. Broderick's easy election to the state senate in 1850, representing San Francisco, was due to his quick action and heroism fighting the Christmas fire of 1849.

The Bowery Boys in San Francisco took up the cause of the poor and the disenfranchised, just as they had in New York. In his first battle with the city's power structure, Broderick fought for the right of squatters on land around Sacramento. This was land owned by real estate speculators that was quickly settled by men returning from the gold fields, many of whom came back with empty pockets. The owners tried to enlist the support of the state to force the illegal settlers off the land. With the motto, "The Public Domain is Free to All," the squatters clashed with police.

Like the distressed industrial workers of the Northeast, the California squatters demanded strong political leadership. Broderick took to the floor of the California Senate in defense of those squatters who had been arrested, some of whom faced the gallows. When he was shouted down by the opposition, Broderick threatened to organize an army of the poor to take the land by force. Broderick became a champion of the underclass in a city that was becoming divided between winners and losers in the California gold rush.

The increasing number of confrontations between rich and poor, the general lawlessness of the city, and a fear of criminal elements emigrating to California from New York, Australia, and elsewhere, led to the formation in 1851 of the San Francisco Committee of Vigilance, made up mostly of the city's merchant and business class. The vigilance committee also set its sights on Broderick, who was building his Democratic Party organization from the same rough, working class elements that constituted the Spartan Band. For Broderick, the Committee of Vigilance was a dictatorship in waiting, intent on taking over the city. The committee largely assumed the duties of the police; established night patrols; and harassed workers, foreigners, and Catholics. Those people whom the committee wanted out of town were left a note on their door that read, "You are hereby warned to leave the city within five days. By order of the Committee of Vigilance." The alternative was the noose.[29]

Broderick's Democratic Party apparatus in San Francisco countered the vigilance committee with its own political machine. In 1853, Broderick forged an alliance with Governor John Bigler, who needed the political style of the New York b'hoys to win reelection. Broderick used all the ballot-stuffing and strong-armed tactics he learned in New York; fraud prevailed and Bigler won by a narrow margin of 1,000 votes. Broderick helped Bigler build up a system of patronage and political payback, and Broderick, for his efforts, received the chairmanship of the State Democratic Committee.

With a far more potent political machine behind him, Broderick was now in a position to oppose the vigilance committee, when the final confrontation came in 1856. The catalyst was the onset of a dramatic downturn in the local economy. The gold fever had reached its peak and the city was feeling the effects of overspeculation in the real-estate market. There were as many as 200 bankruptcies in 1855 and a run on the banks that same year; corruption and lawlessness were on the rise. City merchants, real-estate developers, and members of rival political groups put the blame on Broderick and the Irish Catholics who followed him.

On May 14, 1856, newspaper editor James King, who had been critical of Broderick and corruption in the city government, was assassinated by James Casey, one of Broderick's close associates. Immediately, the San Francisco Committee of Vigilance declared a state of emergency, and as many as 6,000 San Franciscans joined them to rid their city of the corrupt foreign element once and for all. Acting as an unelected government, the vigilance committee set up its own headquarters, armory, and jail. That summer, they started arresting and deporting, one by one, more than twenty-five of Broderick's key loyalists.

Bowery Boy and Spartan street fighter Yankee Bill Sullivan, fearing the worst, slit his wrists in a jail cell and bled to death. Sullivan, whose real name was Frank Ambrose, was always well armed with a two-foot Bowie knife. A fugitive from justice in England, Sullivan had escaped to America stowed aboard a whaling ship. Once in New York, he started up a saloon on Chatham Street and enlisted with Walsh's Spartans, leading the April 1842 Election Day rampage in the Sixth Ward. Sullivan was to Walsh, "a much-loved hero" of the boxing ring, "a brave and generous man."[30]

A professional bare-knuckle fighter, Sullivan was best known for his 1849 championship bout against Tom Hyer, whose Knickerbocker Club aligned with anti-Catholic elements of the Whig party. For many, the fight between Catholic Sullivan and Protestant Hyer, dubbed Young America, crystallized New York's social and ethnic conflicts. Sullivan lost and headed West; Hyer continued his political career, joining the Republican Party and attending the convention in 1860 that nominated Abraham Lincoln.

Back in New York, the respectable classes applauded the vigilance committee's work. George Templeton Strong wrote in an entry to his diary on June 29, 1856, that the vigilance committee had hanged two notorious scoundrels, including Casey, and arrested several more including Sullivan. The committee "claims to represent all the respectability, property and honesty of San Francisco and, if so, I hope its experiment may succeed. One like it will have to be tried in New York within ten years."[31]

An order was issued on July 19, 1856, to seize Broderick, but the vigilance committee was split. Broderick assured the city's vigilantes that his political career was finished and the Bowery Boys were out of the city. The Vigilance Committee was satisfied; they accomplished their major goals— send the Bowery Boys packing and grant temporary relief from creditors to many of the merchants still facing bankruptcy.

For more than a decade, the vigilance committee was firmly in charge of the city, establishing a political organization called the People's Party made up of the Protestant business class. It was not necessarily the end of the line for the shrewd David Broderick. While he lost his power base in San Francisco, he still wielded considerable influence in the State Democratic Party. In 1856, Broderick started to plot the Democrats' return to a majority in the state legislature, which had been lost to the anti-Catholic Know Nothings. Broderick took advantage of the general collapse of the Know Nothing party nationally to engineer a Democratic victory. For their part, the grateful California Democrats nominated Broderick for the U.S. Senate on the first ballot.

David Broderick made good on his promise, returning to visit his friends in New York as U.S. Senator from California. Broderick, Walsh, and Wilkes—Bowery Boys, political operatives, friends of the working class, and barroom brawlers—met together for the last time on St. Patrick's Day 1859.

chapter 7

Boss Rule and the Eclipse of the Bowery Boys

By the time Mike Walsh and the veterans of his Spartan Association met for a final night on the town in 1859, the Bowery Boys were no longer a loud and potent force in the political life of New York's working-class wards. The Bowery Boys were the victim of a growing and maturing city that saw the establishment of professional fire and police departments, as well as the emergence of the strong Democratic Party boss with little patience for neighborhood bullies and upstart clubhouses.

After his single term in the U.S. Congress, Walsh was finished with electoral politics, spending more time in saloons than at the helm of his proletarian faction. Walsh was defeated for a second term by John Kelly by a razor-thin margin. Walsh at first contested the results, but Kelly threatened to reveal that the Bowery Boy leader serving in Congress was not a U.S. citizen. Although Kelly's accusation was never definitively proven, Walsh's quick retreat indicates that he may have been the only member of Congress to hold that distinction.

Through the middle 1850s, Walsh worked on behalf of his close friend and New York shipbuilder George Steers. When Walsh was in Congress, he had tried to amend the law to allow private firms to build warships. With Steers in mind for the navy contracts, he praised the builder of the Yacht *America* in typical Walsh fashion as the "Napoleon of American naval architecture."

In 1855, Steers sent Walsh to Russia during the final days of the Crimean War to arrange a shipbuilding contract. Although armed with letters of introduction from Secretary of the Navy James Dobbin, plenty of spending money, and the promise of a hefty commission, nothing came of the venture except

Walsh's considerable expenses and bar tab. He traveled throughout the continent visiting Sevastopol and Constantinople, presumably to meet combatants of the Crimean War. Walsh, said one observer, "fell into a riotous living in Europe and spent the remittance of his employers." Broke, Walsh raised enough money from American diplomats in Constantinople to make it to Liverpool, and finally boarded a steamship to New York.[1]

The rest of Walsh's career, until his death in 1859, is more mystery than record. It is likely that he served as an unofficial government courier, traveling to Mexico in 1858, but the details of his missions are not recorded. One fact is certain regarding the last few years of Walsh's life—he drank more and more. Even in Congress, an inebriated Walsh "was so disgracefully besotted" that he had to be helped to his feet to cast his vote on the Kansas-Nebraska Act. He did take a brief temperance pledge a decade earlier as a favor to his old friend George Henry Evans, and Walsh even acknowledged that alcohol "retards the emancipation of the working class." Yet Walsh and the Bowery Boys were a part of the nineteenth-century saloon culture that rejected do-good reformers and "puritanical zealots," while glorifying hard drinking pugilists.[2]

After a typical night of revelry on St. Patrick's Day 1859, Walsh headed to his home at 208 West Twenty-first Street. It was about 2:00 a.m. He was discovered by a policeman a few hours later, lying face down in an alley on Eighth Avenue. He had a wound on his scalp and his gold watch and diamond ring were missing.

Murder was never proven, and some surmised he had fallen and later been stripped of his valuables. George Wilkes thought it was murder, telling the coroner he had seen Walsh walk safely home far drunker than on the night of his death. According to his obituary, Walsh was survived by his wife Catherine Wiley; a fifteen-year-old daughter, Catherine; and a twenty-year-old son, George Steers Walsh. An infant daughter, Leonora, died in 1855, "a death that was severely felt by her father."

Mike Walsh was remembered as a persistent and colorful advocate for those on the lowest rungs of the economic and social ladder. Although many regarded Walsh as a dynamic leader with "a powerful hold on the popular mind" who fought in the toughest arenas of New York City politics, he was ill-equipped to serve in public office. He had, as one newspaper editorialist noted, an "erratic mind that throws off all sorts of things with ... wildness and confusion."[3]

Although unpredictable and often thoroughly self-serving, Walsh led the Bowery Boys, in the two decades before the Civil War, from a brawling gang to a proletarian faction aligned with some of the leading figures of the Jacksonian Left. Even while serving in Congress far from his working-class base, Walsh could say proudly that he knew firsthand the aspirations of the people, unlike his colleagues, who "have learned their politics in liveried carriages."

A uniquely eccentric bunch, many of the old Spartans faded into obscurity as the Civil War approached. Others continued to press for labor and social-ist causes: Evans remained committed to his frontier ideals until his death in 1856. John Commerford took his case for organized labor into the middle 1850s—during the depths of a depression that threw thousands out of work. In 1855, he led rallies at Tompkins Square and throughout the city, demand-ing public employment, and he called for converting vacant uptown lots into affordable housing.

Long after the eclipse of the Bowery Boys, Walsh's onetime partner in the *Subterranean*, George Wilkes, continued to argue for socialism in America. As early as the 1840s, he was making a case for abolishing the death penalty and for progressive prison reform in his *Police Gazette*, saying "as no human tribu-nals are perfect in their judgments, they have no right to inflict a penalty which, if proved to be unjust, is beyond their reach and remedy.... Any system is monstrous by which an innocent man can die." On prison reform, Wilkes opposed incarceration behind bars where "men wilt and dwindle under a false condition ... and [which] leads to death." Instead, he proposed turning the nation's convicts into farmers, far from the vices of the city.

By the early 1870s, Wilkes was making the case for communism with his *Defense of the Paris Commune* and *The Internationale: Its Principles and Purposes*. These self-published pamphlets put Wilkes firmly in the Marxist camp, argu-ing for working-class solidarity across national borders. Wilkes was in Paris in 1871 when workers raised the red flag and declared a government based on communist principles. In the same year, echoing the not-quite-forgotten platform of the Working Men's Party, Wilkes advocated universal education "of both sexes ... without the infusion of religious creeds." Among the other points of his radical program were proposals for a one-term president and a remarkably progressive system of international law that would use economic sanctions over military force to ensure world peace.[4]

Mike Walsh's compact with Tammany and his subsequent election to Congress in 1852 removed him from the center of the battles for power in the lower east side wards. The leadership of the Bowery Boys passed to Butcher Bill Poole, who could better awaken the shirtless democrats than Walsh, sitting in Washington at Tammany's behest. Like Walsh, Poole ar-ticulated working-class resentment against low wages and miserable condi-tions in the city's sweated trades. During the particularly harsh depression that started in the winter of 1855, thousands crowded into New York's soup kitchens, protected by lines of police. In the Sixth Ward, on a single day, these kitchens provided food for 6,000 people. In January 1855, approxi-mately 11,000 families received assistance from the Association for Improv-ing the Condition of the Poor, compared with about 4,000 a year earlier. This profound economic distress left many Protestant, native-born workers

searching for a cause of their suffering; they found the enemy in both capitalists and Catholics.[5]

Unlike Walsh, who sought common ground with Catholics against real
and perceived class enemies, Poole allied with the more solidly Protestant
Whigs as their Ninth Ward boss. Poole even joined the militantly anti-
Catholic Order of United Americans that chafed at the Catholics' rising
influence in the Democratic Party. Operating a clubhouse out of his saloon
on Howard Street and Broadway, Poole also controlled the streets of the
ward through his leadership of the traditional Bowery Boy fire brigade,
Howard Engine Company No. 34.

It was in his death at the hands of a rival Irish Catholic gang that Bill
Poole rose to fame as a Bowery Boy folk hero. On February 24, 1855, at the
newly opened Stanwix Hall saloon on Broadway, Poole and partisans of the
Tammany-allied John Morrissey traded insults, and finally, gunfire. Poole,
age twenty-six, was shot in the chest several times at close range by one
Lewis Baker. Lingering for eleven days, Poole died suddenly on March 8
allegedly with the final words "Good-bye boys, I die a true American."

Thousands crowded the streets of New York for Poole's burial in Brooklyn's
Greenwood Cemetery. The funeral procession, with its fifty-two-piece
band and hearse drawn by four white horses, stretched for two miles, from
his residence on Christopher Street. Boats ferried thousands across the East
River to Brooklyn where the parade continued. Fraternal organizations,
such as the Poole Guards and Poole Associations, were spontaneously formed
throughout the city and as far away as Baltimore and Philadelphia to join the
mourners. The banner of the Order of United Americans was draped across
his chest in the open casket, and in the Ninth Ward Poole was proclaimed
"the ready and consistent friend of the workingmen."[6]

With Poole's death the Bowery Boys' decline began. Several factors
were at work, including the absence of a charismatic leader of the caliber of
Walsh and Poole; the election in 1854 and again in 1856 of Mayor Fernando
Wood, who brought an unprecedented discipline to the Democratic Party
apparatus; and rapid urban growth that demanded reforms, including modern fire and police protection. By the end of the 1850s, freewheeling gangs
no longer had the political and social space with which to operate.

More than any other political figure in New York's history, Fernando
Wood was responsible for creating the kind of strong rule—many said dictatorial rule—that shaped the character of the big-city boss. Wood's mastery
over the Democratic Party, particularly his efforts to build effective party
organizations in the wards, left little room for men like Mike Walsh to raise
the banner of insurgency.

Wood emerged from the same Democratic ward politics of the 1840s as the
Bowery Boys. Like Walsh, Levi Slamm, Isaiah Rynders, and Bill Poole, Wood

As mayor of New York, Fernando Wood brought the Democratic Party organization down to the ward level, spelling the end of insurgent political clubhouses like Walsh's Spartan Association. (Courtesy of the Library of Congress)

put himself squarely in the working-class camp. Fernando Wood's goal was to make loyal Democrats out of the city's laborers and immigrants. This, of course, undercut those who would claim the Democratic Party did not represent their interests. Wood's first campaign for mayor in 1850 prompted diarist Philip Hone to comment, "the dregs have risen to the top of the pot."[7]

Recognizing early on that the Irish Catholic vote would be essential to future political victories in New York, Wood accelerated Tammany's aggressive effort to naturalize immigrants off the boat. By 1855, the Irish constituted over a third of the city's electorate. In preparing for his reelection campaign, Wood had more than 16,000 immigrants naturalized in 1856—a record.

In sharp distinction from his predecessors, Mayor Wood threw the full weight of the government behind aiding the poor by putting the unemployed to work and delivering food or coal to the needy. "Wood pioneered the idea of government intervention to alleviate human injustice," said Wood's modern biographer Jerome Mushkat. Taking a page from Mike Walsh's social-democratic program, Wood also pressed for free higher education for the sons and daughters of the working class. The measure, however, was defeated by a hostile Common Council.

During the depths of the depression, as federal troops guarded the subtreasury building on Wall Street, Wood hastened the construction of Central Park and initiated public works projects such as street paving. He proposed to pay workers partly in cash, and also with food, and he employed 125 men daily to tear down the old city hall. Workers rotated the shifts giving each man a day's work every week.

Mushkat says that with an eye to higher office, Wood staked his reputation on making New York a model of urban administration: "New York was ready for a reform-minded innovative leader, a man with an overarching and compelling vision of a better society, a city builder to make the government respond to the needs which other mayors had not acknowledged, let alone addressed."[8]

To accomplish the daunting task of creating even a workable government, Wood said he needed to exert "one-man rule" to bring city departments and corrupt aldermen under his control. Taming an unruly New York put Wood at odds with both the Common Council and a state government fearful of his consolidating power. In some cases, the council sabotaged his efforts to address the conditions of the working class. Opponents in Albany called him a despot who pandered to the dangerous classes. Simply putting the unemployed on public works projects was to some a "monstrous doctrine [of] revolutionary France."[9]

Believing that state-imposed measures were necessary to check Wood's hold on the politics and government of the city, New York's Republican governor John King made the first moves with a revised municipal charter and temperance legislation. The Municipal Charter of 1857 undermined the mayor's authority over key city departments and deprived Wood of a role in city contracts. The goal was to rob Wood of his most important political tool—patronage.

The temperance measures, including the 1855 Maine Law and an excise law two years later, closed saloons on Sundays, barred the sale of alcohol from groceries, and made it more difficult to obtain liquor licenses. Irish and German immigrants, as well as saloon owners in the poorer wards, were hardest hit; reformers and Republicans were hoping to curtail the number of saloons that were instrumental in rallying the Democratic vote.

Citing his defense of home rule, Wood ignored the state's dictates. Governor King then signed the Metropolitan Police Act, essentially taking the police out of the mayor's jurisdiction. Wood refused to recognize the state-imposed Metropolitan Police force, and his now-loyal immigrant constituency backed him against Albany's police thugs set on raiding the corner tavern. By June 1857, the city had two rival police forces, neither exerting any real authority. Fights broke out, including a melee of more than 300 policemen on the steps of city hall when Wood refused to accept Albany's choice for city street commissioner. It took a court ruling by the state on July 2 and the threat of military intervention to convince Wood to accept the Metropolitan Police Act as law, but it was too late to avoid the violence that was building up in the streets. The conditions for gang warfare were ideal in the summer of 1857.

After Poole's death, the confrontation between Protestants and Catholics steadily sharpened. Defenders of the Protestant working class referred to "gangs of foreign marauders" and "Irish assassins targeting men whose hearts are sanctuaries of Americanism." In addition, the economy was at its worst. As the mayor and governor clashed over who controlled the police, the city was left unprotected, and the gangs, including the Bowery Boys, were ready to take full advantage of the situation; "these ruffians emerged from their dens like a horde of wild beasts and disgraced our city," the *New York Times* observed.[10]

By 1857, the leadership of the main Bowery Boy faction passed to one Pat Matthews, a saloonkeeper who opposed Wood on the grounds that the mayor was favoring immigrant Irish at a time when native-born workers were facing starvation. On July 4, several Catholic gang members of the so-called Dead Rabbits assaulted two police officers, who sought refuge in Matthews's saloon. The policemen were native-born Americans, and the Bowery Boys were eager to come to their defense.

Soon the streets were mobbed with young men and adolescents, many under the age of sixteen, engaged in bottle and brick throwing, with the center of the confrontation at Bayard Street. Another Bowery Boy saloon, the Green Dragon on Broome Street, was looted. Police called to restore order were beaten back by both sides, with women and children hurling bricks from the rooftops. The rioting also took on the character of an attack on private property as Dead Rabbits and Bowery Boys directed their anger at the respectable classes. Shops and homes were ransacked, and citizens took up arms to protect their property.

An appeal for peace from Isaiah Rynders, standing between barricades erected from horse carts near Mulberry Street, was ignored. While National Guard regiments were mobilized and a relative calm settled over the evening, rumors spread of plans to attack St. Patrick's Cathedral. Fighting resumed on July 5th between young men divided predominately between Catholic and native-born Protestant.

The police, outnumbered twenty to one, could only stand on the sidelines as the Eighth and Seventy-first Regiments finally intervened and confiscated weapons, including a quantity of muskets and a small cannon. In the end, as many as ten people were killed and well over one hundred injured. The death toll may have been far higher, as there were rumors that some of the dead were secretly buried in tenement backyards. It was the worst rioting the city had seen since the Astor Theater disturbances in 1849.

The battle between the Bowery Boys and the Dead Rabbits has passed into the lore of the city, memorialized in print and most recently on screen. Whether the Catholic gang paraded through the streets with a dead rabbit impaled on a stick is a matter of conjecture, but accounts of ethnic and class warfare during the summer of 1857, including a separate anti-police riot among German youth the week of July 13th, shows a city in desperate need of law and order.

Commenting on the breakdown in public order among working-class youth drawn into the gang culture of the lower east side, the *New York Tribune* editorialized, "Ruffianism and crime are rampant in our city. Our young mechanics and laborers are taught to scoff at religion and make sport of morality. The Bowery Boy is almost never innocent of the knowledge of all debasing vices."[11]

Fernando Wood, and the men who followed him as Tammany boss, continued to build the web of social services that addressed cyclical joblessness and the dismal living conditions of many New Yorkers. Wood affirmed the notion that city hall and Tammany Hall were responsible for addressing misery during hard times, and hence controlling discontent at the neighborhood level.

Gangs like the Bowery Boys and their politicized clubhouses were nourished in a power vacuum. Richard Stott, in his *Workers in the Metropolis*, explains that until men like Wood and John Kelly brought citywide discipline to the Democratic Party, New York "had numerous local bosses, each with personal followings." With the Democratic Party extending its political organization down to the ward level, the Bowery Boys' influence and authority dissolved. Recognizing the saloon's double identity as a nursery for insurgent politics, Wood opened workingmen's social clubs and meeting halls in taverns under strict Democratic Party control.

It is significant that Wood concentrated his efforts on building a year-round Democratic Party ward organization and that he consolidated power as both mayor and leader of the party in power. As Jerome Mushkat writes, Wood abandoned Tammany's collective leadership in 1857 "to become the first man to serve simultaneously as mayor and apparently the head of

Tammany ... he [dominated] the lines of authority from City Hall through the [Tammany] General Committee to neighborhood precincts."

Amy Bridges, in her study of antebellum New York, notes that by making the ward politically meaningful, Wood gave a formal role inside the Democratic Party to the men who earlier built an informal political machine through the fire brigades and saloons. Wood also brought school decisions down to the ward, empowering more Catholic voters. Most importantly, Tammany increased the share of patronage at the ward level, forging a strong bond on the streets to the Democratic machine.[12]

The fractious Democratic Party still had its share of schisms. Tammany broke with Wood, fed up with the mayor's dictatorial style and his emotional appeals to workers. Wood formed the rival Mozart Hall organization, and again rallying his labor and immigrant constituency, he returned to city hall for a third term in 1860; Mozart Hall was reunited with a politically predominant Tammany by 1868.

Wood's successors, such as Boss William Tweed and John Kelly, continued to build a modern political machine through the 1860s and 1870s that prevented the return of political freebooters like Walsh's Spartans. Kelly instilled greater party discipline by requiring candidates to finance their campaigns out of a common fund. Kelly also continued the practice, started with Wood, of bringing the Irish more fully into the political life of the city, as well as assisting the poor. John Kelly, the man who ended Mike Walsh's political career, made sure that Tammany—not the labor unions nor the Bowery Boys—would see to the needs of the working class. This is not to say that the Democratic Party under Wood and his successors became a labor party. As Bridges observes, rather than making it a workers' party, the party made the workers faithful Democrats.[13]

Along the way Tweed and Kelly modernized the police force and other city services. In 1865 New York eliminated the volunteer fire brigades and created a professional force free from gangs and political manipulation. The Bowery Boys vanished as a political force, in part, because they no longer had the base of operations, organization, and prestige that the firehouses offered.

Tammany also realized by this time that while respecting the aspirations of the working class and immigrants, they had to bring the middle class back to full participation in the political life of the city. When he took the helm at Tammany in 1871, John Kelly saw that merchant, reformer, and laborer were all involved in governing a city that was on its way to becoming a world-class commercial capital. With Kelly's support, sugar merchant William Havemeyer, first elected mayor in 1845 and 1848, returned to City Hall in 1873 with a vigorous attack on official corruption. In 1880 Kelly helped put shipping magnate William R. Grace into city hall.

Born in New York in 1822, Kelly was given the title Honest John for his opposition to corruption. As a city alderman and Catholic, Kelly battled the Know Nothings in the streets and at the ballot box. He even earned the respect of Boss Tweed, who said Kelly was the most successful New York City politician in thirty years. "New York politics was dishonest long before my time," said Tweed at the end of his career. "There was never a time when you couldn't buy the Board of Aldermen. If it wasn't for John Kelly's severity, you could buy them now."[14]

The Bowery Boy and his subterranean democracy was born out of that uniquely American revolution tied to the name of Andrew Jackson. In the 1840s, Mike Walsh defined his Bowery Boys as the honest factory lads led by the nose by "idle and dishonest capitalists" and the political wire pullers seeking their share of the patronage spoils. It was a forceful message to those excluded from the economic and political fruits of a growing metropolis.

As historian Bridges observes, men like Walsh were able to organize the disenfranchised because they could speak the language of the streets. Walt Whitman could look back on Walsh's life and write, "What a career! A New York b'hoy ... fond of his friends and they idolizing him."

When roused to action by men like Walsh, Slamm, Ming, Buntline, and Rynders, New York's urban proletariat was a threatening force. The Astor Theater riot in 1849 and the gang war of 1857 proved to New York's respectable classes that there was much to fear in the "multitude of youth neglected and under constant temptation ... to govern elections and plunder the city."[15]

As the Civil War approached, the b'hoy was increasingly irrelevant in a city of complex political and economic connections that stretched far beyond the island of Manhattan itself. Such a city demanded effective governance, and that meant bringing the subculture of gangs and fire brigades into line with the political establishment. New York was ready for men like Fernando Wood, who could co-opt the style and substance of the Bowery Boy to win his constituency. By the time of the Civil War, the city was long overdue for more enlightened political leaders like John Kelly who understood that stability depended on accommodation with both the dangerous and the respectable classes of New York.

Notes

INTRODUCTION

1. D. T. Valentine, *Manual of the Corporation of the City of New York*, McSpedon & Baker, New York, 1850, pp. 385, 399; I. N. Phelps Stokes, *The Iconography of Manhattan Island 1498–1909*, vol. 3, Arno Press, New York, 1967, pp. 517–522; Robert Ernst, *Immigrant Life in New York City: 1825–1863*, King's Crown Press, New York, 1949, p. 20.

2. Ernst, *Immigrant Life in New York*, pp. 40–47; *New York Herald*, August 7, 1843.

3. *New York Evening Post*, July 16, 1842; James F. Richardson, "The Struggle to Establish a London-Style Police Force for New York City," New York Historical Society Quarterly 49 (April 1965): 175–185; Stokes, *Iconography*, pp. 642–643; *American Citizen*, July 1, 1835; *New York Herald*, August 3, 1844.

4. Luc Sante, *Low Life: Lures and Snares of Old New York*, Farrar, Straus, Giroux, New York, 1991, p. 292: quotes from *An Account of Colonel Crockett's Tour to the North and Down East*, 1835.

5. Ernst, *Immigrant Life in New York*, pp. 49–52; *New York Tribune*, June 10, 1850; Edward Martin, *Secrets of the Great City: Virtues and the Vices, the Mysteries, Miseries and Crimes of New York City*, Jones Brothers & Co., Philadelphia, 1868, pp. 190–191, 245.

6. Edward K. Spann, *The New Metropolis: New York City 1840–1850*, Columbia University Press, New York, 1981, pp. 123, 156, 462; Stokes, *Iconography*, p. 523; *Subterranean*, November 8, 1845; *Subterranean*, September 26, 1846; *Subterranean*, April 24, 1847.

7. Edward Z. C. Judson [Ned Buntline], *The Mysteries and Miseries of New York*, Berford and Company, New York, 1848, pp. 74–75; Abram Dayton, *Last Days of Knickerbocker Life in New York*, George W. Harlan Publishers, New York, 1882, p. 141.

8. *New York Tribune*, February 20, 1855; Martin, *Secrets of the Great City*, p. 50; John Griscom, *The Sanitary Condition of the Laboring Classes of New York*, reprint of 1845 edition, Arno Press, New York, 1970, pp. 2–24.

9. Richard B. Stott, *Workers in the Metropolis: Class, Ethnicity, and Youth in Antebellum New York City*, Cornell University Press, Ithaca, NY, 1990, p. 74; Charles Loring Brace, *The Dangerous Classes of New York and Twenty Years Work Among Them*, Wynkoop and Hallenbeck, New York, 1880, pp. 317–318.

10. Michael Walsh, *Sketches of the Speeches and Writings of Michael Walsh*, Thomas McSpedon Publisher, New York, 1843, p. 18; David S. Reynolds, *Walt Whitman's America*, Vintage Books, New York, 1995, pp. 102–105; *New York Tribune*, March 10, 1855; *Subterranean*, February 27, 1847.

11. *New York Tribune*, March 12, 1855.

12. Arthur M. Schlesinger Jr., *Age of Jackson*, Little Brown, New York, 1945, pp. 408–409; *Subterranean*, October 25, 1845.

13. Schlesinger, *Age of Jackson*, p. 508; Matthew P. Breen, *Thirty Years of New York Politics Up-to-Date*, John Polhemus Printing Co., New York, 1899, p. 302.

14. Robert Ernst, "The One and Only Mike Walsh," New York Historical Society Quarterly, 36, January 1952: 44–47; Breen, *Thirty Years of New York*, p. 302–303; *New York Tribune*, November 23, 1846; M. R. Werner, *Tammany Hall*, Doubleday, Doran & Co., New York, 1928, pp. 44–45.

15. Breen, *Thirty Years of New York*, p. 303; Walsh, *Sketches*, p. vii.

16. Mike Walsh papers, New York Historical Society, New York; *Congressional Globe*, 33rd Congress, 1st session, John Rives Printing, Washington, 1854, p. 1231.

17. *Subterranean*, October 25, 1845; Walsh, *Sketches*, pp. 90–104; *New York Aurora*, December 13, 1842. Typical of his self-promotional style, Walsh mentions the death of Francis Scott Key in the *Aurora* of January 10, 1843, claiming that the author of "The Star-Spangled Banner" was an admirer and supporter. "Never will I forget his last words to me," Walsh recounts in the *Aurora*, "'Mike, my boy, persevere in the course you have pursued ... and you are sure to succeed.... You have truth, patriotism and humanity on your side.'"

18. Walsh, *Sketches*, p. 101; Wolcott quoted in Lee Benson, *The Concept of Jacksonian Democracy: New York as a Test Case*, Princeton University Press, Princeton, NJ, 1973, p. 3.

CHAPTER 1

1. Walsh, *Sketches*, p. v.

2. Ernst, "One and Only," p. 51; *New York Herald*, November 14, 1843.

3. Reynolds, *Walt Whitman's America*, p. 103; Walsh, *Sketches*, p. 18; Sean Wilentz, *Chants Democratic: New York & the Rise of the American Working Class 1788–1850*, Oxford University Press, New York, 1984, pp. 328–329.

4. Wilentz, *Chants Democratic*, p. 332; Amy Bridges, *A City in the Republic: Antebellum New York and the Origin of Machine Politics*, Cambridge University Press, Cambridge, 1984, pp. 11, 114–115.

5. William Gover, *The Tammany Hall Democracy in the City of New York*, Martin R. Brown Printers, New York, 1875, p. 10; J. T. Headley, *The Great Riots of New York*, E. B. Treat & Co., New York, 1873, pp. 72–74; Paul O. Weinbaum, *Mobs and Demagogues*, UMI Research Press, New York, 1977, pp. 1–9.

6. George G. Foster, *New York in Slices*, W. F. Burgess, N.Y., 1849, p. 49.

7. *New York Tribune*, March 12, 1855; *New York Evening Post*, September 13, 1838; Stokes, *Iconography*, p. 666; Alvin F. Harlow, *Old Bowery Days*, D. Appleton & Co., New York, 1931, p. 288.

8. Philip Hone, *The Diary of Philip Hone, 1828–1851*, Dodd, Mead & Company, New York, 1936, p. 189; *New York Evening Post*, October 29, 1841; Wilentz, *Chants Democratic*, p. 328.

9. *New York Tribune*, April 12, 1842; *New York Tribune*, April 14, 1842; *New York Tribune*, April 15, 1842; *New York Tribune*, May 11, 1842.

10. *New York Tribune*, April 14, 1842; Walsh, *Sketches*, p. 25; Gustavus Myers, *The History of Tammany Hall*, Boni & Liveright, New York, 1917, p. 132.

11. *New York Herald*, August 31, 1842; *New York Herald*, October 18, 1842; *New York Herald*, October 27, 1842; *New York Herald*, November 2, 1843.

12. *New York Herald*, November 2, 1843; *New York Herald*, November 6, 1843; *New York Herald*, November 14, 1843; Jerome Mushkat, *Tammany: The Evolution of a Political Machine, 1789–1865*, Syracuse University Press, Syracuse, NY, 1971, pp. 210–211; *New York Tribune*, July 12, 1842; *New York Herald*, January 18, 1843.

13. *New York Herald*, August 19, 1843; *New York Commercial Advertiser*, March 16, 1843; *New York Tribune*, March 5, 1853.

14. Bridges, *A City in the Republic*, pp. 74–75; Edward Pessen, "Who Governed the Nation's Cities," Political Science Quarterly 87 (December 1972): 591–614; Edward Pessen, "Political Democracy and the Distribution of Power in Antebellum New York City," in *Essays in the History of New York City*, edited by Irwin Yellowitz, Kennikat Press, Port Washington, NY, 1978, pp. 21–25.

15. *New York Tribune*, July 30, 1852; *New York Tribune*, August 27, 1852; *New York Tribune*, August 28, 1852; *Subterranean*, October 4, 1845; *Subterranean*, September 19, 1846; Spann, *The New Metropolis*, p. 353.

16. *National Police Gazette*, March 27, 1847; Ira M. Leonard, "The Politics of Charter Revision in New York City, 1845–1847," New York Historical Society Quarterly 62 (January 1978): 44; *New York Tribune*, October 7, 1846; *New York Tribune*, November 23, 1846; *New York Tribune*, July 8, 1852; *New York Tribune*, August 31, 1852.

17. *Subterranean*, March 27, 1847; *Subterranean*, April 24, 1847.

18. Walsh, *Sketches*, pp. 10–30; Ernst, "One and Only," pp. 47–49; *National Police Gazette*, August 7, 1847; *Subterranean*, November 21, 1846.

19. *National Police Gazette*, November 2, 1850; *New York Herald*, November 2, 1843; *Subterranean*, April 11, 1846; *Subterranean*, May 30, 1846; Walsh, *Sketches*, pp. 12, 27.

20. *New York Evening Post*, April 12, 1834 quoted in Weinbaum, *Mobs and Demagogues*, p. 14; Walsh, *Sketches*, p. 20.

21. *New York Herald*, October 18, 1842; *Progressive Democrat*, November 21,1846; *Progressive Democrat*, December 5, 1846; Foster, *New York in Slices*, p. 44; *The Man*, February 18, 1834.

22. Mushkat, *Tammany*, p. 208; Hone, *The Diary*, p. 434; Stott, *Workers In The Metropolis*, pp. 263–264; *New York Herald*, August 7, 1843; *The Man*, April 2, 1834.

23. M. R. Werner, *Tammany Hall*, p. 63; Wilentz, *Chants Democratic*, p. 53; Spann, *The New Metropolis*, p. 348; Ronald Bayor and Timothy Meagher, *The New York Irish*, The Johns Hopkins University Press, Baltimore, 1996, p. 119; Foster, *New York in Slices*, p. 83.

24. Stephen Ginsberg, "Above the Law: Volunteer Firemen in New York City, 1836–1837," New York History 50 (April 1969): 165–170; Frank J. Kernan, *Reminiscences of the Old Fire Laddies*, M. Crane Publisher, New York, 1885, pp. 127–129.

25. Ginsberg, "Above the Law," pp. 171–182; Lowell Limpus, *History of the New York Fire Department*, E. P. Dutton and Co., New York, 1940, pp. 162–168; Augustine Costello, *Our Firemen: The History of the New York Fire Departments*, A. E. Costello, New York, 1887. [reprinted 1997 by Knickerbocker Press, New York], pp. 225–227.

26. Wilentz, *Chants Democratic*, p. 260; *New York Aurora*, September 25, 1843; *New York Herald*, July 11, 1843; *New York Herald*, July 17, 1843.

27. *New York Evening Post*, January 11, 1841; Spann, *The New Metropolis*, p. 353; Costello, *Our Firemen*, pp. 118, 796.

28. Costello, *Our Firemen*, pp. 118–124; Limpus, *History of the New York Fire Department*, pp. 181–182, 188–202.

29. *New Era*, October 30, 1839; Costello, *Our Firemen*, p. 360.

30. Paul Boyer, *Urban Masses and Moral Order in America 1820–1920*, Harvard University Press, Cambridge, 1978, pp. 96–97.

CHAPTER 2

1. Reynolds, *Walt Whitman's America*, pp. 131–132, p. 141; Walsh, *Sketches*, p. 102; *Working Man's Advocate*, October 19, 1844.

2. *Subterranean*, October 25, 1845; Edward Pessen, "Who Has Power in the Democratic Capitalistic Community? Reflections on Antebellum New York City," New York History 58 (April 1977): 149–152; Edward Pessen, "The Egalitarian Myth and the American Social Reality: Wealth, Mobility, and Equality in the 'Era of the Common Man,'" American Historical Review 76 (October 1971): 1017–1023; Wilentz, *Chants Democratic*, p. 109.

3. Walsh, *Sketches*, p. 30.

4. Astor quoted in Spann, *The New Metropolis*, p. 208.

5. Bridges, *A City In the Republic*, p. 57; *Voice of Industry*, August 6, 1847 quoted in Norman Ware, *The Industrial Worker 1840–1860*, Houghton Mifflin, Boston, 1924, pp. xx–xxii, 1–7; Ernst, *Immigrant Life in New York*, p. 18.

6. *Working Man's Advocate*, May 11, 1844; *Albany Argus*, January 27, 1848; John R. Commons, *History of Labour in the United States*, vol. 1, Augustus M. Kelley Publishers, New York, 1966, pp. 456–457; *Albany Argus*, January 27, 1848; Douglas Miller, *Jacksonian Aristocracy: Class and Democracy in New York 1830–1860*, Oxford University Press, New York, 1967, pp. 128–133; Wilentz, *Chants Democratic*, p. 117.

7. *Subterranean*, May 2, 1846; *Subterranean*, February 13, 1847; Ware, *The Industrial Worker*, p. 31; Ernst, *Immigrant Life in New York*, pp. 49–50; *New York Tribune*, July 18, 1843.

8. Headley, *The Great Riots*, pp. 100–104; Weinbaum, *Mobs and Demagogues*, pp. 85–87; Commons, *History of Labour*, p. 464; Walter Hugins, *Jacksonian Democracy and the Working Class*, Stanford University Press, Stanford, CA, 1960, p. 91.

9. *Subterranean*, April 17, 1847; *New York Tribune*, January 13, 1855; *Subterranean*, February 27, 1847.

10. Gansevoort Melville to James Polk, October 26, 1844, *Correspondence of James K. Polk*, vol. 8, ed. Wayne Cutler, University of Tennessee Press, Knoxville, TN, 1993, pp. 227–230; Henry Osborn to James Polk, March 17, 1845, Henry Osborn quoted in *Correspondence of James K. Polk*, vol. 9, p. 201; E. J. Edwards, "Tammany and the Reign of the Plug-Uglies," *McClure's Magazine* (May 1895): 580; *Subterranean*, October 3, 1846.

11. Ernst, *Immigrant Life in New York*, pp. 102–103; *Subterranean*, April 17, 1847.

12. *Subterranean*, February 27, 1847; *Subterranean*, March 6, 1847; Spann, *The New Metropolis*, pp. 336, 430; Bayor and Meagher, *The New York Irish*, pp. 91–93; Stott, *Workers In The Metropolis*, p. 72; Ernst, *Immigrant Life in New York*, pp. 193–194; Valentine, *Manual*, p. 399; *New York Tribune*, September 2, 1852.

13. Spann, *The New Metropolis*, p. 316; George Templeton Strong, *The Diary of George Templeton Strong*, ed. Allan Nevins and Milton Halsey Thomas, University of Washington Press, Seattle, 1988, p. 52; Hone, *The Diary*, p. 190; *Subterranean*, May 2, 1846.

14. Lewis Masquerier, *Sociology or the Reconstruction of Society, Government and Property*, [reprint of 1877 edition by Greenwood Press, Westport, CT, 1970], p. 107; Wilentz, *Chants Democratic*, pp. 315–316; *New York Herald*, November 6, 1843; *New York Herald*, November 8, 1843; *Subterranean*, February 28, 1846.

15. *Subterranean*, September 19, 1846; Ernst, *Immigrant Life in New York*, p. 169; George Henry Evans quoted in Hugins, *Jacksonian Democracy*, p. 132; *The Radical*, November 1841.

16. *Working Man's Advocate*, March 16, 1844; *Subterranean*, March 27, 1847.

17. Bridges, *A City in the Republic*, p. 76; Ernst, *Immigrant Life in New York*, pp. 128–129; Alvin F. Harlow, *Old Bowery Days*, pp. 280–284; *Subterranean*, October 31, 1846.

18. *The Man*, July 11, 1834; Paul Gilje, *The Road to Mobocracy: Popular Disorder in New York City, 1763–1834*, University of North Carolina, Chapel Hill, NC, 1987, pp. 248–252.

19. *Subterranean*, April 3, 1847; Hone, *The Diary*, p. 876.

20. H. M. Ranney, *Account of the Terrific and Fatal Riot at the New York Astor Place Opera House*, H. M. Ranney Publishers, New York, 1849, pp. 10–19.

21. Richard Moody, *Astor Place Riot*, Indiana University Press, Bloomington, Indiana, 1958, pp. 158–167; *New York Tribune*, May 12, 1849; *New York Herald*, May 12, 1849; Ranney, *Account*, pp. 23–26; Iver Bernstein, *The New York City Draft Riots*, Oxford University Press, New York, 1990, p. 149.

22. Moody, *Astor Place Riot*, pp. 188–194; *New York Tribune*, May 12, 1849.

23. Moody, *Astor Place Riot*, p. 201.

24. *The Home Journal*, May 12, 1849 quoted in Moody, *Astor Place Riot*, p. 228; *New York Tribune*, May 14, 1849; *New York Herald*, May 14, 1849.

25. *The Home Journal*, May 12, 1849 quoted in Moody, *Astor Place Riot*, p. 228; Ranney, *Account*, p. 32; *New York Tribune*, July 8, 1857.

26. Ranney, *Account*, p. 32; Strong, *The Diary*, p. 18.

27. David Grimsted, "Rioting in Its Jacksonian Setting," American Historical Review 77 (April 1972): 364–365; Weinbaum, *Mobs and Demagogues*, p. 53; *New York Times*, July 7, 1857.

CHAPTER 3

1. *Providence Daily Journal*, March 19, 1842.

2. William Wiecek, "Popular Sovereignty in the Dorr War—Conservative Counterblast," Rhode Island History 32 (May 1973): 38.

3. Wiecek, "Popular Sovereignty," p. 37; Peter Magrath, "Optimistic Democrat: Thomas W. Dorr and the Case of Luther vs. Borden," Rhode Island History 29 (August–November 1970): 94; John McClernand, *Speech to the U.S. House of Representatives*, March 19, 1844, Congressional Globe, Washington DC, 1844, p. 3; Peter J. Coleman, *The Transformation of Rhode Island 1790–1860*, Brown University Press, Providence, RI, 1963, pp. 270–271.

4. Irving Richman, *Rhode Island: A Study in Separatism*, Houghton Mifflin & Co., New York, 1905, pp. 292–293; Coleman, *The Transformation of Rhode Island*, pp. 274–275.

5. Magrath, "Optimistic Democrat," p. 106.

6. *Providence Daily Journal*, January 1, 1842; Elisha Potter, *Rhode Island Memorial*, delivered to the U.S. House of Representatives June 17, 1844, Congressional Globe, Washington DC, 1844, p. 6.

7. Wiecek, "Popular Sovereignty," p. 50.

8. *Providence Daily Journal*, February 18, 1842; *Providence Daily Journal*, February 28, 1842; *Providence Daily Journal*, March 16, 1842.

9. *Providence Daily Journal*, May 17, 1842; *Boston Daily Atlas*, May 17, 1842.

10. *Providence Daily Journal*, March 19, 1842; George Rathbun, *Speech to U.S. House of Representatives*, March 9, 1844, Congressional Globe, Washington DC, 1844, p. 5; Wiecek, "Popular Sovereignty," p. 49.

11. *Providence Daily Journal*, March 17, 1842.

12. George Dennison, *The Dorr War: Republicanism on Trial 1831–1861*, University of Kentucky Press, Lexington, 1976, p. 75.

13. Arthur Mowry, "Tammany Hall and the Dorr Rebellion," *American Historical Review* 3 (January 1898): 295; Hone, *The Diary*, p. 603.

14. *Providence Daily Journal*, May 30, 1842.

15. *Providence Daily Journal*, May 16, 1842; *Providence Daily Journal*, May 17, 1842; Arthur Mowry, *The Dorr War*, Preston & Rounds Co., Providence, RI, 1901, p. 169.

16. *New York Post*, May 17, 1842; *Bay State Democrat*, May 18, 1842; Mowry, *The Dorr War*, pp. 171–173; *New York Tribune*, May 16, 1842; Mowry, "Tammany Hall and the Dorr Rebellion," pp. 296–297; *Providence Daily Journal*, May 17, 1842.

17. *New York Herald*, May 13, 1842; *New York Herald*, May 24, 1842; *New York Courier and Enquirer* quoted in *Providence Daily Journal*, May 18, 1842.

18. Mowry, *The Dorr War*, p. 179; Mowry, "Tammany Hall and the Dorr Rebellion," pp. 296–297.

19. Mowry, *The Dorr War*, pp. 176–178; Marvin Gettleman, *The Dorr Rebellion: A Study in American Radicalism*, Random House, New York, 1972, pp. 116–118.

20. *Providence Daily Journal*, May 17, 1842; *Providence Express*, May 16, 1842.

21. Gettleman, *The Dorr Rebellion*, pp. 121–123; Dennison, *The Dorr War*, p. 86.

22. *New York Tribune*, May 20, 1842; *New York Tribune*, May 21, 1842.

23. Mowry, "Tammany Hall and the Dorr Rebellion," pp. 299–300; *New York Tribune*, May 19, 1842; *Bay State Democrat*, May 19, 1842.

24. Mowry, "Tammany Hall and the Dorr Rebellion," p. 301; *The Liberator*, July 22, 1842; Thomas Dorr to Aaron White, May 27, 1842, May 28, 1842, Dorr Papers, Brown University.

25. E. Barrington to Senator James Fowler, June 6, 1842, Simmons Papers, Library of Congress; *New York Herald*, May 20, 1842.

26. *Providence Daily Journal*, June 4, 1842.

27. Dan King, *The Life and Times of Thomas Wilson Dorr*, 1859; [reprinted by Books for Libraries Press, Freeport, NY, 1969], pp. 247–248.

28. *Working Man's Advocate*, July 6, 1844; *Working Man's Advocate*, August 17, 1844; *Working Man's Advocate*, September 7, 1844.

29. *Subterranean*, June 21, 1845.

CHAPTER 4

1. Walt Whitman quoted in Wilentz, *Chants Democratic*, p. 389; John R. Commons, "Horace Greeley and the Working Class Origins of the Republican Party," Political Science Quarterly 24 (September 1909): 468–469.

2. Hugins, *Jacksonian Democracy*, pp. 12–15; *The Radical*, January 1842; Edward Pessen, "The Workingmen's Movement of the Jacksonian Era," Mississippi Valley Historical Review 43 (December 1956): 428–443.

3. *The Radical*, April 1843.

4. *The Radical*, April 1843; David Harris, *Socialist Origins in the United States*, Internationaal Instituut Voor Sociale Geschiedenis, Amsterdam, 1966, pp. 95–105, 133.

5. *Working Man's Advocate*, October 4, 1834; *Subterranean*, May 30, 1846; *The Radical*, April 1841; *The Radical*, January 1842.

6. *The Radical*, January 1841; Walsh, *Sketches*, p. 31, 66–70.

7. *Subterranean*, April 3, 1847; Edward Martin, *The Secrets of the Great City: Virtues and the Vices, the Mysteries, Miseries and Crimes of New York City*, Jones Brothers & Co., Philadelphia, 1868, p. 222; Spann, *The New Metropolis*, pp. 228–229.

8. Hugins, *Jacksonian Democracy*, pp. 131–134; *Subterranean*, May 15, 1847; *Subterranean*, April 3, 1847; *The Radical*, April 1843.

9. Commons, *History of Labour*, pp. 178–179; Walsh, *Sketches*, p. 31.

10. *Albany Argus*, February 3, 1847; *Subterranean*, October 17, 1846.

11. *The Radical*, February 1842; Wilentz, *Chants Democratic*, p. 206.

12. *Working Man's Advocate*, March 21, 1835; *New York Evening Post*, December 31, 1842; *Plebian*, October 25, 1842; *Progressive Democrat*, December 5, 1846; *Subterranean*, November 8, 1845; *Subterranean*, July 25, 1846.

13. *Working Man's Advocate*, October 11, 1834.

14. *New York Planet*, May 4, 1840.

15. *Subterranean*, May 9, 1846; *Subterranean*, December 13, 1845; *Subterranean*, March 13, 1847.

16. *Working Man's Advocate*, August 29, 1835; *The Man*, August 18, 1834; *Working Man's Advocate*, December 13, 1834; *Working Man's Advocate*, April 18, 1835.

17. *Working Man's Advocate*, December 13, 1834; Hugins, *Jacksonian Democracy*, pp. 165–166.

18. Robert V. Remini, *Andrew Jackson and the Bank War*, W.W. Norton & Co., New York, 1967, pp. 38–44.

19. *Working Man's Advocate*, April 2, 1831; *The Man*, March 19, 1834; *The Man*, March 25, 1834; *The Man*, April 4, 1834.

20. *Subterranean*, May 30, 1846; Mushkat, *Tammany*, p. 215; *New York Herald*, November 2, 1843; *Plebian*, July 2, 1842

21. A popular movement in England, Scotland and Wales during the 1840s, Chartism was based on a so-called People's Charter, published in 1838. The Chartist program was similar to the New York Working Men, calling for universal male suffrage, abolition of property qualifications for a seat in Parliament, and generally greater democratization in public life. Aside from political reform, Chartism was also a movement of the industrial proletariat that included experiments in cooperatives and trade union building. Chartists devised a land program quite similar to Evans's and put it into practice in the Land Cooperative Society of 1845. Chartist exiles like Thomas Devyr joined Evans and Walsh in the land reform movement in the United States, but Evans parted with the Chartists on the issue of slavery. Like most New York workers, Evans thought southern slavery was a problem that could only be discussed after the emancipation of the white wage laborer of the north. Said Evans, "The [Chartist] *Northern Star* does not seem to understand the difficulty of the slavery system which British rule imposed on this country. We sympathize with the black slave and we sympathize with the factory worker in England who has even less subsistence. *Working Man's Advocate*, October 8, 1831; *Working Man's Advocate*,

December 24, 1831; *Young America*, April 5, 1845; *New York Tribune*, May 2, 1850; *New York Evening Post*, October 22, 1842; *Subterranean*, February 28, 1846.

22. *National Police Gazette*, December 5, 1846; Hugins, *Jacksonian Democracy*, p. 62; Wilentz, *Chants Democratic*, p. 291; Commons, *History of Labour*, pp. 372–373; Hone, *The Diary*, p. 200.

23. Wilentz, *Chants Democratic*, p. 239; Walter E. Hugins, "Ely Moore: The Case History of a Jacksonian Labor Leader," Political Science Quarterly 65 (March 1950): 116.

24. The duration of the depression following the panic of 1837 is a matter of debate. John Commons, in his *History of Labour in the United States*, claims the depression lasted until the gold discoveries of 1849. Norman Ware, in *The Industrial Worker 1840–1860*, says that prosperity returned in 1843 and is demonstrated by the revival of the labor movement, as workers returned to employment and could exercise leverage over their employers for better wages. But regardless of when the depression actually lifted, workers' wages never fully recovered and in many sectors, remained depressed through most of the decade, as prices generally climbed upward. Ware, *The Industrial Worker*, p. 3; Wilentz, *Chants Democratic*, p. 221; Maurice Neufeld, *The Size of the Jacksonian Labor Movement: A Cautionary Account*, Labor History 23 (1982): 599–607; *Working Man's Advocate*, September 19, 1835; Commons, *History of Labour*, pp. 432–433.

25. *Working Man's Advocate*, August 3, 1844.

26. Ware, *The Industrial Worker*, p. xxv; Richard T. Ely, *The Labor Movement in America*, 1886 [reprinted 1969 by Arno Press, New York], pp. 57–58; *Subterranean*, May 8, 1847; *National Police Gazette*, August 7, 1847.

27. *Working Man's Advocate*, July 6, 1844.

28. *Working Man's Advocate*, September 19, 1835; *Subterranean*, May 8, 1847.

CHAPTER 5

1. *Subterranean*, March 23, 1844.

2. *Working Man's Advocate*, September 21, 1844; *Working Man's Advocate*, October 12, 1844; *Working Man's Advocate*, December 21, 1844; Ernst, "One and Only," p. 50.

3. *Working Man's Advocate*, July 6, 1844; *Working Man's Advocate*, April 20, 1844; *Working Man's Advocate*, March 30, 1844; *Working Man's Advocate*, May 4, 1844; *Working Man's Advocate*, September 7, 1844; Helene Zahler, *Eastern Workingmen and National Land Policy, 1829–1862*, Columbia University Press, New York, 1941, p. 43.

4. *Working Man's Advocate*, July 6, 1844; John R. Commons, *A Documentary History of American Industrial Society*, vol. 7, Russell & Russell, New York,1958, pp. 305–307.

5. *Working Man's Advocate*, March 16, 1844; *Working Man's Advocate*, July 6, 1844; *The Radical*, June 1841; *The Radical*, February 1841; Masquerier, *Sociology*, p. 19; *Subterranean*, June 6, 1846.

6. *The Radical*, June 1841; Masquerier, *Sociology*, pp. 20–21.

7. *Working Man's Advocate*, May 18, 1844; *Working Man's Advocate*, November 30, 1844; *The Radical*, February 1841; *Subterranean*, April 24, 1847; Richard K. Matthews, *The Radical Politics of Thomas Jefferson*, University Press of Kansas, Lawrence, KS, 1984, pp. 80–85.

8. *Subterranean*, March 23, 1844.

9. *Working Man's Advocate*, April 20, 1844; *New York Tribune*, May 21, 1850.

10. *Working Man's Advocate*, May 16, 1835; *Working Man's Advocate*, April 27, 1844; *Working Man's Advocate*, May 5, 1844; *The Radical*, June 1841.

11. *New York Tribune*, March 29, 1842; *New York Tribune*, April 2, 1842; *New York Tribune*, April 16, 1842; *New York Tribune*, August 4, 1842.

12. *Plebian*, July 2, 1842; *Plebian*, January 27, 1844; *Plebian*, April 8, 1844.

13. *Working Man's Advocate*, April 20, 1844; Commons, *A Documentary History*, Vol. 7, pp. 327–331, 341.

14. Commons, *A Documentary History*, Vol. 7, p. 237; *Subterranean*, July 25, 1846; Carl Guarneri, *The Utopian Alternative: Fourierism in Nineteenth Century America*, Cornell University Press, Ithaca, NY, 1991, p. 341.

15. Commons, *History of Labour*, pp. 534–535; *Volks-Tribun*, September 26, 1846 and *Volks-Tribun*, May 9, 1846 quoted in Commons, *A Documentary History*, Vol. 7, pp. 229–231, 92–93; *Young America*, November 8, 1845.

16. Karl Marx and Friedrich Engels, *Collected Works 1845–1848*, vol. 6, Progress Publishers, Moscow, 1984, p. 35; Robert Weiner, "Karl Marx's Vision of America: A Biographical and Bibliographical Sketch," The Review of Politics 42 (October 1980): 482; Karl Marx and Friedrich Engels, *Marx and Engels on the United States*, edited by Progress Publishers, Moscow, 1979, p. 48.

17. Marx and Engels, *Marx and Engels on the United States*, p. 49.

18. "Circular Against Kriege" in Marx and Engels, *Collected Works*, pp. 35–45.

19. Commons, *History of Labour*, p. 535; Stanley Nadel, "From the Barricades of Paris to the Sidewalks of New York: German Artisans and the European Roots of American Labor Radicalism," Labor History 30 (Winter 1989): 54–56; *Volks-Tribun*, November 7, 1846 quoted in Hermann Kriege, Documentation of a Transformation from Revolutionary to Democrat. Writings and Speeches of Hermann Kriege, edited by Heinrich Schlueter and Alfred Wesselmann, Der Andere Verlag, Berlin, 2002, pp. 604–607; *Subterranean*, November 7, 1846; *Subterranean*, November 28, 1846.

20. Karl Marx and Friedrich Engels, *Letters to Americans 1848–1895*, International Publishers, New York, 1953, pp. 25–26; Carl Wittke, *The Utopian Communist: A Biography of Wilhelm Weitling*, Louisiana State University Press, Baton Rouge, 1950, p. 116.

21. Walsh often expressed crude anti-Semitic views consistent with working-class radicals, referring, for example, to "the Jews of Wall Street." In one case Walsh attacked Fifth Ward alderman Mann Hart as a "licentious Israelite [whose descendants] pressed the crown of thorns on Christ's head." *Subterranean*, January 3, 1846; *Working Man's Advocate*, March 30, 1844; *New York Sun* quoted in *Working Man's Advocate*, February 15, 1845; Werner, *Tammany Hall*, p. 52; *Subterranean*, May 15, 1847.

22. *Working Man's Advocate*, October 19, 1844.

23. *Boston Investigator* quoted in *Working Man's Advocate*, October 26, 1844.

24. *Voice of Industry* July 3, 1845 quoted in Commons, *A Documentary History*, Vol. 8, pp. 111–113; *Subterranean*, January 10, 1846.

25. *Subterranean*, March 6, 1847; Wilentz, *Chants Democratic*, pp. 377–379.

26. *Subterranean*, May 15, 1847.

27. Wilentz, *Chants Democratic*, p. 373; Marx and Engels, *Letters to Americans*, p. 79; *Congressional Globe*, April 22, 1852 quoted in Commons, *A Documentary History*, Vol. 8, pp. 67–70.

28. *New York Herald*, July 16, 1850; Bernstein, *The New York City Draft Riots*, pp. 86–87; Wilentz, *Chants Democratic*, pp. 374–375.

29. Bernstein, *The New York City Draft Riots*, pp. 90–91; Commons, *History of Labour*, pp. 560–561; *New York Herald*, July 16, 1850; Commons, *A Documentary History*, Vol. 8, p. 340.

30. Commons, *History of Labour*, pp. 613–617.

31. *Subterranean*, April 17, 1847; *Subterranean*, May 8, 1847.

CHAPTER 6

1. *Subterranean*, February 28, 1846; *Subterranean*, November 14, 1846.

2. *New York Tribune*, November 23, 1846; *Subterranean*, November 21, 1846; *Albany Argus*, January 25, 1847.

3. Mushkat, *Tammany*, p. 244.

4. Mushkat, *Tammany*, p. 226; *Albany Argus*, March 12, 1847; Ernst, "One and Only," p. 58.

5. *Albany Argus*, February 3, 1848; *Albany Argus*, February 10, 1848.

6. *Congressional Globe*, 33rd Congress, Session 1, John Rives Printing, Washington, 1854, p. 191.

7. *Albany Argus*, April 23, 1847; *Albany Argus*, January 25, 1847; *Subterranean*, March 13, 1847.

8. *Albany Argus*, January 18, 1848; *Albany Argus*, January 17, 1852; *Albany Argus*, March 9, 1852.

9. Walsh claimed to have a particularly large following among the women of Albany who viewed him as a gentleman in a chamber of drunks and louts who propped their feet on their desks while colleagues spoke. *Subterranean*, May 20, 1847; *Subterranean*, May 22, 1847; *Subterranean*, March 20, 1847; *Subterranean*, April 3, 1847; *Albany Argus*, January 20, 1847.

10. *Subterranean*, April 3, 1847.

11. *The Man*, June 28, 1834; *The Radical*, February 1841.

12. *Albany Argus*, March 17, 1847; *Subterranean*, March 20, 1847; *Subterranean*, May 22, 1847.

13. *New York Tribune*, August 27, 1852; *New York Tribune*, August 30, 1852; *New York Tribune*, September 4, 1852; Mushkat, *Tammany*, p. 259.

14. *New York Times*, January 2, 1854; *Congressional Globe*, 33rd Congress, Session 1, p. 1691; *New York Times*, May 24, 1854.

15. *Congressional Globe*, 33rd Congress, Session 2, p. 287; *Congressional Globe*, 33rd Congress, Session 1, p. 1097.

16. Schlesinger, *Age of Jackson*, p. 492.

17. Edward Spann, "Gotham in Congress: New York's Representatives and the National Government, 1840–1854," New York History 67 (July 1986): 323–325; *New York Times*, May 10, 1854; *New York Times*, May 23, 1854; *New York Times*, May 24, 1854.

18. *Congressional Globe*, 33rd Congress, Session 1, p. 1232; *Albany Argus*, February 3, 1847.

19. *New York Tribune*, January 10, 1855.

20. *Volks-Tribun*, November 21, 1846; Friedrich Engels, "Principles of Communism," in Marx and Engel, *Collected Works*, vol. 6, p. 343; *Congressional Globe*, 33rd Congress, Session 1, p. 1232; *The Radical*, March 1841; *Young America*, June 7, 1845.

21. *The Radical*, March 1841; *Young America*, June 7, 1845; *Young America*, September 23, 1848.

22. *The Liberator*, March 19, 1847.

23. John Calhoun, *The Works of John Calhoun*, vol. 6, D. Appleton and Company, New York, 1855, p. 317.

24. From Virgil Maxcy to John Calhoun, September 14, 1843, *The Papers of John C. Calhoun*, vol. 17, edited by Clyde Wilson, University of South Carolina Press, Columbia, SC, 1986, pp. 445–446; *Subterranean*, April 24, 1847; *Young America*, December 13, 1845; *Young America*, September 13, 1845; *Subterranean*, January 10, 1846.

25. Working Man's Advocate, April 27, 1844; *Weekly Plebian*, June 1, 1844; *Working Man's Advocate*, May 11, 1844.

26. Walt Whitman quoted in Schlesinger, *Age of Jackson*, p. 450; *Subterranean*, May 1, 1847; John O'Sullivan, "Our Manifest Destiny," United States Magazine and Democratic Review, July 1845.

27. Philip Foner, *A History of Cuba and its Relations with the United States*, vol. 2, International Publishers, New York, 1963, pp. 86–95; *Subterranean*, April 3, 1847; *Subterranean*, May 8, 1847; *Albany Argus*, January 23, 1852; *Subterranean*, May 2, 1846.

28. *National Police Gazette*, July 21, 1846; *National Police Gazette*, August 1, 1846; James O'Meara, *Broderick and Gwin*, Bacon & Company Printers, San Francisco, 1881, pp. 18–21.

29. Arthur Quinn, *The Rivals*, Library of the American West, Crown Publishers Inc., New York, 1994, p. 117.

30. *New York Tribune*, September 26, 1842; *Subterranean*, October 25, 1845.

31. Strong, *The Diary*, p. 99.

CHAPTER 7

1. Walsh papers, *New York Herald*, March 18, 1859; *Congressional Globe*, 33rd Congress, Session 1, p. 830; James Fairfax McLaughlin, *The Life and Times of*

John Kelly, Tribune of the People, The American News Company, New York, 1885, p. 152; Ernst, "One and Only," pp. 62–63.

2. *New York Times*, May 23, 1854; *Working Man's Advocate*, September 21, 1844; *Subterranean*, October 4, 1845.

3. *New York Herald*, March 18, 1859; *New York Herald*, November 17, 1842; McLaughlin, *The Life and Times of John Kelly*, p. 152.

4. *National Police Gazette*, May 9, 1846; *National Police Gazette*, March 13, 1847; George Wilkes, *The Internationale: Its Principles and Purposes*, George Wilkes, New York, 1871, pp. 17–22; Timothy Messer-Kruse, *The Yankee International: Marxism and the American Reform Tradition, 1848–1876*, University of North Carolina Press, Chapel Hill, NC, 1998, pp. 100–104.

5. *New York Tribune*, January 15, 1855; *New York Tribune*, January 20, 1855; *New York Tribune*, January 23, 1855.

6. Elliott J. Gorn, "'Good Bye Boys, I Die A True American': Homicide, Nativism, and Working-Class Culture in Antebellum New York City," Journal of American History 74 (1987): 390–391; *New York Tribune*, March 10, 1855; *New York Tribune*, March 12, 1855.

7. Hone, *The Diary*, p. 927.

8. Leonard Chalmers, "Fernando Wood and Tammany Hall: The First Phase," New York Historical Society Quarterly 52 (October 1968): 393; Jerome Mushkat, *Fernando Wood: A Political Biography*, The Kent State University Press, Kent, OH, 1990, pp. 77, 38; Stokes, *Iconography*, p. 675; *New York Tribune*, January 23, 1855.

9. Mushkat, *Fernando Wood*, p. 40; *New York Evening Post*, November 10, 1857 quoted in Bridges, *A City in the Republic*, p. 118.

10. Gorn, "Good Bye Boys," p. 397; *New York Times*, July 6, 1857; *New York Tribune*, July 7, 1857.

11. Harlow, *Old Bowery Days*, pp. 309–311; *New York Tribune*, July 6, 1857; *New York Tribune*, July 7, 1857; *New York Tribune*, July 8, 1857; *New York Tribune*, July 10, 1857.

12. Stott, *Workers in the Metropolis*, p. 237; Bridges, *A City in the Republic*, pp. 121, 147; Mushkat, *Fernando Wood*, pp. 61–62.

13. William V. Shannon, *The American Irish*, Macmillan Publishing Company, New York, 1963, pp. 72–73; Bridges, *A City in the Republic*, p. 124.

14. Bridges, *A City in the Republic*, pp. 126, 144–145; Shannon, *The American Irish*, pp. 72–73; McLaughlin, *The Life and Times of John Kelly*, p. 23.

15. *New York Tribune*, July 8, 1857.

Bibliography

BOOKS AND JOURNALS

Allen, Irving Lewis. *The City in Slang*. Oxford University Press, New York, 1993.

Allen, Oliver. *The Tiger: The Rise and Fall of Tammany Hall*. Addison-Wesley Publishing Co., Reading, MA, 1993.

Asbury, Herbert. *The Gangs of New York*. A. A. Knopf, New York & London, 1928.

Ashworth, John. *Agrarians and Aristocrats: Party Political Ideology in the United States, 1837–1846*. Royal Historical Society, London, 1983.

Baker, Benjamin. *A Glance at New York*. S. French and Son, New York, 1890.

Bales, William. *Tiger in the Streets*. Dodd, Mead & Co., New York, 1962.

Bayor, Ronald, and Timothy Meagher, eds. *The New York Irish*. The Johns Hopkins University Press, Baltimore, 1996.

Benson, Lee. *The Concept of Jacksonian Democracy: New York as a Test Case*. Princeton University Press, Princeton, NJ, 1973.

Bernstein, Iver. *The New York City Draft Riots*. Oxford University Press, New York, 1990.

Bestor, Arthur. *Backwoods Utopias*. University of Pennsylvania Press, Philadelphia, 1950.

Blau, Joseph L., ed. *Social Theories of Jacksonian Democracy*. Bobbs-Merrill Co., New York, 1954.

Boyer, Paul. *Urban Masses and Moral Order in America, 1820–1920*. Harvard University Press, Cambridge, 1978.

Brace, Charles Loring. *The Dangerous Classes of New York and Twenty Years Work Among Them*. Wynkoop and Hallenbeck, New York, 1880.

Breen, Matthew P. *Thirty Years of New York Politics Up-to-Date*. John Polhemus Printing Co., New York, 1899.

Bridges, Amy. *A City In the Republic: Antebellum New York and the Origins of Machine Politics*. Cambridge University Press, Cambridge, 1984.

Burrows, Edwin G., and Mike Wallace, eds. *Gotham: A History of New York City to 1898*. Oxford University Press, New York, 1999.

Calhoun, John C. *The Works of John Calhoun*. Vol. 6, D. Appleton & Co., New York, 1855.

Causin, John M. S. *U.S. House Select Committee on Rhode Island Minority Report*. 28th Cong., 1st sess., June 17, 1844.

Chalmers, Leonard. "Fernando Wood and Tammany Hall: The First Phase." New York Historical Society Quarterly 52 (October 1968): 379–402.

Ciaburri, Robert L. "The Dorr Rebellion in Rhode Island: The Moderate Phase." Rhode Island History 26 (July 1967): 73–87.

Coit, Margaret L. *John C. Calhoun*. American Portrait, Houghton Mifflin & Co., Boston, 1950.

Coleman, Peter J. *The Transformation of Rhode Island 1790–1860*. Brown University Press, Providence, RI, 1963.

Commons, John R., ed. *A Documentary History of American Industrial Society*. Vol. 7 and Vol. 8. Russell & Russell, New York, 1958.

Commons, John R. *History of Labour in the United States*. Vol. 1. Augustus M. Kelley Publishers, New York, 1966.

Commons, John R. "Horace Greeley and the Working Class Origins of the Republican Party." Political Science Quarterly 24 (September 1909): 468–488.

Connable, Alfred, and Edward Silberfarb. *Tigers of Tammany*. Holt, Rinehart and Winston, New York, 1967.

Costello, Augustine E. *Our Firemen: The History of the New York Fire Departments*. A. E. Costello, New York, 1887. Reprint, Knickerbocker Press, New York, 1997.

Current, Richard Nelson. "John C. Calhoun, Philosopher of Reaction." Antioch Review 3 (Summer 1943): 223–234.

Dayton, Abram C. *Last Days of Knickerbocker Life In New York*. George W. Harlan Publishers, New York, 1882.

Degler, Carl. "The Loco Focos: Urban 'Agrarians.'" The Journal of Economic History 16 (September 1956): 322–333.

Dennison, George M. *The Dorr War: Republicanism on Trial 1831–1861*. University Press of Kentucky, Lexington, KY, 1976.

Edwards, E. J. "Tammany and the Reign of the Plug-Uglies." McClure's Magazine (May 1895): 577–580.

Ely, Richard T. *The Labor Movement in America*. 1886. Reprint, Arno Press, New York, 1969.

Ernst, Robert. *Immigrant Life in New York City: 1825–1863*. King's Crown Press, New York, 1949.

Ernst, Robert. "The One and Only Mike Walsh." New York Historical Society Quarterly 36 (January 1952): 43–65.

Feldberg, Michael. *The Turbulent Era: Riot and Disorder in Jacksonian America*. Oxford University Press, New York, 1980.

Feuer, Lewis S., "The Influence of the American Communist Colonies on Engels and Marx." Western Political Quarterly 19 (September 1966): 456–474.

Fish, Carl Russell. *The Rise of the Common Man*. The Macmillan Co., New York, 1927.

Foner, Philip. *A History of Cuba and Its Relations with the United States*. Vol. 2. International Publishers, New York, 1963.

Foster, George G. *New York by Gaslight*. Dewitt and Davenport , New York, 1850.

Foster, George G. *New York in Slices*. W. F. Burgess, New York, 1849.

Fox, Dixon Ryan. *The Decline of Aristocracy in the Politics of New York*. Columbia University Press, New York, 1919.

Francis, John W. *Old New York: Reminiscences of the Past Sixty Years*. Charles Roe, New York, 1858.

Frieze, Jacob. *Concise History of the Efforts to Obtain an Extension of Suffrage in Rhode Island From the Year 1811–1842*. Benjamin Moore, Providence, 1842.

Gersuny, Carl. "Seth Luther—The Road From Chepachet." Rhode Island History 33 (May 1974): 46–55.

Gettleman, Marvin E. *The Dorr Rebellion: A Study in American Radicalism: 1833–1849*. Random House, New York, 1972.

Gettleman, Marvin E., and Noel P. Conlon, eds. "Responses to the Rhode Island Workingmen's Reform Agitation of 1833." Rhode Island History 28 (August 1969): 75–94.

Gilbert, Amos. "A Sketch of the Life of Thomas Skidmore." Free Enquirer (March 30, 1834); (April 6, 1834); (April 13, 1834).

Gilje, Paul A. *The Road to Mobocracy: Popular Disorder in New York City, 1763–1834*. University of North Carolina, Chapel Hill, NC, 1987.

Ginsberg, Stephen F. "Above the Law: Volunteer Firemen in New York City, 1836–1837." New York History 50 (April 1969): 165–186.

Gorn, Elliott J. "'Good Bye Boys, I Die A True American': Homicide, Nativism, and Working-Class Culture in Antebellum New York City." Journal of American History 74 (September 1987): 388–410.

Gorn, Elliott J. *The Manly Art: Bare-Knuckle Prize Fighting in America*. Cornell University Press, Ithaca, NY, 1986.

Gover, William C. *The Tammany Hall Democracy of the City of New York*. Martin R. Brown Printer, New York, 1875.

Grimsted, David. *American Mobbing, 1828–1861*. Oxford University Press, New York, 1998.

Grimsted, David. "Rioting in its Jacksonian Setting." American Historical Review 77 (April 1972): 361–397.

Griscom, John H. *The Sanitary Condition of the Laboring Classes of New York* (reprint 1845 edition). Arno Press, New York, 1970.

Guarneri, Carl J. *The Utopian Alternative: Fourierism in Nineteenth Century America*. Cornell University Press, Ithaca, NY, 1991.

Hammond, Jabez. *The History of Political Parties in the State of New York*. Vol. 2, C. Van Benthuysen, Albany, NY, 1842.

Harlow, Alvin F. *Old Bowery Days.* D. Appleton & Co., New York, 1931.

Harris, David. *Socialist Origins in the United States: American Forerunners of Marx 1817–1832.* Internationaal Instituut voor Sociale Geschiedenis, Amsterdam, 1966.

Headley, J. T. *The Great Riots of New York.* E. B. Treat & Co., New York, 1873.

Herreshoff, David. *American Disciples of Marx: From the Age of Jackson to the Progressive Era.* Wayne State University Press, Detroit, 1967.

Hobsbawm, E. J. *Primitive Rebels.* W. W. Norton & Co., New York, 1965.

Hofstadter, Richard. *The American Political Tradition.* Alfred A. Knopf, New York, 1948.

Holloway, Mark. *Heavens on Earth: Utopian Communities in America 1680–1880.* Dover Publications, New York, 1966.

Hugins, Walter E. "Ely Moore: The Case History of a Jacksonian Labor Leader," Political Science Quarterly 65 (March 1950): 105–125.

Hugins, Walter E. *Jacksonian Democracy and the Working Class.* Stanford University Press, Stanford, CA, 1960.

Hugins, Walter E., ed. *The Reform Impulse 1825–1850.* Harper & Row Publishers, New York, 1972.

Jackson, Kenneth T., ed. *The Encyclopedia of New York.* Yale University Press, New Haven, CT, 1995.

Jenkins, John. *History of Political Parties in the State of New York.* Alden & Parsons, New York, 1849.

Johnson, David. *Policing the Underworld.* Temple University Press, Philadelphia, 1979.

Judson, Edward Z. C. *The Mysteries and Miseries of New York.* Berford and Company, New York, 1848.

Kernan, Frank J. *Reminiscences of the Old Fire Laddies.* M. Crane Publisher, New York, 1885.

King, Dan. *The Life and Times of Thomas Wilson Dorr.* 1859. Reprint, Books for Libraries Press, Freeport, NY, 1969.

Leggett, William. *Democratick Editorials: Essays in Jacksonian Political Economy.* Edited by Lawrence H. White. Liberty Press, Indianapolis, IN, 1984.

Lens, Sidney. *Radicalism in America.* Thomas Y. Crowell Co., New York, 1966.

Leonard, Ira M. "The Politics of Charter Revision in New York City, 1845–1847." New York Historical Society Quarterly 62 (January 1978): 43–70.

Leonard, Ira M. "The Politics of Charter Revision in New York City, 1847–1849." New York Historical Society Quarterly 63 (January 1979): 7–23.

Leonard, Ira M. "The Rise and Fall of the American Republican Party in New York City, 1843–1845." New York Historical Society Quarterly 50 (April 1966): 151–192.

Limpus, Lowell. *History of the New York Fire Department.* E. P. Dutton and Co., New York, 1940.

Lipset, Seymour Martin, and Gary Marks. *It Didn't Happen Here: Why Socialism Failed in the United States.* W. W. Norton & Co., New York, 2000.

Magrath, Peter C. "Optimistic Democrat: Thomas W. Dorr and the Case of Luther vs. Borden." Rhode Island History 29 (August–November 1970): 941–112.

Martin, Edward W. *The Secrets of the Great City: Virtues and the Vices, the Mysteries, Miseries and Crimes of New York City*. Jones Brothers & Co., Philadelphia, 1868.

Marx, Karl, and Friedrich Engels. *Collected Works 1845–1848*. Vol. 6. Progress Publishers, Moscow, 1984.

Marx, Karl, and Friedrich Engels. *Marx and Engels on the United States*. Progress Publishers, Moscow, 1979.

Masquerier, Lewis. *Sociology or the Reconstruction of Society, Government and Property*. 1877. Reprint, Greenwood Press, Westport, CT, 1970.

Mathews, Cornelius. *Pen and Ink Panorama of New York City*. John S. Taylor, New York, 1853.

Mathews, Mitford, ed. *A Dictionary of Americanisms*. University of Chicago Press, Chicago, IL, 1951.

Matthews, Richard K. *The Radical Politics of Thomas Jefferson*. University Press of Kansas, Lawrence, KS, 1984.

McCabe, James D. *New York by Sunlight and Gaslight*. Hubbard Brothers Publishers, Philadelphia, PA, 1883.

McGrane, Reginald. *The Panic of 1837*. University of Chicago Press, Chicago, 1924.

McLaughlin, James Fairfax. *The Life and Times of John Kelly, Tribune of the People*. The American News Company, New York, 1885.

Messer-Kruse, Timothy. *The Yankee International: Marxism and the American Reform Tradition, 1848–1876*. University of North Carolina Press, Chapel Hill, NC, 1998.

Miller, Douglas T. *Jacksonian Aristocracy: Class and Democracy in New York 1830–1860*. Oxford University Press, New York, 1967.

Miner, Margaret, and Hugh Rawson. *American Heritage Dictionary of American Quotations*. Penguin Books, New York, 1997.

Monaghan, Jay. *The Great Rascal: The Life and Adventures of Ned Buntline*. Little Brown and Company, Boston, 1952.

Moody, Richard. *Astor Place Riot*. Indiana University Press, Bloomington, IN, 1958.

Mowry, Arthur. *The Dorr War*. Preston & Rounds Co., Providence, RI, 1901.

Mowry, Arthur. "Tammany Hall and the Dorr Rebellion." American Historical Review 3 (January 1898): 292–301.

Mushkat, Jerome. *Fernando Wood: A Political Biography*. The Kent State University Press, Kent, OH, 1990.

Mushkat, Jerome. *Tammany: The Evolution of a Political Machine 1789–1865*. Syracuse University Press, Syracuse, NY, 1971.

Myers, Gustavus. *The History of Tammany Hall*. Boni & Liveright, New York, 1917.

Nadel, Stanley. "From the Barricades of Paris to the Sidewalks of New York: German Artisans and the European Roots of American Labor Radicalism," Labor History 30 (Winter 1989): 47–75.

Neufeld, Maurice. "The Size of the Jacksonian Labor Movement: A Cautionary Account." Labor History 23 (Fall 1982): 599–607.

Norcross, Frank W. *A History of the New York Swamp*. The Chiswick Press, New York, 1901.

Nordhoff, Charles. *The Communistic Societies of the United States.* Dover Publications, New York, 1966.

Noyes, John Humphrey. *History of American Socialisms.* J. B. Lippincott & Co., Philadelphia, 1870.

O'Meara, James. *Broderick and Gwin.* Bacon & Company Printers, San Francisco, 1881.

Pessen, Edward. "The Egalitarian Myth and the American Social Reality: Wealth, Mobility, and Equality in the 'Era of the Common Man.'" American Historical Review 76 (October 1971): 989–1034.

Pessen, Edward. *Most Uncommon Jacksonians: The Radical Leaders of the Early Labor Movement.* State University of New York Press, Albany, NY, 1967.

Pessen, Edward. "Political Democracy and the Distribution of Power in Antebellum New York City." In *Essays in the History of New York City: A Memorial to Sidney Pomerantz,* edited by Irwin Yellowitz, National University Publications, Kennikat Press, Port Washington, NY, 1978, pp. 21–42.

Pessen, Edward. *Riches, Class, and Power Before the Civil War.* D. C. Heath and Company, Lexington, MA, 1973.

Pessen, Edward. "A Variety of Panaceas: The 'Social Problem' and Proposed Solutions to it in Mid-Nineteenth Century New York State," New York History 59 (April 1978): 198–222.

Pessen, Edward. "The Wealthiest New Yorkers of the Jacksonian Era: A New List." New York Historical Society Quarterly 54 (April 1970): 145–155.

Pessen, Edward "Who Governed the Nation's Cities." Political Science Quarterly 87 (December 1972): 591–614.

Pessen, Edward. "Who Has Power in the Democratic Capitalistic Community? Reflections on Antebellum New York City." New York History 58 (April 1977): 129–155.

Pessen, Edward. "The Workingmen's Movement of the Jacksonian Era." Mississippi Valley Historical Review 43 (December 1956): 428–443.

Peterson, Merrill D. *The Great Triumvirate: Webster, Clay and Calhoun.* Oxford University Press, New York, 1987.

Quinn, Arthur. *The Rivals.* Library of the American West, Crown Publishers Inc., New York, 1994.

Rae, John B. "Democrats and the Dorr Rebellion." The New England Quarterly IX (September 1936): 476–483.

Ranney, H. M. *Account of the Terrific and Fatal Riot at the New York Astor Place Opera House.* H. M. Ranney Publishers, New York, 1849.

Remini, Robert. *Andrew Jackson and the Bank War.* W. W. Norton & Co., New York, 1967.

Reynolds, David S. *Walt Whitman's America.* Vintage Books, New York, 1995.

Rezneck, Samuel. "The Social History of an American Depression 1837–1843." American Historical Review 40 (July 1935): 662–687.

Richardson, James F. "The Struggle to Establish a London–Style Police Force for New York City." New York Historical Society Quarterly 49 (April 1965): 175–197.

Richman, Irving Berdine. *Rhode Island: A Study in Separatism*. Houghton Mifflin & Co., New York, Boston, 1905.

Rosenberg, Carroll S. "Protestants and Five Pointers: The Five Points House of Industry, 1850–1870." New York Historical Society Quarterly 48 (October 1964): 327–347.

Sante, Luc. *Low Life: Lures and Snares of Old New York*. Farrar, Straus, and Giroux, New York, 1991.

Schlesinger, Arthur M. *The Age of Jackson*. Little, Brown & Company, New York, 1945.

Shannon, William V. *The American Irish*. Macmillan Publishing Co., New York, 1963.

Spann, Edward K. "Gotham in Congress: New York's Representatives and the National Government, 1840–1854." New York History 67 (July 1986): 305–329.

Spann, Edward K. *The New Metropolis: New York City 1840–1857*. Columbia University Press, New York, 1981.

Stokes, I. N. Phelps. *The Iconography of Manhattan Island 1498–1909*. Vol. 3. Arno Press, New York, 1967.

Stott, Richard. *Workers In The Metropolis*. Cornell University Press, Ithaca, NY, 1990.

Taylor, George. "Gaslight Foster: A New York "Journeyman Journalist" at Mid-Century." New York History 58 (July 1977): 297–312.

Thompson, Dorothy. *The Chartists: Popular Politics in the Industrial Revolution*. Wildwood House Ltd., Hampshire, England, 1986.

Trimble, William. "Diverging Tendencies in the New York Democracy in the Period of the Locofocos." American Historical Review 24 (April 1919): 396–421.

Trimble, William. "The Social Philosophy of the Locofoco Democracy." American Journal of Sociology 26 (May 1921): 705–715.

Valentine, D. T. *Manual of the Corporation of the City of New York*. McSpedon & Baker, New York, 1850.

Walsh, Michael. *Sketches of the Speeches and Writings of Michael Walsh*. Thomas McSpedon Publisher, New York, 1843.

Walters, Ronald G. *American Reformers 1815–1860*. Hill and Wang, New York, 1978.

Ware, Norman. *The Industrial Worker 1840–1860*. Houghton Mifflin & Co., Boston, 1924.

Watson, Harry L. *Liberty and Power: The Politics of Jacksonian America*. Farrar, Straus and Giroux, New York, 1990.

Weinbaum, Paul O. *Mobs and Demagogues: The New York Response to Collective Violence in the Early Nineteenth Century*. UMI Research Press, 1977.

Weinbaum, Paul O. "Temperance, Politics, and the New York City Riots of 1857." New York Historical Society Quarterly 59 (July 1975): 246–270.

Weiner, Robert. "Karl Marx's Vision of America: A Biographical and Bibliographical Sketch." The Review of Politics 42 (October 1980): 465–503.

Wennersten, John, R., *Parke Godwin, Utopian Socialism, and the Politics of Antislavery*. New York Historical Society Quarterly, Vol. LX, July 1976, pp. 107–127.

Werner, M. R. *Tammany Hall*, Doubleday, Doran & Co., New York, 1928.

Wiecek, William M. *Popular Sovereignty in the Dorr War - Conservative Counterblast*, Rhode Island History, Vol. 32, May 1973, pp. 34–51.

Wilentz, Sean. *Chants Democratic: New York City & the Rise of the American Working Class 1788–1850*. Oxford University Press, New York, 1984.

Wilkes, George. *The Internationale: Its Principles and Purposes*. George Wilkes, New York, 1871.

Williams, David A. *David C. Broderick: A Political Portrait*. The Huntington Library, San Marino, California, 1969.

Wittke, Carl. *The Utopian Communist: A Biography of Wilhelm Weitling*. Louisiana State University Press, Baton Rouge, LA, 1950.

Zahler, Helene. *Eastern Workingmen and National Land Policy, 1829–1862*. Columbia University Press, New York, 1941.

NEWSPAPERS

Albany Argus, 1847–1848, 1852–1853
The American Citizen, 1835
Bay State Democrat, 1842
Boston Daily Atlas, 1842
Boston Morning Post, 1842
The Bunker Hill, 1844
The Liberator, 1842
The Man, 1834
National Police Gazette, 1845–1850
New Era, 1837, 1839, 1842
New York Advertiser and Express: 1837
New York American, 1842
New York Atlas, 1840
New York Aurora, 1842–1843
New York Commercial Advertiser, 1842–1843
New York Evening Post, 1838–1844
New York Herald, 1842–1846, 1859
New York Planet, 1840
New York Times, 1851–1854, 1857
New York Tribune, 1842–1857
New York Weekly Plebian, 1842, 1844
The Progressive Democrat, 1846
Providence Chronicle, 1842
Providence Daily Journal, 1842
Providence Express, 1842
Providence Herald, 1842
The Radical, 1841–1843
Subterranean, 1843–1847
United States Magazine and Democratic Review, 1844, 1845

The Working Man's Advocate, 1830–1835, 1844–1845
Young America, 1845–1848

MANUSCRIPTS, SPEECHES, AND COLLECTIONS

Calhoun, John C. *The Papers of John C. Calhoun*. Vol. 17. ed. Clyde N.Wilson, University of South Carolina Press, Columbia, SC, 1986.

Congressional Globe, 33d Congress, 1st session, 1854.

Congressional Globe, 33d Congress, 2nd session, 1854.

Dorr Manuscripts. Brown University, Providence, RI.

Hone, Philip. *The Diary of Philip Hone 1828–1851*. Dodd, Mead & Company, New York, 1936.

Kriege, Hermann. *Documentation of a Transformation from Revolutionary to Democrat: Writings and Speeches of Hermann Kriege*, ed. Heinrich Schlueter and Alfred Wesselmann, Der Andere Verlag, Berlin, 2002.

Marx, Karl, and Friedrich Engels. *Letters to Americans 1848–1895*. International Publishers, New York, 1953.

McClernand, John Alexander. *Speech of Mr. McClernand of Illinois on the resolution authorizing the committee on the Rhode Island controversy to send for persons and papers*. U.S. House, March 19, 1844. Globe Printing Office, Washington DC, 1844.

Polk, James K. *The Correspondence of James K. Polk*. Vols. 8, 9. ed. Wayne Cutler, University of Tennessee Press, Knoxville, TN, 1993

Potter, Elisha R. *Speech of Mr. Potter delivered in the House of Representatives, March 7, 9, and 12, 1844*. Globe Printing Office, Washington DC, 1844.

Rathbun, George Oscar. *Speech of Mr. Rathbun of New York on the resolution authorizing the committee on the Rhode Island controversy to send for persons and papers*. U.S. House, March 9, 1844. Globe Printing Office, Washington DC, 1844.

Simmons, James Fowler. Papers. Manuscripts Division, Library of Congress.

Strong, George Templeton. *The Diary of George Templeton Strong*, eds. Allan Nevins and Milton Halsey Thomas, University of Washington Press, Seattle, WA, 1988.

Walsh, Mike. Papers. New York Historical Society, New York.

Weed, Thurlow. Papers. Manuscripts Division, Library of Congress.

Woodbury, Levi. Papers. Manuscripts Division, Library of Congress.

Index

Abolition: and Dorr, 48; and effects on northern wage workers, 114–118, 121; Evans on, 117, 120; and Kansas-Nebraska Act, 114–115; Kriege and Engels on, 117; and New York gangs, 40, 114–115, 116–117; and racism, 89, 114–115; Walsh on, 99, 108, 114–115
Anderson, Joshua, 39
Anti-clericalism, 67–68, 96, 136
Armstrong, John, 37
Association for Improving the Condition of the Poor, 131
Astor, John Jacob, 26, 27, 39, 67
Astor Theater riot, 37–45, 57, 136; and Walsh, 37, 43

Baker, Lewis, 132
Bank of the United States, 73–74; and Locofocos, 73–74
Bennett, James Gordon, 102, 103, 104

Benton, Thomas Hart, 58
Bernstein, Iver, 103
Bigler, John, 126–127
Blackwell's Island, 1, 2, 6, 44, 57, 76, 78, 125
Bowery Boys' culture and characteristics, xv–xxi
Brace, Charles Loring; and Children's Aid Society, 23–24, 89–90
Bridges, Amy, 3, 5, 137, 138
Brisbane, Albert, 91–92, 93, 94, 98
Broderick, David, 10, 123–128; defense of the poor, 126; and Democratic Party, 125; and San Francisco Committee of Vigilance, 126–128; and Walsh, 123–125
Brownson, Orestes, 51–52, 115
Buntline, Ned (aka Edward Z. C. Judson), 30, 32, 33, 40, 42, 43, 44, 100, 123, 138
Butchers, 18, 30, 33–34, 37; and Bill Harrington, 18
Butler, Benjamin, 31

About the Author

PETER ADAMS is a freelance writer. A former journalist, his work has appeared in newspapers for the Gannett chain, including *USA Today*, as well as in publications that specialize in national security issues. He lives in the Washington, DC, area.